WEB RULES

WEB RULES

How the Internet Is Changing the Way Consumers Make Choices

TOM MURPHY

DEARBORN™
A **Kaplan Professional** Company

This publication is designed to provide accurate and authoritative information in regard to the subject matter covered. It is sold with the understanding that the publisher is not engaged in rendering legal, accounting, or other professional service. If legal advice or other expert assistance is required, the services of a competent professional should be sought.

Acquisitions Editor: Jean Iversen
Managing Editor: Jack Kiburz
Project Editor: Trey Thoelcke
Interior Design: Lucy Jenkins
Cover Design: Jody Billert
Typesetting: Elizabeth Pitts

© 2000 by Dearborn Financial Publishing, Inc.

Published by Dearborn
A Kaplan Professional Company

Printed in the United States of America

00 01 02 10 9 8 7 6 5 4 3 2 1

Library of Congress Cataloging-in-Publication Data

Murphy, Tom, 1953–
    Web rules : how the Internet is changing the way consumers make choices
    / Tom Murphy.
        p.   cm.
    Includes index.
    ISBN 0-7931-3613-X (hb)
    1. Internet marketing.   2. Consumers.   I. Title.
    HF5415.1265.M87   2000
    380.1'0285'4678—dc21
                                                                            99-086718

Dearborn books are available at special quantity discounts to use as premiums and sales promotions, or for use in corporate training programs. For more information, please call the Special Sales Manager at 800-621-9621, ext. 4514, or write to Dearborn Financial Publishing, Inc., 155 N. Wacker Drive, Chicago, IL 60606-1719.

DEDICATION

For Pam, who's inspired me in all things
for a quarter century.

CONTENTS

ACKNOWLEDGMENTS

I'd like to express my sincere gratitude to my mother, family, and friends, for their support and encouragement; to my readers for their interest; and to all others who lent their thoughts, time, and expertise. I'm especially grateful to Mike Bloomberg, Jerry Brown, Barry Diller, Rebecca Eisenberg, Paul Erdman, Andy Grove, Trip Hawkins, Paul Saffo, Jerry Yang, and Ann Winblad for so generously sharing their personal thoughts about the amazing time in which we live. Thanks, also, to Daren Marhula, David Roddy, and Burton Malkiel, whose comments and analyses were very helpful.

Special thanks to my editor, Jean Iversen, and the great team at Dearborn; to Eric Risberg, a great photographer and an even better friend; and to Elizabeth Armstrong, Adrienne Becker, Karen Greene, Holly Hartz, Howard High, Diane Hunt, Stacey Wells, and, of course, the amazing Wildfire.

Many thanks to J. Peter Bardwick at infoUSA for his enthusiastic support of my work. I'd also like to thank *all* my former colleagues at CBS.MarketWatch.com, particularly Jean Atelsek, Larry Kramer, Shawn Sabin, Bill Bishop, Alexander Davis, and David Callaway. Their cooperation made it possible to pursue this project. I'm very proud to have worked with these people on a daily basis.

We should all be grateful to the myriad men and women who work very long hours on technologies that empower us. I wish they all could become Internet millionaires, but most end up with little more than the simple satisfaction of participating in something great. The Internet reflects their greatness.

PART ONE

INTRODUCTION
The Powerful Consumer

We're witnessing the greatest transition of power in history, one that will take power away from the mightiest corporations and social institutions and give it to . . . *consumers.*

That's right, the consumer: you and me; our neighbors, parents, and friends; even our enemies. In fact, we're already very powerful. Individual consumers are gaining the power to shake corporate giants, to force politicians to respond to our concerns, to demand a better bargain in the marketplace, and to shape what's in the media.

It's about time. More specifically, it's about the remarkable time in which we live—the Information Age. This period represents an enormous challenge—and opportunity—for the companies and institutions that have held the power to this point. Smart merchants will seize this opportunity to offer spectacular customer service, low prices, and great product selection in an effort to attract this new breed of consumers. Web entrepreneurs are already busy setting up shop in virtual malls, hoping to steal customers from corporations weighed down by the brick-and-mortar storefronts.

Stubborn corporations who resist this change, or shrug it off, will learn quickly that their powerful customers don't need them anymore.

Information, as the adage goes, is power. When you know something, you have the ability to make a better choice. If you know it will rain tomorrow, you'll take your rain coat with you. If you know a car dealer in the next town is selling the model you want at a lower price, you can save money.

Until recently, the consumer's power was limited. Individuals could try to find the best bargain, but their ability to find it depended on their access to reliable information and the time they could afford to invest. Now those obstacles are gone. Consumers can find the best value in a few minutes on the World Wide Web. They can even ask a software robot to search for them.

The Internet has suddenly empowered everyone with access to it to get all the information they need to make better decisions and to influence the decisions made by others. For example, you can get specific answers to health questions, find out the latest score for your favorite teams, analyze a stock with the precision of a Wall Street analyst, and send e-mails instantly across an ocean. This is power.

Voters can find out how congressional representatives voted on the issues that matter most to them. Homebuyers can get the lowest rate on a 30-year mortgage from a bank three states away so that they can buy a cute little bungalow down the street. People interested in e-commerce can buy this book at the lowest possible price and even post their own reviews. And if one retailer treats them poorly, they can find another retailer who treats them better, all without leaving the comfort of home. This is power.

Consumers still may want to drive to the mall, but they need not shop there. They can inspect the goods at their local stores and then go home and order them at a lower price online. That way they can get lower prices. They don't even have to carry packages; theirs will be delivered to their doors the next day. This is power.

One might argue that this revolution began with the personal computer a generation ago, but that isn't the case. Having computers that couldn't communicate with one another was like having telephones that couldn't reach out to touch anyone. What the Internet has done for computers is like connecting all the telephones in the world. Suddenly, everyone has discovered this wonderful thing at the same time.

POWERFUL INDIVIDUALS

The Information Age—characterized by cheap, ubiquitous access to information—is upon us. Where the past few decades could be symbolized by powerful multinational corporations, the Information Age is all about the consumer, the all-powerful individual. It's about what they know and what they want and what they need. It's about their fantasies and realities, their health and happiness, their beliefs and curiosities.

Though these changes have only just begun, the Information Age promises to have a very short infancy. At the start of the 1990s, the only people using the Internet were a few thousand university researchers, technophiles, and defense agency employees. Today, more than 100 million people in the United States alone use the Internet, mostly for simply sending e-mail to friends, checking a stock price, researching a term paper, playing games, or catching up with some sports news. Some folks chat semianonymously over a modern-day party line.

When tens of millions of people fully embrace the notion of spending hundreds or thousands of dollars each per year over the Internet, corporations will compete savagely to get that business. The power of the consumer will soar.

Companies that want that business will have to earn it with something a lot more meaningful than a snazzy advertisement or a catchy jingle. Loyalty to a favorite brand will take a back seat to price, ease of use, and service.

3

NEW COMPETITION

This is a new technology and it is filled with new brands like Amazon, Yahoo!, and eBay. Consumers *expect* to try new brands, including some yet to be created. The old brands will be there, but their strength will be challenged by hundreds of new competitors with lower overhead and a business model better geared toward the Internet.

Electronic commerce (e-commerce)—virtually nonexistent just a few years ago—will account for $3 trillion in sales by 2005, and could represent a quarter of the world's economy by the year 2010, according to Cisco Systems chairman John Chambers. Indeed, Chambers' company, which makes many of the switches and other gear that tie computers to the Internet, has seen its revenues growing by 40 percent or more in recent years, while its stock price has more than tripled. Its growth, like that of most companies supplying equipment to the Internet market, has been accelerating exponentially.

Even if Chambers' estimate is high—and some people would argue it is, you can bet that virtually every large company is going to go after the vast market emerging in cyberspace. They won't be alone. On the Internet, virtually any scrappy entrepreneur with a Web site, some business sense, and a little moxie can get into the ring with the biggest opponent and have a fighting chance to win. As Chambers put it during a speech at the 1999 Internet World Conference, "This levels the playing field between companies in a global way we haven't seen before."

Witness Amazon.com, which emerged early as a model for Internet companies. This is a "bookstore" that didn't exist until 1995. Today, more than 2.5 million customers browse through its more than 10 million selections. Barnes & Noble, long the dominant national chain, now must fight for its life to catch up through barnesandnoble.com. Amazon, in the meantime, has moved into music sales, videos, toys, electronics, auctions, and other lucrative areas. The competition is so fierce that Amazon's brash move into auctions challenged another cyber pioneer—

eBay. Just two years earlier, eBay created the Internet auction category; now it suddenly had to fend off a savvy new rival in Amazon.

Corporate warfare is imminent in cyberspace. Alliances are being forged. Huge fortunes are being spent. Strategies are being drawn. And why? Because all these companies want consumers to like them, to spend their hard-earned dollars on their sites, to remain loyal to them. The new competitors have so little to lose: the time of their founders, perhaps a small investment of seed money, and perhaps some venture funding. Corporations that control traditional markets face a very difficult adjustment if they are to survive. They must be as nimble as their smallest traditional rival, as technologically savvy as fast-growing Silicon Valley powerhouses, and as ready to compete on price as their new cyber-rivals that have much lower overhead costs.

INTERNET MODEL

During a conference about technology stocks, money manager Steve Demirjian of Westfield Capital summed up the importance of the Internet: "If you're not looking at changing your business to an Internet model, you're in trouble."

In the corporate battle for the eyes of Web viewers, corporations are spending freely on advertising, hoping to capture the loyalty of a share of the market before their competitors. According to a research report from PricewaterhouseCoopers, Internet advertising already accounts for more than $1.9 billion, and is rising fast. That's about 20 percent more than the total spending on "outdoor" advertising—billboards, bus shelters, and the like. Global online advertising is projected to reach $33 billion by 2004, according to Forrester Research Inc.

Beyond e-commerce, this sea change is also washing over the media. At a seminar at the University of California, Bruce Koon, managing editor of Knight-Ridder's online venture, the Mercury Center, said most online readers for the *San Jose Mer-*

cury News don't live in the San Francisco Bay area. Readers all over the world go to the site for the latest technology news.

New York Times CEO Arthur Sulzberger, speaking at an advertising conference in San Francisco, said his paper's online effort isn't just an offshoot of "the old gray lady," as the paper is known, but is "fundamental" to its present and future. "Our challenge is to adapt our valuable franchise to this new medium," said Sulzberger, noting that three out of five online readers have never held a print copy of the *Times*.

In a national election, you can expect e-mail blitzes, online chats with the candidates, instant polls, and extensive advertising. But smart voters will use the medium to their own advantage, seeking out position papers, voting records, campaign finance information, and other data that can help them select their candidate. The era of the seven-second sound byte on the evening news isn't quite over, but it is quickly becoming irrelevant to anyone who surfs the Net.

Where does this leave us? At the beginning. In the chapters ahead, we'll visit the not-too-distant past, before our choices were limited to the growth of retail chains. We'll look at the breadth of choice available today on the Internet. We'll see how the Nintendo generation is growing up. We'll meet some of the visionaries who are leading this change.

Change is good. It's making consumers ever more powerful. And it will force corporations to follow a new set of rules— the Web rules.

CHAPTER 1

PAST IS PROLOGUE
The Customer Is Right, Again

In the late 1950s, Ike was president, TV was black and white, and Williston Park, New York, was as typical a suburb as you could find. The families who lived there were headed by a generation that survived two World Wars, the Korean Conflict, and the Depression. And there was an overriding sense that we were very, very lucky compared to the rest of the world, that these were the good times that followed so much pain and anguish.

My mother regularly shopped for groceries in the five-aisle Sunkist Market, now a store that sells chi-chi kitchenware. I clearly remember going with her to that store when I was about five or six. Every time we went to the butcher counter, it was as if my mother was meeting an old friend. The butcher would smile and say something like: "Hello, Mrs. Murphy. How are you? I see you brought Thomas with you today. You think he'd like a little nibble of salami? What can I get you? We have some nice plump chickens that just came in, and at such a good price."

We never shopped at the new supermarket. My mother would explain that the older market had fresher vegetables, riper fruit, better meat. "And they're nice people," she'd say.

And she was right. I still remember all those details because shopping there was such a pleasant thing to do.

That was a time when consumers had power. They expected to be treated well. They expected top-quality goods. They expected the best possible prices. Customers—we didn't know the word "consumers" then—were kings and queens. The customer was *always* right. And a merchant who didn't respect those rules wasn't a merchant very long.

A lot has been lost over the past four decades, but it's about to change back. Why? Because technology has advanced to the point where almost anyone can afford a high-speed computer that puts them and, perhaps, their business, in a position of enormous power. The Internet and related technologies already give consumers nearly unlimited choices of goods from around the corner or around the world. During the next few years, these choices will grow exponentially and the technology will become as ubiquitous as a telephone is today.

There are already some clear, early signs that the negative trends of the past 40 years can be reversed, if we demand it. Compare a few of my memories of the 1950s to some of the promising services already on the Web:

- In the '50s, my family doctor made house calls and could recall when each of my siblings had the mumps or the measles. Today, several health vendors offer to store your family's health history while offering medical advice and even online access to physicians—right from your home.
- In the '50s, a bread truck with a friendly driver brought fresh baked goods to our door. Fresh dairy items also were delivered. Today, you can have groceries delivered by companies like Peapod and WebVan.
- In the '50s, my father bought four daily newspapers, choosing from a dozen that were available. Today, you can read hundreds of newspapers from around the world on the Internet, most of them for free.

It's premature and perhaps naïve to call this a new, golden age of consumerism. But these are powerful new technologies with a very real potential of influencing culture well beyond the Internet as consumers awake to their new-found freedoms. If consumers flex those muscles, it could influence politics, religion, global economics, the fates of mighty corporations, distributions of wealth, and—most importantly—concentrations of power. Consumers are becoming very powerful, and each company must learn to respect that.

To better understand the foundation of this new era, it helps to take a look at our not-so-distant past. It's a dark journey, but it leads to a bright future. We need to examine the delicate balance of freedom and power in the consumer arena in a broad context before we can understand the underpinnings of the cyber revolution. Power brings with it a responsibility to exercise it wisely and to respect the rights of others, a principle that is often lost when too much power falls into the hands of too few.

For you to gain power, someone has to lose it. In the case of the Internet, consumers and small businesses will gain control at the expense of some of today's largest corporations. Consumers like you will decide the magnitude of that power shift with the click of a mouse.

WHEN DID THINGS GET SO BAD?

One doesn't need to be a historian to see the tug of war between individual freedom and dominating systems, whether social, economic, or both. Social control has existed only when power was concentrated in the hands of the few, whether Roman senators, medieval nobles, Nazis, cold war superpowers, or the multinational corporations. When that control becomes too oppressive, revolution ensues. The human spirit has always prized freedom, often over life itself. New Hampshire even captured that in its state motto: "Live free or die."

Why did our ancestors come to the New World? They wanted to be free of oppression, to pursue happiness, to seek spiritual fulfillment through worship, and to seek out wealth.

Once here, the idealistic pursued the dream. Entrepreneurs bet their meager savings on new businesses to challenge the status quo. From Tom Paine's *Common Sense* to this morning's *New York Times*, journalists have struggled so that society may be guided by informed choice instead of blind submission. Writers, poets, artists, musicians, dancers, and actors explored deep recesses of the soul, often sacrificing wealth for the sake of their art. Ordinary folks have put down farm tools and picked up the tools of war to defend freedom.

In the twentieth century, we've witnessed horrid events, up to and including the Holocaust. Even now we ask how could that have happened? We pledge: "Never again."

Now take a good look around you. What do you see?

- Toxic chemicals are leaking into our groundwater.
- 30,000 deaths occur a year from second-hand smoke.
- 16,000 deaths occur from alcohol-related accidents in the United States alone.
- Murder is the leading cause of death for young African Americans.
- Children shoot children while gun makers lobby Congress.
- Some scientists believe degradation of the ozone layer is melting the ice caps.

These should be very disturbing facts in a country that is guided by the will of its people. How did we get to this point?

We did it ourselves. We elected the leaders. We sat by as corporations exerted control over what we read and eat and do. We drove past poor neighborhoods. We chose to cut taxes rather than support the public schools that Ben Franklin said were fundamental to our freedom. We drank and smoked and ate more fat, salt, and sugar than our doctors advised. And when critics questioned our actions, we shrugged and said: "I guess you're right, but what can I do about it? I'm too busy."

We didn't even stop to ask *why* we're so busy, *why* we're under so much stress. *Why* does it take two wage earners to support a family now? *Why* are so many of us working 50 or even 70 hours a week to *maintain* our standard of living? *Why* do so many people have to work a second or third job to find the ever-more-elusive American dream? Do *you* own your home? Probably not.

Reversing those trends won't be easy, but it's possible. Technology alone won't do it, but it's a powerful tool that can help each of us regain control of our lives. And it can help all of us regain control of society and the marketplace. The Internet and related interactive technologies give us the time, information, and control we need to start reversing many of these problems. In effect, we're all getting a second chance.

We can see clearly how this revolution has begun by looking at the treatment of consumers by retailers who depend on us to make their livings. Most of this book centers on Internet consumers and on the things corporations will have to do to keep their business. These are issues that are critical to our economy and quality of life. Hopefully, these lessons also will be learned by the political and educational establishments in years to come. To be sure, that will be a longer, more difficult struggle.

There are still pockets—mostly in wealthy suburbs or rural settings—where the small-town feel exists, where shopkeepers know your name and take pride in their wares, where a mechanic won't tune your car unless it needs work. But it's the exception to the rule, isn't it? If you live in such a place, consider yourself lucky.

Today, it's more likely that a CVS drug store, Starbucks, Home Depot, Wal-Mart, and a Noah's Bagel have replaced many mom-and-pop shops. The local market is now 16 or 20 aisles wide and carries tens of thousands of items with a razor-thin retail mark-up. But you could play softball with the tomatoes, and you really don't want to know how they process the chickens.

How did we end up with so many large chains? In a word: mergers.

Let's take a closer look at why companies merge, what it means to consumers, and what is the government's role. We'll also look at some technology company mergers, leading up to the blockbuster merger of America Online (AOL) and Time Warner. It's a grand example of how consumer choice can have powerful, even unintended, effects.

MERGER MANIA

Companies merge because it makes good business sense. Customers support the merged company out of choice, even though they may regret the long-term outcome. In most mergers, companies increase profits. In most mergers, customers end up with fewer stores to shop in and, sometimes, higher prices due to reduced competition. Power shifts from the individual to the corporation.

This is a critical point in understanding what is happening on the Web. On the Web, thousands of new businesses are opening, providing consumers with myriad new choices, and, frequently, lower prices due to the increase in competition. Power is shifting away from large corporations back to the individual.

Consider this example. It's simple logic that if you and Joe and I have shoe stores in the same town, you and I can pool our resources and become more price- and cost-efficient than Joe. We can combine bookkeeping and other administrative functions, eliminating redundant jobs in the process. We can combine inventories, expand our selection, and still reduce our prices because we order in greater volumes. We can combine marketing expenses. In the long run, we can sell shoes more cheaply than Joe. He can try to compete by offering more service, but that will merely drive his prices higher.

Of course, if we have shareholders, they'll expect us to increase profit. If low price is our main attraction, we'll have to find ways to save, like firing that nice middle-age clerk who's been with us for a decade and replacing her with someone new at minimum wage with no benefits. Sure, the old clerk knew a lot of the customers, but business is business.

Once Joe goes out of business, we can buy his store and inventory at a song, offer his ex-employees minimum wage jobs, and find even greater efficiencies. And we can raise our prices slightly because Joe's not there to compete any more. Then we can push on into the next town, and repeat the process. The consumers? Hey, they're getting a wider variety of shoes at prices that are still lower than before the merger. This is a pro-consumer move, right?

Whether its shoes, or household goods, or books, or pizza, this scenario and many variations of it have been repeated over and over and over again for decades in the United States and many other countries as companies merged.

From mighty department stores that anchor vast malls to 30-foot-wide storefronts on the street where you catch the morning bus, chain retailers have rushed into neighborhoods and villages undermining local shops, plastering corporate logos everywhere, and supporting it all with mighty advertising campaigns that small businesses simply can't afford. This is progress, this is good business, this is good for the consumer . . . right? Maybe not.

Three key elements of a purchase are (1) individualized customer service, (2) selection, and (3) price. I think most consumers and retailers would agree those are pretty fundamental to a satisfying shopping experience. Now, think of any trendy clothing chain and estimate in your own mind how it matches up against those three standards.

In the area of selection, does the chain you're thinking of carry clothes that are appropriate for regional tastes and needs? Or does it sell the same shirts and pants in hot and dusty Flagstaff that you'd find in the cool and rainy clime of Portland? In the area of price, is it charging a huge mark-up on simple styles that were made in an offshore factory? If you've been in the store more than a few times, does the clerk know you? Does the clerk

13

seem committed to the merchandise and your satisfaction, or more on getting you through the store quickly?

I can't think of one chain clothing store I've visited in the past decade that would pass this test. That's because chain stores tend to focus more on icons than on the products consumers need.

Compare that to going into an independent boutique where the owner has personally stocked goods that she thinks would appeal to the kind of people who come into her store. She's conscious she has to compete against the chains in price, but doesn't put a lot into marketing or store design. Odds are, the employees in such a store are likely to take more interest in matching customers with products.

When you go into a large chain bookstore, the selection is broad, but it doesn't vary much from store to store. Compare that to visiting an independent bookstore, where the owners of each store order books specifically for their clientele. Is there a more pleasurable way to spend a rainy afternoon in Seattle than to wander through the Elliot Bay bookstore and discover what's hidden high on this shelf or that? You just don't get that kind of feeling in a Borders or Barnes & Noble.

Where can you get a really great pizza? Where can you get a tasty deli sandwich? Where did you last enjoy a really good steak? Now, how many of you named Domino's, Subway, or Outback?

Big movie chains like United Artists or AMC can put the same film in front of millions of viewers over a single weekend, while a small independent theatre will take a chance screening a new Italian film with subtitles, hoping it will satisfy a choosier clientele. In the long run, the big movie chain ends up helping to form social tastes by deciding what should be shown.

Financial Web sites and newspapers are filled with stories of the latest multibillion-dollar merger. While they may have become routine in the past few decades, mergers are rife with the potential to harm consumer interests. Corporate spin doctors will argue they result in greater efficiencies that mean lower prices and choice for consumers. Bunk. It's always been bunk, and it's still bunk.

THE VIRTUAL MALL

Now, imagine that a thousand boutiques suddenly opened around one large chain store, but the boutiques didn't have to pay rent. Suddenly, the consumer has enormous choice and the boutiques, because of their lower operating costs, can charge less for products. In essence, that is what's happening on the Internet, and it is undermining the business models of the world's largest corporations. Suddenly, power is shifting from the large corporations back to the consumer.

Of course, large retailers also can operate stores in cyberspace. But, in many ways, they'll be just one more competitor. Plus, they still have to pay rent on all their stores, their "brick-and-mortar" assets.

The analysts love to debate which model—virtual stores reached through mouse clicks or traditional brick-and-mortar stores—works best. The truth is that some combination—a variation known as clicks-and-mortar—will probably be the most efficient model. But during this transitional stage, consumers will have enormous power to pick the winners and the losers, and it's a choice they should use wisely if they hope to reverse the trends wrought by mergers.

Clearly, legislators have been unable to deflect the anticonsumer effects of mergers. And, as we'll see in the AOL-Netscape case, the actions of consumers themselves sometimes have unforeseen effects.

It was precisely because of the anticonsumer effects of mergers that Congress enacted the Clayton Act of 1914. But that legislation had a fatal flaw—it didn't require corporations to announce a merger before it was consummated. If the government thought the merger would be detrimental to consumers, it could file a legal complaint to undo the damage. The problem was that the legal actions took so long to resolve that consumers had suffered considerable damage by the time any remedy took place.

The classic case involved El Paso Natural Gas Co., which acquired Pacific Northwest Pipeline. Pacific Northwest shipped natural gas throughout the northwest United States and wanted to sell gas in California, where El Paso was the only supplier. So El Paso bought the company. The government objected, and seven years later, the Supreme Court said El Paso couldn't buy Pacific Northwest. But the actual divestiture took another decade. Over the 17-year history of the case, it's estimated El Paso earned an extra $170 million as a result of an acquisition that should never have taken place.

In 1976, Congress enacted the Hart-Scott-Rodino Act, requiring among other things, advance notification of any mergers. Rest assured, this was no easy sell. Corporations opposed it, saying the United States could fall victim to global competition. However, it passed and has since saved consumers hundreds of millions of dollars.

But don't think for a second the law slowed the pace of mergers. In the first year after the act was passed, there were about 860 merger applications filed with the government. Twenty years later, there were nearly 3,100. More recently, the pace has increased to about 8,000 mergers a year, transactions with a total value approaching $500 billion. Nowhere is the pace of acquisitions quicker than in the technology arena, where corporate acquisition has become a game corporations must play to avoid losing market share.

Consider just this short sampling of the many, many marriages of a single recent year—1998: HBO & Co–McKesson; AMP–Tyco; Bay Networks–Northern Telecom; Digital Equipment–Compaq; DSC Communications–Alcatel; AOL–Netscape; General Signal–SPX; Seagate Software–Veritas; Texas Instruments–Micron Technology; Boole & Babbage–BMC Software; Stratus Computer–Ascend Communications; Xerox–XL Connect.

What's stunning about that list—aside from the many obvious factors such as the number, size, values, and competitive threats to smaller companies—is the crossover from one area of technology into another, or into an entirely new industry. HBO, for example, made health care software while McKesson distributed pharmaceuticals, and the strange marriage came back to haunt McKesson. Xerox ("the Document Company") wanted XL Connect, a networking services firm, so it could network systems that produce documents. Compaq and DEC merged, bringing desktop computers together with a higher life form—the bigger machines that serve data over networks.

YOU'VE GOT NETSCAPE!

By far, however, the most dramatic merger in the context of this book is the acquisition of Netscape Communications by America Online. More than any single merger, even AOL's subsequent merger with Time Warner, this marriage reflects the online consumer's power to alter the corporate landscape.

Curiously, it took place while Microsoft was on trial for alleged antitrust violations. Remember, those antitrust allegations were largely pushed by Netscape, which claimed it couldn't compete with Microsoft. And key testimony came from AOL, which once shunned Netscape to form an alliance with Microsoft.

The AOL–Netscape merger brought together the world's two largest groups of Web subscribers, forming a company serving some 17 million Web users, the vast majority of them AOL customers. Yet this union faced only a cursory federal review and no serious objection from federal regulators because it was considered a "vertical" integration; that is, it matched two companies whose technologies complemented one another instead of competed with one another.

"The battle between individual expression and freedom, and corporate domination and greed on the Web, just got uglier," media critic Jon Katz told The Associated Press the day the merger was announced.

While the transaction can be viewed from a number of perspectives, one of the most interesting is to look at it as an example of the power of consumers. Both companies offered a way to get onto the Internet at a time that millions of consumers wanted to do just that. But their business models were very different.

AOL made it very easy for people to get onto its private network, but charged them for it. It cost nothing (other than a subscription to an Internet Service Provider, or ISP) to surf the Net with Netscape, but it was harder to get online the first time. Ultimately, while AOL's paid network services grew, Netscape's one-time monopoly of the browser market eroded to the point that it was forced to merge with a larger company.

The story began in 1993 when a University of Illinois student named Marc Andreesen created a program called Mosaic, which he promptly gave away over the Internet. Mosaic was a key that unlocked the potential of the World Wide Web, the brainchild of Tim Berners-Lee. Suddenly, this obtuse worldwide network that had been the private domain of technophiles and the education and defense establishments was an easily accessible public network on which anyone—that's very important: ANYONE—could publish any information they wanted and make it available immediately to anyone else anywhere in the world.

And he gave it away. Imagine that.

Andreesen joined up with Silicon Valley veteran Jim Clark to start a company called Mosaic. The company became Netscape Communications Corp. and went public in an offering that made both men, and many of the start-up's employees, rich beyond their dreams. Still, Netscape struggled to find a business model.

First it tried to sell software to companies so that they could develop products for the Web that would be best viewed through Netscape's browser. It tried charging for new versions of the browser, although test versions of its even-better products were still available for free. Netscape then turned to the business market, hoping to cash in on the surging demand for so-called intranets.

Meanwhile, Microsoft had been ignoring the Internet during the early 1990s as if it was just another CB radio craze. But it suddenly woke from a deep slumber in December 1995 and announced it would spend $2 billion on developing products for the Internet, including its own browser called Internet Explorer.

Three thousand miles away, AOL had built a private dial-up network that was derided by Internet aficionados. It had become extremely popular with new computer users, however, because of its simplicity of use. AOL was marketed with flawless precision, with access disks packed with new computers, stuffed into computer magazines, and jammed into mailboxes across North America and much of Europe.

AOL was very user-friendly. Anyone who could follow the instructions to insert a disk or CD into their computer could install AOL in minutes and then sign up for service following extremely simple on-screen instructions.

Finally, AOL did something very clever: It *talked*. It was corny—so silly that AOL critics made it a running joke—but when you signed onto AOL, the network said "Welcome!" And on a really happy day, you also heard: "You've got mail!"

Alas, Netscape never said a word. Worse, the techno-elitist Netscape crowd never quite realized how difficult it was for the average person to figure out how to

- buy the right type of computer,
- sign up for Internet access through some poorly advertised ISP,
- install the ISP's program and adjust the computer's parameters,
- learn to use the Internet without formal instruction, presumably a browser supplied by the ISP, and
- somehow download Netscape's browser over the Internet and set that as the default browser for that computer.

For a population that couldn't program a VCR clock, the technical obstacles to using Netscape's e-mail was comparable to learning Russian without a tutor.

MICROSOFT'S ROLE

AOL continued adding millions of subscribers and collecting billions of dollars in revenue while Netscape's fans laughed. Microsoft, meanwhile, produced a very good browser and began giving away its own product, packing it with new computers just like AOL had, but offering its own nationwide access service as a gateway to the Internet.

Because almost all new personal computers already came with Microsoft's Windows operating system, they now also came with Internet Explorer. Then AOL adopted Internet Explorer as its "default" browser, signaling the beginning of the end for Netscape.

Netscape then attempted yet another business model, trying to become an ad-supported online network. It developed a large audience, but competition from other Web portals, notably Yahoo!, stood in Netscape's way. It was too late. Netscape was doomed.

The end result was that a company that started out by giving away a great product was bought by an industry titan that had always charged for its own service.

In the end, the fate of Netscape didn't hinge on its technology, which was excellent. It was determined by consumers who shunned the difficult-to-use Netscape model in favor of the everything's-done-for-you simplicity of America Online.

That same philosophy is bound to dominate as AOL moves into the cable TV and content arenas through the merger with Time Warner. The new company, AOL Time Warner, will make it very simple for tens of millions of Americans to switch to broadband Internet service through AOL.

It comes down to this: It no longer matters if a company has 100 percent of the market share. It doesn't matter if the company's motivation is altruistic or commercial. It doesn't even matter whether its technology is more advanced than a competitor's. What matters is that the company's leaders recognize the power of consumers and serve them to the fullest extent possible. If they do that, the company will prosper. Any merchant that doesn't, won't be a merchant very long.

CHAPTER 2

REAL-TIME MEDIA
Then and Now

One of the most intriguing things about working in the news business, particularly at a wire service, is that you know about events as soon as they happen. So it was at The Associated Press (AP), where I spent the 1980s. When an earthquake hit Mexico, I watched the bulletins come in. When John Lennon was murdered, I knew it in minutes. When jets crashed, or a pitcher hurled a no-hitter, or a big merger was announced, we heard about it first.

You also had more information. In addition to the 30 or 40 stories you might see in the local paper, the AP puts out thousands of other stories that most people outside the media never see. And while there might be a dozen or so stories in a newspaper's business section, PR Newswire and BusinessWire published thousands of company announcements each day, including hundreds with market-moving potential.

I'd see these stories long before most of my fellow citizens. I felt privileged—past tense. That privilege no longer belongs to a few thousand people working in the media. It belongs to all of us, thanks to the Internet. And it's only the first stage of a media revolution that will change the way we live our daily lives.

Welcome to the world of real-time media, a world we've been orbiting for more than a century. We've had real-time one-to-one long-distance communication since the telegraph. The telephone refined that and added a human voice. The radio allowed instant one-way communication with large audiences, and the TV added picture to the sound. We're all familiar with the social impacts those media have had.

But now we have something new: a way for many people to *interact* with many other people—or with just one person—with print, images, sound, and/or moving pictures. Initially, that means people have the power to pick and choose what they want to read from myriad sources. Eventually, those choices will expand dramatically and include multimedia products like interactive television.

The Internet is the most significant advance in mass communications since Gutenberg invented his press. But its long-term impact remains largely unknown. When we wonder about how quickly the Net will be fully integrated in our lives, and how it will enhance our power, it's helpful to look at the way similar technologies developed.

In the early 1990s, industry gurus spun romantic visions of how we'd all be zipping along the "information superhighway" by 1997. These folks weren't wrong about much except the time of arrival for certain technologies, such as the ability to interact with real-time TV images. Within a few years, you'll be able to change the camera angle while watching a basketball game online as you can today with DVD technology.

We are moving steadily toward such advances, but at a leisurely walk rather than a quick gallop—and that shouldn't be surprising. It took many years for the public and corporate interests to warm up to radio, TV, and then color TV, so we should expect a moderate transition to the Internet, and that's just what we're seeing.

With the cost of advanced personal computers now well below $1,000, and the number of sophisticated online attractions growing at a frantic rate, it appears clear this is not a fleeting craze like CB radio. This is here to stay, just like the printing press, telegraph, telephone, radio, and TV. And just like those other media, the Internet and its interactive successors will empower consumers by changing the way we all work, play, vote, learn, and live.

Later in this chapter, we'll look at some of the impacts of this new medium. First, let's look into the past to see how carefully society adapts to new technologies.

THE TELEGRAPH

Samuel Morse sent his first telegraph messages in 1837. The first actual telegram wasn't sent for another seven years, an excellent example of how long it takes for technology to move from the lab to practical use. Of course, the first devices had little resemblance to the machines we see in the train stations of old cowboy movies. Morse's problem was that his telegraph had a range of only about 15–20 miles. (Today we call this problem scalability.) Soon it became obvious you could extend the range by creating relays.

A second problem with early telegraphy was it could only send one message at a time—the dits and dots would get mixed up if two messages were sent at once. (In today's world, this problem is known as a lack of bandwidth.) Other inventors, including Thomas Edison, came up with ways to send messages in both directions, and to increase the number that could be sent simultaneously—a process still known as multiplexing.

In the ensuing decades, telegraphy evolved, particularly with the widespread use of microwave transmissions following World War II and the emergence of facsimile systems—the precursor to the modern fax—that allowed the transmission of images and documents.

So it was more than a century after Morse sent his first transmission that telegraphy became a communication system widely used by average citizens for sending urgent messages, birth announcements, and so on. Of course, by then, it was possible to speak to someone over the phone or to hear important news over a radio.

The telegraph had a powerful impact on the stock market, government, defense, and other social sectors with access to it. It delivered information in real time to many points at the same time—the first medium beyond devices like smoke signals or jungle drums capable of doing that. It meant that an investor could learn of a business deal and buy into the stock before the news became widespread. It meant a government could learn immediately that enemy forces were attacking. But for most ordinary consumers, it remained a novelty that was never incorporated into their day-to-day lives.

THE RADIO

Until the Internet, I would argue the radio was the most important advance in mass communications since the printing press. That is probably one reason why the name Marconi is written into every grade school history book. But any reader who can say when Marconi sent his transmission, and what the nature of that broadcast was, deserves a gold star. It was 1894 and Marconi sent a wireless telegraph—not a human voice. Like Morse, he had a limited range; the first signals went just a mile or so. Improvements to his system, however, came much more rapidly than Morse's. By 1899, Marconi had beamed a signal across the English channel. Two years later, he sent a signal from England to Newfoundland.

But when did voice transmissions begin? Radio as we know it today really began in 1906 when Reginald Fessenden broadcast his voice on a wireless telegraph on Christmas Eve, quite to the astonishment of wireless telegraphers who heard it loud and clear. Fessenden's fame never came close to that of Marconi, who received a Nobel prize. Though it may not have had the scientific impact of Marconi's work, Fessenden's contribution had a far greater social impact. In geek-speak, the sound of a human voice was the "killer ap" of radio, the application that made the radio a must-have technology for tens of millions of people.

Even so, a decade passed before David Sarnoff would go to his superiors at the American Marconi Company and try to convince them that there was a consumer market for radio devices. By then, thousands of "early adopters" had made their own radios from crude antennas, ground wires, and a piece of crystal. My father, then a small boy, used to recall fondly how his family got a primitive crystal radio set and put the earphone in a ceramic bowl to amplify the sound. They'd sit around the bowl to hear the sound while tuning the crystal with the help of a straight pin. What they heard was the sound of amateur broadcasts from radio pioneers (communications similar to some of the early, noncommercial Web sites).

One of the pioneers was an engineer named Frank Conrad, who used to play Victrola recordings over the air. Not only was Conrad among the first disc jockeys, but in 1920 he became the first radio newscaster by announcing the election of Warren Harding as president on a transmitter he built for his employer, Westinghouse Electric Corporation. Five million radios were sold by 1926 and Congress established the Federal Radio Commission—precursor to the FCC—a year later.

Networks formed. Entertainers became superstars. By 1930, 24 years after Fessenden made history, radio was ubiquitous. Comedy and music helped the world struggle through the Depression. On December 7, 1941, Franklin Roosevelt delivered the most dramatic radio broadcast in history with his "day of infamy" announcement that Pearl Harbor had been attacked by Japan. For the first time in history, within seconds millions of people learned their nation was at war. Radio had gone from a national craze to an indispensable technology that is as vital today as it was then. There are still a surprising number of homes in the United States that don't have a telephone, but it's extremely difficult to find a family without a radio.

Alas, radio has its limits. Again, bandwidth is a limitation; there are only so many programs that will fit on the frequencies available to the public. Also, with the exception of call-in talk shows, which actually reflect the marriage of the two communications media, radio and telephone, the mass market radio networks aren't interactive.

So while radio has enormous social power, that power at least initially was concentrated in the hands of the broadcasters, who chose what to air. Eventually, consumers gained small shares of that power by tuning in programming they liked and tuning out programs they didn't like.

This level of control is somewhat comparable to the ability today for Web surfers to leave a site if it doesn't please them, but there are critical differences. For one thing, radio offers a limited range of frequencies available to the public while the Internet knows no such bounds. For another, it requires governmental approval to broadcast legally, but there is no legal restriction on publishing on the Web (aside from prohibiting child pornography or certain other types of antisocial behavior, and even those laws are difficult to enforce). Finally, consolidation of media has left some large media chains in control of several radio stations within a single market, further limiting consumer control of the medium. That is something that can't happen on the Internet because, even as large media organizations produce programming, countless other alternatives will continue to be available and the technology to create them is becoming cheaper day by day.

Anyone can become a Frank Conrad on the Net, and hundreds of thousands of people already have by creating their own Web sites. Small businesses have generated big revenue by recognizing the commercial potential of the Internet.

Large U.S. corporations were painfully slow to recognize the potential of radio. Remember, it was 26 years between the time of Marconi's first wireless telegraph and Conrad's announcement of the Harding victory. Similarly, it was 25 years from the inception of the Internet before the first large-scale commercial Web site opened.

TELEVISION

In 1927, the same year the Federal Radio Commission was born, Philo Farnsworth developed a new type of vacuum tube that became the heart of television and erased much of the remaining skepticism about the practicality of transmitting images via radio waves. A year later, the first broadcast took place in upstate New York, although few people saw it.

But it would be a very long 11 years later that RCA debuted a prototype of TV at the New York World's Fair of 1939. And the all-consuming war that followed delayed the arrival of television on the mass market until 1945—18 years after Farnsworth's discovery—when it took off with the same sort of frenzy we see today over the Internet. By 1948, government regulators grew so concerned about the growth that they stopped issuing new licenses for stations.

The ban lasted four years, but there was no stopping TV. A decade after the end of World War II, two-thirds of American households had televisions. By the mid-1960s, the figure was about 95 percent. Today, about 97 percent of U.S. households have a television, and the average family watches seven hours of TV a day.

After a half-century of broadcasting, TV is still heavily criticized for failing to reach its potential. Instead of unlocking the doors to the world's greatest performing arts, education, information about health, and other social benefits, it is cluttered with mindless sitcoms, bloody police dramas, talk shows that appeal to the lowest common denominator, and reruns of reruns of reruns.

While hardly anyone with a grain of self-respect would say they think TV programming is high in quality, the truth is that these programs wouldn't be on if we didn't watch them. When publicly owned TV stations broadcast a classical concert, hardly anyone watches. But when "Seinfeld" goes off the air, it gets more press coverage than the death of a former president.

The United States has already started a transition from analog TV signals to digital, an evolution that will be complete by 2006. What does that mean? Well, it means that by 2006, a TV will really be a computer that downloads signals much the way a personal computer does today—reading data in digits of 0 and 1 instead of wavelengths. It also means that consumers will have the potential to pull down any programming available, including anything from the Internet. Instead of choosing from four VHF networks, a few UHF stations, and a poorly funded public broadcast, viewers will have a virtually unlimited choice of programming from "Frank Conrads" around the world. The technical quality of that programming will range from the amateurish to the highly professional. I believe, however, that viewers will be guided more by their personal preferences than by technical glitz, just as millions of people today choose to watch static Web pages instead of moronic TV shows that have higher technical quality.

If the Internet today were merely the haven for a handful of intellectuals, political extremists, and such, it would be a poor indicator of things to come. But, as we've discussed, there are already tens of millions of people using the Internet and showing interest in an extremely broad range of subjects—personal finance, news, and myriad special interests ranging from bicycling to crocheting to alternative medicines. Yes, there is also mass interest in sex, computer games, risqué chat rooms, and commercial media icons. So be it. Consumers are now in control of what they want to see.

THE INTERNET AND THE FUTURE

My good friend Eric Benson caught my interest with something he said in the early 1990s when the investment community was abuzz with talk of the information superhighway. He scoffed: "The information superhighway is already here! It's called the Internet."

Though I wasn't so sure at the time, Eric knew whereof he spoke, and he's done well with the knowledge. He later went to work for Netscape and, just as that company reached its peak, he and his wife—who also worked for Netscape—quit to help start an online bookstore called Amazon.com.

Other real-time media have spawned vast business opportunities, of course. The telegraph gave birth to Western Union. The telephone begat Ma Bell. The radio gave us RCA. And the television brought forth the networks.

The Net is likely to have much broader impacts because it is the first real-time mass medium that also offers interactivity on an individual level. So far, the Internet has given birth to a few huge companies, notably Amazon, Yahoo!, and AOL. But that is only a first step in a dance that eventually will include virtually every company doing business today. It's already clear that the telephone companies, TV networks, cable giants, radio companies, and most major technology companies—from chips to computers to software—are scrambling to find their niche in a brave new world of interactive media. When they're finished, all bets will be off. The Net will change the nature of profit margins, competition, service, employment, real estate, and virtually every other aspect of doing business today.

Princeton University economist Burton Malkiel, the author of one of my perennially favorite books on investment, "A Random Walk down Wall Street," said of the interactive future: "I think there's no question that we are in the middle of an information revolution that is probably as important as the industrial revolution of the last century. I don't think there's any question about that."

One of the most curious observers of the current revolution is none other than Federal Reserve chairman Alan Greenspan, who for years has generously credited technology for contributing to the economic conditions for which he and the other Fed governors are frequently given thanks. In one speech, for example, Greenspan talked about the impact of technology for improving productivity in everything from modern medicine to agriculture. "The newest innovations, which we label information technologies, have begun to alter the manner in which we do business and create value, often in ways not readily foreseeable even five years ago," he said.

This is potent stuff. Let's look at just one factor of value: profit growth. Productivity improvements generate greater profits. As the chairman pointed out, in the mid-1990s analysts surveyed by the Institutional Brokers Estimate System predicted profit growth of about 11 percent. A comparable group surveyed five years later predicted profit growth of 13.5 percent. Nowhere is this being seen more dramatically than in technology, where the year-over-year profit growth rate is three to four times faster.

Even so, you'll rarely find an economist who's completely sold on the power of the Internet. Most Net-based companies are years away from turning a profit. And it's difficult to find a direct link between Web technologies and productivity gains. Even Greenspan, in the same speech, threw a bucket of cold water on the technology bonfire.

"I do not say we are in a new era, because I have experienced too many alleged new eras in my lifetime that have come and gone," he said. "We are far more likely, instead, to be experiencing a structural shift similar to those that have visited our economy from time to time in the past."

That structural shift will pay the greatest dividends to consumers. The clearest illustration I can think of has to do with books. You may recall that giant book chains grew in the mid-1990s, threatening smaller merchants by offering books at prices well below their suggested retail price. Amazon did them one better. Because it had much lower overhead costs—more comparable to a mail-order house than a brick-and-mortar retailer— Amazon was able to slash prices by up to 40 percent. A week before the barnesandnoble.com initial public offering in spring 1999, Amazon cut the price of *New York Times* bestsellers to 50 percent of the cover price.

So what happens when a Web startup with even lower overhead than Amazon decides to cut prices by 60 percent, as Books-a-Million did a week or so later? Price competition is inevitable on the Web as the number of competitors rise and the price of technology falls, and the end result is a razor-thin profit margin—perhaps as small as 1 or 2 percent, like the margin we see today in the food retailing industry, instead of the 40 to 60 percent markup one traditionally associates with bookstores.

Or, as Malkiel put it: "What Economics 101 teaches you is when there's perfect competition, when anyone can get into the market, profit margins shrink to just about zero."

This is terrific for consumers, *particularly* in the short term. It means that the price of a book that would have sold for $30 could fall 60 percent to just $12. That is a *permanent* reduction in the profit margin. After that short-term shift, the price then will start to rise again over the longer term. And that's probably why Greenspan—the sworn enemy of inflation—says he expects old patterns to reemerge over time. Similarly, the productivity gains related to the Net will become part of a new and predictable structure, creating a sense of normalcy over time and returning us to traditional methods of valuing securities.

WEB PROFITS

We talked about the price of books dropping in the short term. That's not all. Virtually anything that can be sold over the Net has seen similar price reductions. That includes shampoo, CDs, airline tickets, some types of clothing, and myriad other items.

Some things won't see a dramatic price reduction, and probably won't sell well over the Net. What about cars? If you know you want a forest green, two-door Saturn with a tan interior, you can order it over the Web. You probably can recall that TV commercial where a college student in a dorm orders his Saturn that way and has it delivered to his dorm room like a pizza. You shouldn't expect the price of the car to drop 60 percent. Saturn is still going to get as much for the car as it did before, you're still going to have to pay for transporting the car from the plant

31

to your town, and the dealer is still going to take a cut. So the biggest costs are fixed.

As Saturn does in the commercial, you can compare it to a pizza. The pizza costs the same, whether you have it in the restaurant or in your house. The overhead associated with staffing a dining room is transferred to the overhead of delivering the pizza. So you won't see a big price shift there, either.

I already mentioned the razor-thin margin on groceries in supermarkets. So you have to ask yourself if a can of soup can be cheaper delivered to your door than on a grocer's shelf. And there are some groceries that many folks would rather go pick out by themselves—fruit, meat, and vegetables, for example. Even so, the enormous convenience of having food delivered to your home is likely to become a very popular feature.

Many services, notably financial services and medicine, are likely to change dramatically because of the Web. Your TV could become the bank of the future, helping you with any transaction except dispensing cash. But then, you'll probably use a lot less cash in the future anyway. And you probably will be able to add a cash-like credit to a "cash card" or e-wallet—a device you can carry with you to pay for a newspaper or a dozen eggs at the market. If you want to buy or sell securities, well, we've already seen an enormous growth in e-brokers, and that trend is very likely to continue as exchanges move toward a 24-hour trading day.

Medical care also is likely to change when you can consult an online questionnaire to determine what's ailing you. A computer may not be able to match the bedside manner of a good physician, but it probably can help to make sure that all alternatives have been considered before a diagnosis is made.

There are many other services that I believe will remain in traditional settings, from car repair to education. But even these can be augmented online. The Net can help a teacher prepare a teaching plan, or can help a mechanic obtain the schematic diagram for a 20-year-old carburetor.

The bottom line here is that the success of retailing and services on the Web will vary from product to product depending on the existing profit margin on the product and the distribution of costs associated with its manufacture, display, and delivery.

POLITICS

Where does your senator stand on gun control? On abortion? On taxes? Do you often take time to sit down and write to your representatives in Congress, or on the state assembly, or down at city hall?

How easy is it for you to check the fund-raising records of the politicians on your ballot? Would you vote more often if you could do it on your television?

These are just some of the questions that should run through your mind as you ponder the Internet's potential impact on politics. To be sure, it would take an enormous change in social attitude to get citizens to take an active role in politics online. But, from time to time, we have seen massive social movements start with a single person like Rosa Parks or Mahatma Gandhi. Imagine the impact the Internet could have—for good or bad—in mobilizing like-minded people.

In the meantime, I have to think candidates today are either silly or have something to hide if they don't create a Web site that clearly describes their positions on key issues or provides an e-mail link so that constituents can express opinions easily, perhaps even engaging in a dialog. For hot issues, the Web offers the potential of conducting an online "town hall" meeting (although the real-life version probably remains a better venue than cyberspace for dissecting complex, emotional issues).

On a higher level, there is the two-edged sword of how instant communications could affect global politics. On the hopeful side, improved communications should help the world avoid many crises. Certainly the Web has the effect of "shrinking" the world, of driving home the message that we are all the same no matter who we are or what country we happen to call home. By providing competing viewpoints, it can help diffuse some of the propaganda put out by one government to sell its policies to a gullible public. And it can serve as a forum for protest that has a far lower potential for violence than the traditional form of street protest.

The downside is that the Web is instantaneous, and rage can be spread around the world in milliseconds. As more nations gain the technologies of mass destruction—chemical, biological, and atomic weapons—there are times when a "cooling off" period might be preferable to the idea of an immediate, public confrontation. When U.S. war planes dropped bombs on the Chinese consulate in Belgrade, there was an almost immediate outpouring of rage from within China, including violent demonstrations outside U.S. buildings. The Internet will not only enhance the distribution of images like those, but may create a tier of semipro media in which the reporting is done by groups with less interest in good journalism and a larger interest in promoting an agenda.

ENTERTAINMENT

Entertainment is such a big part of our leisure time that it's worthwhile to offer a sneak preview of how the Internet is likely to alter that part of our lives. In short, the difference is choice, bandwidth allowing. But what does that mean?

The Web opens up thousands of new possibilities. Suddenly, you can get programming—relatively crude for now, but improving—in virtually any language from anywhere in the world. And this trend is likely to grow dramatically *if* two things happen:

1. The broadcaster must find a motivation to deliver the programming. Most broadcasts today are supported by commercials directed to a target audience. With a global broadcast, this will be difficult because products may not be available in different areas, or may go by different brand names. For example, a consumer may have a hard time finding, say, Budweiser beer in Germany. Of course, the broadcaster may want to beam out

the show for some other altruistic reason, like education. But there must be some motivation.

2. There must be adequate bandwidth to deliver the messages that broadcasters want to send and consumers want to receive. The lack of bandwidth could continue to be a limiting factor for the Web just as it has been for the wireless telegraph, telephone, radio, and TV. While it's widely assumed by most corporations that adequate bandwidth will be available, history offers many reasons to question that belief. Data-intensive applications, like interactive multimedia programming, will gobble up available bandwidth rapidly. While there are plans to create more bandwidth, it does not yet exist.

The question of creating adequate bandwidth for Web applications is comparable to the growth of the auto industry in the 1950s when there was a general assumption there would always be enough highways. That was before words like "traffic jam" and "gridlock" existed.

Without adequate bandwidth, we can't achieve true real-time media, now or ever.

CHAPTER 3

GADGETS
The Future and Getting There

You've seen those cell phones that are about half the size of Capt. Kirk's communicator. Although we're still a couple of centuries away from the maiden voyage of the Starship Enterprise, Motorola figured out long ago that anyone who's ever seen Star Trek wants one of those darn things. So, right now, you can own one. Oh, you might have a bit of trouble reaching Mr. Spock when he's beyond Earth's radiation belt, but it works just fine, say, between San Francisco and Paris.

It's pretty hard to say where we'll go from here, and it's hard even to know what more we might possibly want. But this much is certain: We're going to see smaller, cheaper gizmos in the years ahead and the best of them—including cell phones— will connect with the Internet. We're rapidly gaining the bandwidth that will allow these devices to work efficiently. We're also going to see the expansion of software to give us intangible tools to manipulate Web information to our advantage. We'll have robotic "steam shovels" to do our digging for us in the vast universe of data on the Internet. All of this will give the consumer tremendous power to access information, find bargains, and interact in real time with merchants and other "netizens" around the world through written words, the spoken voice, and visual contact.

There is no crystal ball to give us a list of what we'll have in the future. Many have tried to do so and ended up looking foolish. Instead, we'll suggest some possibilities of how we may tap into the Internet through small, cheap, ubiquitous, and frighteningly intelligent devices and software. If enough of us want these things, someone will almost certainly make them. And if they make them, we will want them.

First, we need to get a sense of our momentum going forward, for this instant is only a link in a long, long chain that began 40 years ago. Maybe you've seen pictures of the early computers from back in the 1950s and 1960s. Some of us saw them in person. Somewhere back around 1962, my father brought me along to the bank where he worked one day and proudly showed off the latest thing in technology. It was a computer that, I was told, could do the work of several people and would work around the clock. The vacuum-tube beast filled a room the size of a typical classroom. An array of noisy fans dissipated the heat. It cost more than $100,000—a fortune at that time.

It's frightening to think that was state of the art in computing at the time of the Cuban missile crisis. It's amazing to think we somehow stumbled onto the moon later that same decade when NASA scientists still used slide rules for most calculations.

I'm writing this book on a 200-megahertz computer that is almost immeasurably superior to that old clunker in my father's bank. It sits on my desk and cost $2,000. Two years after I got that machine, I bought a three-pound subnotebook computer that is more powerful than my desktop computer but costs less than half as much.

There are now wireless computers the size of a book that give you instant access to personalized Web services like your stock portfolio or the local weather from anywhere.

What we've seen over the past few decades is the shadow of that well-known principle called Moore's Law, named for Intel Corporation founder Gordon Moore. In 1965, Moore noted the number of transistors on a semiconductor chip doubled every 18 to 24 months. According to Intel, that has meant a 3,200-fold increase during the final quarter of the twentieth century. At the same time, the price of all that processing power has tumbled to the point where a Pentium II chip with 7.5 million transistors costs less than a night in a good hotel. This puts tremendous computing power into the hands of consumers.

TOMORROWLAND

Where are we going? We're heading onto the Internet and taking Moore's Law along for the ride. Once again, consumers are gaining enormous amounts of power.

"This force has the potential to create even more change than the industrial revolution did at the turn of the century," Dr. David Roddy wrote in a 1999 research report for Deloitte Consulting entitled "The New Economics of Transactions." "The consequences of Moore's Law's impact on the capabilities and pricing of personal computers will now extend even further via the Internet."

It's worthy to note at this point that no matter where we end up, virtually every major technology company in the world— Intel, Microsoft, IBM, Novell, Oracle, AT&T, MCI Worldcom, you name it—is focusing its research and development effort on the Internet and related technologies. That's happening for a simple reason: Whatever advances are made in computers and software over the next decade or two, they'll be meaningless if they aren't tied to other computers over a universal medium such as the Internet.

Why is networking so important? Remember what we said about interactivity. We are social beings. We need to interact. And you can't interact with others without a network. And, even if it undergoes substantial refinement or expansion in the future, the Internet represents the concept of the universal network.

Paradoxically, the thing that makes the Internet such a powerful tool for the individual is the number of other people using it. Hence, the power of the Internet rises as it adds users, and as access to the network gets faster. As modem speeds rise, individuals can download information from the Net more rapidly. As processor speeds pass 600 megahertz, all that information could be processed more rapidly. As software like browsers and operating systems became more efficient, that information could be displayed in a fraction of the time it used to take. All of this adds to the power of consumers.

Competition in the technology arena will continue to drive further improvements in all these elements. Technologists generally agree there is no end in sight to this trend. Plus, one of the most remarkable things about technology is the fact that it can leapfrog into the future with the help of a breakthrough, Moore's Law of computing power notwithstanding. For example, if researchers develop a better way to compress audio signals, you'll be able to download better quality sound in real time. The development of CD-ROMs made it possible to store the contents of a dozen floppy disks on one cheap piece of plastic.

Novell, which has been struggling for many years to fend off competitive challenges from Microsoft, may be in the midst of another leap. The company has long held an advantage in a software technology called directory services, which is something like a telephone directory that a computer uses to find information. But Novell is pursuing a strategy that would place the directory in the service of an individual using the Internet, essentially displacing the need for search engines or smart browsers.

Look at it this way: Today, an individual who wants to get information from the Internet generally logs on through a personal computer that must then be configured to personal specifications. If that person uses another computer, the procedure must be repeated. This is because it is the computer, not the individual, that connects to the network. Novell is trying to organize the directory around the individual instead of the computer. That means that someone could use any computer anywhere to connect to the Internet and instantly would have access to all their personal information and customized applications. Instead of carrying around a PDA with one set of data, a cell phone with another, and a laptop with a third, a traveler could simply log onto the Internet from a computer built into an airline seat or from a customer's office to check e-mail, retrieve a report, or check confidential inventory data.

This would almost certainly lead to having computers available almost everywhere, much the way public phones are available today. When you leave your home today, you leave your phone on your desk, knowing that wherever you go, you'll be able to find a phone if you need one. The same could soon be true for computers.

WIRELESS FREEDOM

Your cell phone also will give you access to a wide array of services on the Net. You can already call Paris while riding on a ferry across San Francisco Bay. What could be better? Well, what if the phone spoke French? Voice recognition software is already available that will allow you to dictate reports to your computer. Now that technology is being combined with translation software to allow people to speak to and understand one another, even if they speak different languages.

This isn't necessarily an application that must go through the Internet. It could just as easily go through a satellite system or traditional ground-based phone network. But the argument for using the Internet as a low-cost channel for telecommunications is compelling: Anyone can connect to the Internet from almost anywhere and the quality of audio communications is rapidly rising to a quality above the capabilities of the human ear. Why would anyone want to place a direct call to Paris when you could connect that call at a fraction of the cost through your local Internet service provider?

After you get off the phone from Paris, you might need to send an e-mail. But instead of using a wireless modem and typing the message out on a keyboard, you can just call your computer, have it read new messages to you, and you can dictate any messages you'd like to send. All at the cost of a local call.

Motorola deputy CEO Fred Tucker assured investors at a 1999 Minneapolis stock conference that the company is hard at work developing the "third-generation" cell phone that combines voice and data. While the company is anxious to avoid conflicting phone standards that plagued the first two generations, Tucker said Motorola will make the phones for multiple standards if necessary because it can't pass up the opportunity to provide any kind of communications from anywhere at any time. "The Internet is changing everything and forcing the convergence of voice and data," he said.

WHERE'S THE MONEY?

The Net's also changing the very nature of money—or we should say e-money—because you may not need much cash in the future.

Just a few years ago, I had to go to the bank every week or so to withdraw some cash so that I could pay for groceries, gas for my car, and go out to a movie on Friday night. Today I can easily pay for all that with my ATM or credit card. Soon, I'll be able to pay for it from my e-wallet.

The e-wallet concept under development throughout the '90s and already used commonly in many parts of Europe, allows you to store a small amount of cash on a credit card like device. Then you can scan it at the market, the movie theatre, or just to buy a paper. Because there is no actual cash involved, you would be able to replenish your card by accessing your bank account over the Internet from anywhere in the world. Just as counterfeiters are expanding their craft with the help of color copiers and laserprinters, other technologies are coming close to making cash obsolete.

We've already seen basic e-wallets in the form of phone cards and debit cards. Phone cards, however, are usually purchased with cash and can only be used on phones. Debit cards are little more than ATM cards masquerading as an electronic check. More advanced versions will become commonplace by 2005.

E-wallets could store a lot of other information or property. For example, it might hold your address book, medical records, schedule, and other information that would be handy when you travel. Perhaps it carries a standing prescription for your eyeglasses or a medication you take regularly.

Or, let's say you're heading to San Francisco from New York on business and want to see the ballet while you're there. You simply would slide your e-wallet into your computer, purchase the tickets online, and store them in your e-wallet. When you arrive at the War Memorial Opera House the night of the show, the ticket taker would slide your e-wallet through a device and direct you to your seats.

After watching a four-act Swan Lake, you might want to grab a bite at the Hayes Street Grill, but— uh, oh—forgot to replenish the cash. No problem, the e-wallet also serves as a credit or debit card—your choice. Or you can download the cash you need from the restaurant's Net link.

BANK ON IT

Earlier I talked about the computer in my father's bank; soon we will have banks inside of our computers.

Dr. Roddy points out that the cost of banking transactions in a brick-and-mortar bank cost the bank an average of $1.07 while a transaction on an automated teller machine costs just $.27. But a transaction over the Internet would cost less than $.01. Roddy estimates the cost of reaching 10 million potential customers through branches at $900 million. He puts the cost of reaching the same market through the Internet at $1 million.

Of course, once the banks expand fully into cyberspace, they may find it a tad crowded. There are already cyberbanks that have secured a beachhead by using their lower overhead costs to offer their customers higher interest rates on savings deposits. I wonder how a traditional bank would feel about raising the rate it pays to customers just so it can compete with its e-commerce rivals?

Aside from the cyberbanks, there is another quantum leap that could possibly change everything—e-money. We talked about transferring money through the Internet, but some think this "money" will actually transform into software.

"Banks that survive in cyberspace will come to look more and more like shops of computer programmers than institutions of friendly tellers dispensing cash," said Dr. Roddy. "In fact, there seem to be no major long-term barriers to software companies becoming—or replacing—banks in this process of exchanging value to complete transactions." Roddy also mused about the possibility we might one day auction off mortgages to the highest bidder "in a way similar to those who sell Beanie Baby toys on eBay."

ON THE ROAD

The only transistors in my first car were in the radio. Today, there are more than 60 microprocessors—tiny computers—in the average new car, keeping an eye on everything from the antilock brakes to the fuel injection. Navigation systems built into cars can tell you how to get from here to there. What could be better?

Well, how about a wireless Net device built into the dashboard that—at the push of a button—can show the road ahead, the weather conditions and, oh, any movie ever made. (OK, maybe you can't watch, but the kids can, and it might keep them quiet for a while.) Is it any wonder that Bill Gates is in such a hurry to make Windows CE the dominant system for portable computers, including those in cars?

It's great fun to muse about the gadgets of the future, and most of those I mentioned are already well on their way through the research and development process. We may take many of them for granted within the next decade. And, yes, they will make you even more powerful by giving you access to cash, credit, information, and communication from anywhere at any time. But will they heat your house and cook your dinner?

Glad you asked. Let's say it's 6 PM in the middle of winter and you're still at the office. You dread driving home, walking into that cold, dark house, and facing the task of making dinner. So, instead, you use the Internet to call up your home controls, turn on the furnace, turn on the driveway and front porch lights, and place an order for a meal to be delivered at 7. Most of that is already possible, but the average person doesn't have the technical skills, the time, or the money to install the systems and learn how to use them. The only technology needed here, then, is some company to actively market such services. Some homebuilders are already teaming up with utility companies to construct homes that incorporate remote controls.

ROBOTS AND OTHER 'BOTS'

The idea of robots as physical, mechanical devices has been around even before electricity became widely available a century ago. Some futurists of the nineteenth century thought they would run on steam. Robotic manufacturing equipment has learned to perform many factory jobs, ranging from making cookies to welding an automobile together. But somehow, I doubt we'll see many robots running around our living rooms in the near future, except as amusements.

Why? Because they're silly. Why would you need a robot when virtually everything in your house is a computer connected to the Internet? If you could turn off the TV upstairs simply by asking the computer to do so, why would you need a robot to do that? We already have washing machines, dishwashers, garbage disposals, trash compactors, and a number of other devices to simplify our labor. But I suspect we'll stick with those fixed-place devices and a few others like them for a long while—a quarter century or so—before someone comes up with a device that can stack the dishes, put the wet clothes in the dryer, or fry eggs on the stove. Even R2-D2 couldn't do that.

While there may be no need for *physical* robots, there is clearly a vast potential for *software* robots that can travel rapidly through cyberspace doing tasks for us. These "bots," or intelligent agents, as they are sometimes called, could take care of a great deal of our personal business far more efficiently than we could do it ourselves. For example, let's say you're hoping to find the left taillight for a 1939 Cadillac Sedan de Ville. You could search the Web, but it would take quite a while and your search would likely be incomplete. Moreover, if someone posted such a part for sale just after you completed your search, you wouldn't know it. But if you station a bot in cyberspace and authorize it to buy such a part for you at up to $100 in e-money, it could wait until the part becomes available, conduct the transaction, have the part shipped to you, and notify you of when to expect delivery.

While many people enjoy shopping, I cannot say I am one of them. So I look forward to the day when my bot can study the likes and dislikes of some of my close friends, then cruise the malls during the holiday season to see if there's anything they might like. Of course, in that case, I'd like to get a list of suggestions and make the final decisions myself.

Bots can enhance your personal power, but they can also challenge it. For example, the IRS—if it ever upgrades to faster computers—could use bots to keep track of e-commerce transactions, find delinquent taxpayers, and even block shipments until taxes are paid. It is very likely the U.S. government will use such technologies to keep track of e-commerce, given the difficulty in determining exactly where a particular transaction took place. States could also use bots to find out if they are owed state sales taxes on the purchases.

Theoretically, bots could talk and even take on physical manifestations on the computer screen so you feel like you're speaking to a friend or dedicated servant instead of a piece of software. Technology forecaster Paul Saffo, who we'll speak to later in the book, has a phone system that does that and also schedules his appointments and tracks him down for urgent calls.

Macromedia, which makes software for creating multimedia programs, launched a virtual machine on its Web site, www.shockwave.com, that could store and play any of the multimedia snippets found on the site—cartoons, greeting cards, video games, etc. The machine, which costs $20, is really a software interface that connects the customer to software stored on a server. However, from the user's perspective, the machine looks like a kind of rotary juke box. In essence, it's a robot-like device that doesn't need to exist physically. The user really is paying $20 to store and access data. But the illusion is that they are buying a machine that will do that for them.

MOMENTUM AND INNOVATION

What is it that makes some futuristic visions so plausible and others so untenable? It's momentum. We have been heading in the same direction for about four decades. We started with giant stand-alone computers and soon added "dumb" terminals to create a network. We built personal computers and soon created local and dial-up networks so that they could communicate. Finally, we adapted the Internet so it could distribute text, sound, and graphical images in a manner comparable to applications running on a LAN, or local area network.

Why have we always wanted a network? Because, while many of us feel stress in crowds, we like to be *near* other people. Occasionally we may relish solitude, but most of us don't like being completely alone for long periods. This is reflected in the things we create. A computer network allows you to be connected even when you're "alone."

"Something about the human species is that we are fundamentally social and interactive," Trip Hawkins said when we talked about interactivity. Hawkins founded two of the world's most successful video game companies, Electronic Arts and 3DO. In effect, he's made a career out of building interactivity into software.

Hawkins spun some fantastic futuristic visions in 1993 when launching 3DO. Not all have come true, but there is nothing today that suggests they won't. One idea involved hearing some music you liked on TV, so you decide to listen to more songs by the group. Then you decide you want a CD, so you buy it. And the site where you buy it says, "Oh, by the way, here's another group you might like. And did you know that group is coming to your town? If you'd like to buy tickets, we can sell them to you now."

Those things are possible today—if you have enough computing power and bandwidth. It still requires a fairly complicated system, but—remember Moore's Law—the capabilities of such systems are growing geometrically and their costs drop every day. That 3,200-fold increase in performance over the past 26 years will become a 6,400-fold increase by 2001, and a 12,400-fold increase by the middle of 2003.

As for bandwidth, there are already faster options for connecting to the Internet than a 56k modem. Millions of people already receive a flood of data through cable access services like ExciteAtHome or RoadRunner. Many others receive a slightly lower grade of service through phone companies offering DSL (digital subscriber line) service.

About 65 million U.S. homes are connected to cable—a number that has held relatively stable for the past few years—and cables run past tens of millions more. Roughly 90 million U.S. homes are connected to the Internet, but only a tiny percentage can access the Net over cable. Clearly, the potential to expand access to the Internet over cable is in place. So what's holding it up?

BUILDING BANDWIDTH

Broadband cable isn't a system that can be turned on nationally with the flip of a switch. It will take years to install local systems needed to support local high-speed access to cable. It will take years to market it to the public. It will take years for consumers to acquire the type of equipment that will enhance the high-speed Net experience. And, finally, the Net itself must be upgraded continually to provide the bandwidth vital to its continued growth.

Let's look at each of those four points in more detail: (1) installing cable, (2) marketing services, (3) acquiring equipment, and (4) adding bandwidth.

Installing Cable

Installing the broadband cable system is no done deal. While the system is up and running in some small areas, early installations have been costly and somewhat experimental. The first time anything is done in technology, the cost is many times what it will be at a later date. Engineers learn a tremendous amount from initial installations.

Marketing Services to Consumers

Once the decision is made to expand, the service must be marketed to the public, which is already paying for cable TV, phone service, movie rentals, and Internet access. How much will these people be willing to pay for a broadband cable that will add high-speed Net access? And what will it cost to deliver the service to them? The difference between these two figures is the gross profit per home of high-speed Internet access service. Let's say the Browns are paying $20 a month for Net access. Would they be willing to pay twice as much for high-speed access?

Even if they are, there's a serious question about whether enough of their neighbors would also want to pay that much. It's probably not going to be worthwhile for the cable company to deliver the high-speed service to the neighborhood until enough residents agree. What's needed then is a campaign to convince large numbers of cable subscribers that they also need high-speed Net access. Cable companies are expected to approach that by bundling the Net access with other broadband services, like telephone access, delivery of movies, and interac-

49

tive games. Let's say the Browns are paying $35 a month for phone service, $25 a month to rent movies, $25 for basic cable, $20 for Net access, and an average $20 a month for video games. That's $125 a month. It also means they write at least three checks and have to spend a good amount of time running around from store to store.

What if the cable company could deliver on-demand movies, games, phone service, cable TV, *and* broadband Net access all through the cable for the same price? The Browns would pay one bill, get better Net service, and wouldn't have to go to the store to find video games or movies. From menus right on the TV they could choose from a wide variety.

This concept of unified services is the holy grail of the cable industry. It's one of the big reasons why Time Warner—maker of movies, TV shows, news products, and video games—decided to merge with Turner Communications and later AOL. Turner produces TV shows, movies, CNN, and owns a treasure trove of films. AOL is the world's largest ISP. The combined AOL Time Warner, as the nation's second largest cable network, is positioned to offer anything from Net service to your choice of movies right through a TV cable. Viacom's merger with CBS is another example of this kind of thinking, and you can expect many more marriages of programming and distribution.

But what about telephony? Are cable companies really ready to offer local phone service? Are consumers who've grown used to highly reliable telephone service ready to trade that in for phone access from a cable company? No way. Cable companies, partly due to their rapid growth over the past three decades, have never developed a reputation for reliable service. And, although most states have already cleared the way for different companies to offer local phone service, it doesn't mean any company is going to be as good at it as your current provider. Although we take it for granted, local phone service is extremely complex, requiring extensive switching operations. Cable companies would lease those operations or work with long distance carriers rather than create their own phone network, but they'd still have to switch local phone traffic into the local phone company's network or that of a competing company—even that is an awesome undertaking.

And the local phone companies, which are promoting competing broadband services, aren't making it easy. They're fighting every step of the way, in some cases charging premiums for information services and other amenities that consumers now take for granted. Lawsuits are wending their ways through federal appeals courts, but legal wheels grind slowly. And even after a court rules, implementation of the order can take years.

The good news for cable companies is that content providers will likely be eager to get their movies, video games, and other programs onto an interactive broadband cable system so that consumers can buy from home. In fact, they're likely to be so eager that they'll pay a premium to get there. That's great for the cable companies and should result in greater revenue. Today, Web portals already charge some news companies and other content vendors to put their wares in front of the public.

The result of all this is not so great for consumers. Any added costs faced by content providers will be passed along to consumers, who are already paying for the delivery system— the cable. So, if you want to watch a movie, you'll have to decide if it's cheaper and easier to get it through the cable, or to drive down the local video store and rent it. Nobody knows at this point how these cost factors will balance out, but it may be assumed the price will be as high as the market will bear. That probably means the movie will cost more over your home cable because you'll be paying for the extra convenience.

Let's assume that one day in the not-distant future, the Browns get a phone call at dinner time from the cable company saying: "Hey, folks, now you can have all these services in one cable for $125." How will the Browns react?

I've seen research conducted by the cable and phone companies that come to completely contradictory conclusions on that, so I'll leave it to you to take an educated guess. But basically, I think it will rest on whether the Browns see any compelling reason to make the change. And that's a tough sell, unless the Browns are convinced that they must have broadband Internet access.

New Equipment

The third point involves getting consumers to see a need for new equipment. Forecasters suggest public demand for broadband equipment will rise sharply by 2006 when the FCC has determined the nation will turn off all analog TV signals. That means viewers will need to have a digital TV. Given that such sets currently cost more than $1,000, and given that there are something like a half-billion working analog sets in the United States today, it's mind-boggling to think this will actually take place on the timetable set by the government. But if it does, it will provide a compelling case for consumers to acquire high-speed Net access, because the new TVs will essentially be computers, with a remote control that functions like a computer mouse.

This opens the door to a wide range of advanced Internet services that have yet to be created. Their ability to take advantage of high bandwidth means they could include full-motion video, high-fidelity sound, and graphical elements designed specifically for TV screens. These programs could include such things as:

- Video games that could be played against large numbers of opponents. The best games would probably include the ability to speak to other players over a phone-like network while playing. Less sophisticated games are already popular on narrowband Net services.
- Movies that you can watch like a film in a VCR. That is, you'll have the ability to start or stop the film, or rewind it to repeat a portion.
- Vast selections of TV-like programming, particularly sporting events. Want to go to a ballgame in Boston that isn't being broadcast for free? It'll be on your TV, for a fee.
- Shopping. The big problem with the TV home shopping now is you have to leave the TV and pick up the phone.

Interactive digital TVs will eliminate that need. Just press a button and you can buy that stunning faux pearl necklace for $112.59 right now.

Adding Bandwidth

None of this can be counted on until it appears on your TV, and you can expect to see substantial delays based on debates over access to bandwidth—our fourth factor. That's right, the same issue that delayed the adoption of virtually every other electronic medium of the past century could also delay the growth of services on the Internet.

Until now, many people assumed the Internet has virtually unlimited bandwidth, much the way most residents assume the city's water mains have all the capacity they'll ever need. Neither is true. The Internet is put together like a maze of interconnected data pipes. There are pipes going into businesses, pipes going into your home, and big pipes connecting them all. If the demand to use any of those pipes exceeds capacity, the service slows to a trickle.

Today, most of the applications built for the Web are text and graphics. These have become increasingly sophisticated thanks to advances in software and bandwidth. But the ability to design sophisticated Web pages greatly surpasses the ability to download them on the 56k to 128k modems now in common usage. So Web designers have learned that they'll serve many more pages to consumers if they keep the designs on the simple side.

As we move toward high-speed Web access, Web designers are likely to rapidly ramp up the graphical elements of their designs, including much more sophisticated graphics, video, high-quality audio, and some of the other elements we've talked about. A language translator or a complex virtual machine also require substantial bandwidth to function smoothly.

So the amount of data users will need to transmit through the Internet will rise geometrically at the same time tens of millions of new users will be moving onto the Net. Meanwhile, corporations will be demanding far more from the Net than they have in the past.

Though clearly a minority, many Net engineers believe we are heading for a clogged network. And there are only three things we can do to avoid that:

1. *Don't grow.* This alternative simply won't work because it would require people to voluntarily stay off the Net and to limit the sophistication of their Web sites. The old adage is still true: You can't stop progress.
2. *Prioritize Web usage.* Many people believe we should, in effect, turn the superhighway into a toll road, allocating bandwidth to the highest bidder.
3. *Build more bandwidth.* Obviously, if you can't provide enough water through a four-inch pipe, you could replace it with an eight-inch pipe.

Let's take a look at the idea of charging a premium for priority bandwidth. In his study for Deloitte Research, Dr. Roddy embraces this method: "Bandwidth needed for important IP (Internet protocol) transactions and IP telephony would be sold at a higher price, and the individual packets (of data) would carry the applicable information. Economists point out that such a program would not only ration demand sensibly at peak times, it also would serve as a sensible guide to (and reimbursement for) the optimal investment in additional router and connectivity capacity."

While this argument may make a good deal of sense to some Internet users, I can't think of a better way to derail the revolution taking place in cyberspace. While we have some toll roads today, I think Americans would stage another revolution if the government decided to turn the Interstate highway system into a toll system. Yet this is close to what it would be like to charge for bandwidth on the Internet.

The very thing that makes the Internet so appealing to so many millions of users is that it provides cheap access for everyone to anything on the Internet. While the service itself has nominal costs, you can "surf" there for free at any time. You can send e-mail for free at any time. If we start charging for access to bandwidth, we would remove those benefits. The result is that many people would drop off the Net, and that would, in effect, diminish the value of the Internet.

Fortunately, there are two groups working at building a bigger Web. The first is the Next Generation Internet effort, backed with $300 million in federal funding. The second effort is Internet2, a coalition of 135 universities and businesses. Both are aimed at increasing Web access speeds by up to 1,000 times using fiber-optic lines.

We started this chapter by predicting that people will want the futuristic tools and services of the Internet if they are built, and that they will be built if there is sufficient demand. Of all the futuristic elements we've talked about, bandwidth may not seem very exciting. But as we've seen over and over again during the past century, it is probably the most important.

CHAPTER 4

INTERACTIVITY
Taking Control

Have you ever watched a child play a video game like "Super Mario Brothers" or "Sonic the Hedgehog?" If so, you've probably seen a masterful display of manual dexterity and hand-to-eye coordination. Players at the advanced levels of video games typically issue 200–300 computer commands a minute, all with the idea of manipulating the action on the screen. That's roughly four commands per second.

Try to think of anything that you do that fast. For example, when you drive, you might brake, check the mirror, and turn on a turn signal within a second. When you're cooking, you might lift the lid from a pot and stir the contents. But you do those things for a second at a time, then go back to a slower pace. Imagine if you kept that pace up for a minute, for several minutes, or for hours on end. That can give you a sense of how deeply interactive a video game or other types of media can be.

Now, think about how you read a newspaper or watch TV. You might take in several words or images a second for an extended period of time—remember, the average American watches seven hours of TV a day—but you're passive. People who read books often like to think that they're "engaging their minds" more than people who watch TV, but simply reading anything is a largely passive experience.

When I worked at Electronic Arts (EA), I was fascinated by two things. First, I actually *loved* playing some video games. There was something about it that sucked me in, just like a little kid playing Super Mario. I found myself staying up half the night piloting jet fighters, or playing a round of golf at Pebble Beach, or trying to get to "the next level" in a "twitch" game like Sonic the Hedgehog. And I was 39 years old.

The second thing that fascinated me was the fact that the Nintendo generation was growing up. In our focus groups, we regularly hosted game players in their mid-20s to upper-20s. We also learned many pro baseball players took Sega game consoles on the road so they could play some of the sports games we made. When I introduced my adult friends to games like "PGA Tour Golf" and "John Madden Football," I discovered that many of them would play the games for hours in their first sitting, then want to go back and play more after a short break.

Trip Hawkins had, by that time, started the new company that would become 3DO, but he came to a company meeting at EA one day with a paperback book in his hand. He pointed out that a paperback book was a terrific piece of entertainment software. It was cheap, yet it fully engaged the imagination. It was small and portable, so that you could take it anywhere. It didn't require power or an expensive game console. It lasted for several hours, and you could read it over and over if you desired. You could even flip to your favorite parts easily—something you couldn't do at the time with most video games. What was lacking, he said, was interactivity. And that was the key to making great games.

MEDIA IMPACT

About that time, I realized what interactivity would mean to journalism. These millions of people growing up are not going to be content to sit passively in front of a TV or simply read a broadsheet newspaper. While those, too, are terrific pieces of software, people would enjoy journalism more if they could interact with the medium in the same way one interacts with Super Mario.

So I left EA, intent on pursuing the holy grail of interactive, real-time journalism and sought out kindred spirits. This led me to *Bloomberg Business News*, where Mike Bloomberg—a former head trader from Salomon Brothers—had built a computer network that allowed traders to interact with financial news and data. Bloomberg, who studied both engineering and business, realized long before anyone around him that the trading systems used on Wall Street would be far better if the traders could interact with data at a much deeper level. So, using his own cash and some capital from Merrill Lynch, he built "the Bloomberg."

Given my recent experience, I viewed the Bloomberg as something else—a sort of Nintendo machine for financial professionals. What's more, Bloomberg had started creating its own news and the company was eagerly recruiting journalists like myself. I spent the next four years as the Bloomberg correspondent in San Francisco, mostly covering the emerging interactive multimedia industry, attempts to build the information superhighway, and the effects they both were having on the struggling regional economy.

Over time, something became clear to me. As good as the Bloomberg was at providing information to the world's financial whizzes, the Internet offered a much more fertile development environment for interactive media.

As the information superhighway hype of the early 1990s faded, attention swiftly shifted to the Internet. The event that most completely convinced me that the Internet could succeed came in December 1995 when Microsoft announced it would pour $2 billion into Internet research in the coming year.

Fourteen months later, I left Bloomberg to join a tiny newsroom at Data Broadcasting Corporation as its managing editor. DBC was the leading provider of financial data to individual investors. At DBC, the newsroom was led by vice president Larry Kramer, a veteran of the *San Francisco Examiner* and the

Washington Post. Most of the tiny staff was young and green, with the notable exception of news editor Alec Davis, a veteran of UPI, and news director Thom Calandra. With Davis's dedication to style, Calandra's high energy, and my focus on real-time interactive news, we worked with DBC's engineers, trained the young writers, and designed a financial news service called DBC News, the predecessor to MarketWatch.com.

WHERE ARE WE GOING?

Some people believe the Internet will be dominated by big brands. I don't. There's too much evidence to the contrary. Amazon proved a small company can come out of nowhere and compete with industry giants. MarketWatch competes successfully with such big rivals as Microsoft Money and *The Wall Street Journal.* E-Trade and other online brokers have been so successful that Merrill Lynch and other big firms have moved to add their own online presences.

Some people believe the Internet will turn passive, like television. I don't. The Nintendo generation isn't about to sit in front of a television, and there are already more than 100 million people opting to go online instead.

The Internet is still very new. People come to it expecting— even wanting—to try new things. It's not like movies, TV, radio, newspapers, or wire services. It's a new medium with its own rules, and rule number one is that the consumer is in control.

Think about playing a video game and you'll see the human mind is capable of issuing hundreds of commands a minute while interacting with a medium. The Internet has put the control panel into the hands of the consumer. Now, however, the object of the game isn't about making Mario jump through hoops, it is to live your life more fully by constantly making choices about your health, job, wealth, education, culture, and your world.

SIM CITY

To take the video game metaphor a bit further, I believe the Internet will evolve into something like a giant game of Sim City. For those who've never played it, Sim City is a computer game developed by a company called Maxis in which you rule your own city. You decide whether to protect the environment or push a pro-business agenda. You decide where the housing should go, where the roads should go, where the fire stations should go, and so on. The simulated citizens, or sims, can move into your city, or move out. As your city becomes larger, it becomes more difficult to satisfy all the sims. So, eventually, you're likely to see the sims abandoning your city.

So it goes with the Internet. There are hundreds of thousands of Web sites, and if you expect the Web surfers to hang out on yours, you'd better make it appealing. Of course, real life is still more challenging than any computer game. In the Internet game, each of the so-called "netizens" is an individual who isn't quite like any other netizen. And so, while the sims all move one way or the other, netizens can move in any direction at any time.

Those netizens, those consumers, have already demonstrated their individual and collective powers. Let's look at three success stories: AOL, CBS.MarketWatch, and Amazon.

- More than 20 million netizens like AOL so much that they pay about the same to be members of AOL as they pay for basic cable TV. They visit tens of thousands of Web sites dedicated to such pursuits as research in hieroglyphics to philately.
- MarketWatch competes with more than 2,000 Web sites dedicated to covering financial news and data. It has attained millions of customers by being motivated to stay ahead.
- Amazon.com made the transformation from tiny startup to earth-shaking corporation in three years and, despite its occasional miscues, has become a model for any company planning to conduct retail sales over the Internet.

What do AOL, MarketWatch, and Amazon have in common? They are in three different fields: Web service, financial news, and retail sales. They are very different in size. They have dramatically different corporate cultures. They are located thousands of miles away from one another. Graphically, they are different. Technologically, they are quite different. And their business models couldn't be much further apart.

So what do these three have in common? They're all highly interactive, putting the consumer in complete control of their experience. Their success is entirely dependent on the desire of the netizens to return again and again. Each of these companies provides something that the consumers like better than the alternatives.

The key to success on the Internet—whether for a service, a retail store, a politician, an entertainment site, or any other venture—is to give the customers what they want: control. The customer is always right. That's an easy axiom to toss around, but an extremely difficult and demanding way to do business in a world where corporations have proven themselves so adept at taking control *away* from consumers over the past 40 years.

This is not to say that any Web site that serves its customers well will be successful. That is quite *un*likely. On the other hand, an otherwise good Web site that fails to put the consumer in control has little chance of success on the Internet.

This is just like the 1950s, when a shopkeeper who didn't understand and pander to his clientele would quickly lose them. The customers were in control then, too.

This control isn't limited to business. The same is very likely to follow in politics because all those netizens out there are soon going to expect their candidates to be available for online chats, e-mail exchanges, and open public debate on the issues that matter most to the public. If you want to know how your senator voted on gun control, abortion, or military appropriations, it already is available on the Web. Lobbying groups on both sides have made it easy to get information on who stands where on what, and it is now up to the candidates to explain their positions.

SHOW TIME

The potential for entertainment on the Internet is still largely unknown, although it is widely assumed it will be a massive global market. There is already talk of the day when hit movies will debut on the Internet—bypassing the costs of distribution and making it possible for hundreds of millions of people to watch the same film at the same time. Film is actually the wrong word. There will be no film, just digital images transmitted by computers through a network and into another computer.

For the time being, bandwidth is holding back the development of entertainment in cyberspace. While enough bandwidth exists to play video games, the ability to compress vast amounts of data and distribute that data on a massive scale remains elusive. Even high-speed cable feeds will do little more than add a few bells and whistles to the current state of television.

Entertainment won't hit its true potential in interactive media like the Net until the entertainment experience surpasses the thrill of seeing a blockbuster movie on the big screen amid an audience of similarly energized fans. That involves a great deal more than just piping passive digital images through a quarter-inch coaxial cable.

CYBER YARDSTICKS

Later, we'll look at some of the business models that succeed or fail on the Web. For now, however, let's stick with the basic interactive elements consumers expect from three different types of Web sites: commercial, political, and entertainment. Laying out a few standards now will help us maintain a sense of perspective as we wander into the visually disorienting World Wide Web.

We've already talked about a few Web sites and what makes them successful—I argue it's the way they put the consumer in charge. If you're willing to go along with that thesis, then it follows that the most important thing to understand in your business model is the consumer viewpoint: What do consumers really want when they interact with a Web site?

Make your own list if you want—after all, you're the customer and you know better than I do what you want (and candidly, there's no perfect list).

Here are five basic yardsticks of interactivity I chose, based on what I've heard from consumers, discovered through my own experience, and heard at various business presentations at trade shows, seminars, and stock conferences:

1. *Choice.* Are more choices available somewhere else?
2. *Price.* Does the Web site offer a very competitive price?
3. *Usability.* Is the site engaging? Is it easy to use? Is help readily available?
4. *Personalization.* Is the focus on you individually? Or on the mass market?
5. *Safety.* Is it safe to spend money? Is it safe for kids?

Now, let's see how these yardsticks apply to shopping, political, and entertainment Web sites.

SHOPPING

Choice

The one thing that consumers want over everything is a diverse selection. Even if there are more choices than they can easily evaluate, they want to know they have more choices available to them than they would find elsewhere. If you sell books, you'd better have more titles than anyone else has. If you produce business news, your readers want to know they aren't missing a big story when they choose to read news on your site. If you sell drugstore items, you'd better have every brand of shampoo in every available size, because customers are going to expect it.

Price

This is the greatest unknown about retailing on the Web today. This much is clear: Consumers expect you to give them a competitive price. Even if you offer the convenience of the world's biggest selection, consumers are going to expect you to offer the world's best prices, too. In cyberspace, there's no difference between a shop in a good neighborhood and a shop in a poor one. There's no difference between the product itself. And customers aren't likely to show any brand loyalty if they feel the shopkeeper they're dealing with is charging 10 percent more than a competitor just a mouse click away. If you charge more than competitors, the netizens will march out of your store unless you throw in some extra service or benefits that enhance the value.

We are very likely to see cyberstores competing on razor-thin margins in the future, much in the way that supermarket chains have slashed markups to a fraction of a percent on most items. I predict that Amazon, even if it continues to offer great service and other premiums, eventually will have to compete with other Internet bookstores that mark up books by an average of 2 percent or less.

Usability

So, your site has the best value and the best selection. You win, right? Wrong. They're only part of the equation. Your customers are also going to expect great service. Wouldn't you?

On the Web, service is much more complicated than in the old days when all you needed to do was smile and remember the names of your customers' kids. Service on the Internet involves technical issues similar to the gameplay in video games. How long does it take to download a page? How well designed is your navigational system—the signposts that lead you through your Web site? If a customer wants to find blue shorts instead of green shorts, is it easy? Will it take long? How about a shirt to match the shorts? And some shoes to complete the outfit? Is it easy or hard to bring all that together?

Usability also means you'll need to make the customers feel comfortable while using the site. How easy is it to return merchandise they don't want? Is there help available when they need it, even at 3 AM?

Personalization

Have you ever gone to a store for the same sort of items so frequently that the proprietor knows your likes and dislikes? In one way, that's another form of good service. But in another, it's crafty merchandising. Smart shopkeepers know they can increase their revenues by letting customers know when their favorite items are in stock, or when they have a new item that customers might fancy.

This form of marketing is what's commonly called personalization on the Web, and it's a delicate issue. If you do it right, people tell their friends that they just love the feature. If you go to far, you may anger your customers because they feel their privacy has been invaded. Amazon ran into a problem with that with their "circles" program, and wisely responded by changing the program to meet its customers' demands.

As any experienced consumer knows, there is a fine line between aggressive sales tactics and providing just the proper amount of support. I'm afraid that line may be invisible to many on the Internet, who are so interested in grabbing market share they often forget they're also simultaneously dealing with individual customers. This isn't just a mass medium, like TV; it's a one-on-one medium, like the telephone.

Safety

We've all become familiar, perhaps to the point of boredom, with questions of protecting one's privacy and one's credit cards when shopping on the Web.

A survey by @dtech and Talk City found 42 percent of Internet shoppers listed "security" as a concern; 18 percent said "privacy" was the greatest single deterrent to shopping online.

A Web site that cannot guarantee the security or the privacy of its customers has no business opening shop in cyberspace. The fact that such sites are relatively common is such a huge threat to electronic commerce that I believe it could delay advantages of Web commerce for years.

POLITICAL

The Internet is becoming a bigger part of U.S. election campaigns than kissing babies. What will a successful Internet campaign include? Much of it will need to follow the same guidelines as a commercial business.

Choice

Well, this is what elections are all about, aren't they? You might think a site for a candidate only has one choice—the candidate. But a well-designed political site will become what the user wants it to be. It should be a forum where voters can find what they want. Maybe they want to know where the candidate stands on the sale of assault weapons. Maybe the issue is abortion, or prayer in schools, or war, or taxes.

Whatever the issue, the site must respond to the voter's inquiries with responses on all key issues. Imagine if you went to Joe Candidate's Web site to find out where Joe stood on building a new dam up the river from your home and the Web site said: "Sorry, we are unable to answer your query at this time." You wouldn't accept that, would you?

On the other hand, maybe Joe didn't think of answering that question because the dam is 400 miles up the river in another state, and because he has limited resources, and there are a lot more pressing issues closer to home.

Smart candidates will get around that by offering a highly visible checklist of key issues right up front on the site, and by inviting voters to submit questions on issues that don't appear on the checklist.

Price

We don't like to think our politicians are for sale, do we? Yet we know that a senator is expected to raise up to $10,000 a day while in office to finance a reelection campaign. How does one do that?

This is a great question to answer on a Web site, and a good opportunity to raise funds. Smart candidates will do both. Candidates with nothing to hide will publish a list of all major donors, estimate their own campaign expenses, and solicit donations at the grass roots level. They also may post a list of their rivals' contributors.

Usability

Nobody likes to find all those flyers crammed in the mailbox just before election day that tell you what a splendid job Sally Votegetter did for you in her last term. Instead, wouldn't it be refreshing to find that info on her Web site, when you want it? And smart candidates will replace the hype with cold, hard facts. Consumers don't like fluff—they like the plain truth straight up. Did the candidate vote against gun controls, or not? No justifications, just the truth.

Remember, the key here is to provide interactive elements that let the voters investigate the candidate and the issues that they think are important.

Personalization

We've all gotten those letters just before the election that start off "Dear Thomas Murphy." Aren't they irritating?

But if your congressional representative called you up and asked your name and then asked your opinion on a number of issues, you'd probably cooperate, wouldn't you? Imagine if you had an opportunity to do that on a Web site—less personal, perhaps, but a whole lot more impressive than a form letter jammed in your mail slot three days before the election.

Safety

Just one thought here: pass my name and interests along to other candidates and I'll change my party affiliation. Again.

ENTERTAINMENT

Adjusting to a high degree of interactivity represents a tough challenge for the entertainment industry, which is used to working with passive media like film and videotape. There's still a need to have a compelling story, an engaging cast, an appropriate setting, and good production values. But now you also want to get each member of the audience involved in the drama by having them play some sort of role—either as an actor, a stagehand, or a director. There are a lot of experiments underway in Hollywood and other locales to make the most of the new medium.

The key, ultimately, is to blend the interactive elements of a video game with the richness of a great film. Short of that, interactivity also entails giving viewers enormous power over choice of programming, times, and viewing controls.

Choice

There is absolutely nothing to limit a choice of entertainment on the Web. Right now, when you want a little entertainment, you might go through the listings in a newspaper for the 10 or 20 movies that might be showing in a major metropolitan area on any given weekend, or check the TV-radio page, or maybe check out a list of concerts. Soon you'll instead go to a menu (perhaps through your TV) and choose from TV, radio, film, dance, music, night clubs, games, live events, virtual reality, and several other types of multimedia entertainment. You may have an opportunity to view a film trailer or listen to a music excerpt. If it's a live event, you can buy the tickets in advance. If it's a digitized film, you'll likely have a nearly unlimited choice and will be able to choose when you want to watch it.

Price

Right now when you buy a movie ticket, where does the money go? As you might imagine, only a fraction goes back to the studio that made the film. A good chunk goes to the theater operator and the chain that owns the theater. On the Web, that won't happen. The studio that owns the film may well be the company behind the Web site and, while it may get more money per viewing, the final price to the viewer should be less because there is no markup by a theater owner.

The same principles would apply to CDs ordered through the Web (or music delivered directly on demand, perhaps downloaded from a music company's master recordings onto a disk) or to computer games you buy through the Web instead of through a retailer.

Usability

Entertainment Web sites are all about service, so this category is a slam dunk. It's hard to imagine an entertainment venue that would not try to help you relax and enjoy yourself, and that infers a high level of response to consumer demands.

Personalization

This category is similar to the model in retailing. A good entertainment site will gradually learn your likes and dislikes and, while you'll always retain the opportunity to choose from a vast array of different types of entertainment, a good Web site will suggest features that seem to match your tastes. If you watched two Woody Allen movies, and there's a new film that stars Woody, the site might point that out to you. If you watched the last series the Dodgers played with the Giants, a good entertainment portal should remind you when the next match-up is taking place. Did you buy tickets to go see the Smashing Pumpkins on their last tour? Well, maybe you'd like to see their concert from Paris this weekend.

An even higher level of personalization may come when Hollywood gives viewers the opportunity to actually be in movies. This is, of course, a different kind of entertainment than traditional storytelling and I will regret the day when we have a way to choose a different ending in *Casablanca*.

Safety

There's little to say about Web pornography. It's an important consumer issue and the consumer is the boss. Clearly, a lot of people want adult entertainment on the Web. Clearly, a lot of people don't want their children exposed to it.

Fortunately, it's very easy to use filters to prevent your children being exposed to adult images, violence, bad language, racial epithets, or anything else you wish to block. And any Web site that hopes to find itself used at any hour by any member of a household would be wise to incorporate such filters into its site. In the end, it's easier to screen out smut on the Internet than it is to get it out of traditional media.

CHAPTER 5

POWERSHOPPING
Service, Please!

Ask a historian about Roosevelt Field and you'll hear that's where Charles Lindbergh took off on his famed trans-Atlantic flight in 1927. Ask a retail analyst and he'll tell you Roosevelt Field made history as the first shopping mall. It also happens to be where I bought my first suit.

Gazing into cyberspace, it's easy to see reflections of the past, and the early design of Roosevelt Field comes to mind as I think about the virtual malls of tomorrow. Just as retailing in America went through many phases, we're likely to see e-commerce evolve through many forms over the next decade. It will grow in fits and starts. Some concepts will work, some won't. Sometimes consumers will find bargains, sometimes the prices will be high.

In the end, however, consumers will find they have enormous power as shoppers, and that merchants will have a difficult time keeping up with their demands. By 2010, we'll take that for granted, but we'll see a lot of instability between now and then as merchants learn how to sell things over the Internet, and consumers learn how to buy them. Once again, the best clues about the future lie in our past, but this time the arrival of new technology will alter the finish.

Consider how retailing grew in the past. The first shop-keepers—the butcher, the baker, the candlestick maker—focused on what they did best. This is still the way things are done in much of the world. It's a charming way of life. And, in my experience, the steaks that come from a butcher generally taste better than the ones that come from a supermarket. A pie from a baker is almost always superior to one at a market. And, yes, candle shops have a bigger selection of high-quality candles than you'd find in a variety store. Alas, the individual shops generally charge more for their wares because the bigger stores can buy and sell mediocre goods in a volume that allows them to narrow their profit margin. As a result, we've seen hundreds of thousands of small shops close their doors in the United States over the past four decades. Specialized retailers today tend to cater to the upper middle class and the rich. The middle class mostly shops there on special occasions.

As I mentioned earlier, I recall the delivery services of the 1950s, when bread trucks, produce wagons, milk trucks, and others delivered their wares to your door. I also recall that most markets offered delivery service. These were marvelous services, but their labor-intensive nature, higher prices, and growing consumer expectations for consistent quality gradually undid them.

Department stores have been around for more than a century, often growing out of the general stores that opened in virtually every American town as the nation grew west. Although the quality was sometimes lower than one might expect from a small shop, the variety of wares represented a convenience that consumers still love today. That's why we still have department stores for all economic levels of our society, ranging from Kmart, Target, and Wal-Mart to Saks, Nordstrom, and Neiman-Marcus.

Sears hit pay dirt long ago not only with its department stores, but with a general merchandise catalog business that allowed rural Americans to order tools, shoes, clothes, and other items by placing an order through the mail or a local catalog counter. Importantly, Sears built its reputation by providing consistency in a way that appealed to consumers. A Sears catalog shopper knew the merchandise would be a good value;

without that confidence, the catalog business would never have worked. Myriad catalog companies followed, but Sears catalog outlets became the standard.

In bigger towns, supermarkets—the department stores of food—took the lead over smaller markets like the one I recall from my youth.

Then something funny happened. Sure, supermarkets got bigger and Wal-Marts opened from coast to coast. Yes, drug stores grew into superstores. And malls covered way too much open space with asphalt. But there was something else: specialty shops staged a strong comeback in the form of boutiques.

TODAY'S MALL

Today at the mall, you can expect to see big department stores as anchor tenants. But between them you'll find dozens of small shops, although most of them belong to chains. These stores offer higher levels of personal service, a wider choice of a niche product, and the cost-efficiencies associated with volume pricing on the wholesale level. In the end, the consumer gets more choice, albeit at a slightly higher price.

Finally, we've seen the same thing happen with catalogs. Just as large department stores have seen increased competition from specialty chains, general merchandise catalogs have been challenged, and quite successfully, by specialty catalogs. Millions of consumers order clothes, gifts, books, records, and other specialty items through catalogs because—just like early Sears catalog shoppers—they have a high confidence that the goods they order will be of consistent quality at a fair price.

WHAT'S NEW?

When you look at the early growth of e-commerce, you see so many familiar things that it can help take the surprise out of what happens next. While the press seems alternately confused and amazed by what's happening in the e-tailing arena, it shouldn't be. The only thing new here is that some entrepreneurs have opened shops on the Internet, creating an alternative to mail-order catalogs. Big deal!

Over the past few years, we started hearing about small shops that sell things over the Internet. IBM even featured the concept in its advertisement that showed an American couple buying olive oil from an elderly Italian woman. She explained she shipped oil all over the world because of orders from her Web site.

Given the astonishingly low overhead of putting up a Web site, it would be surprising only if small businesses *didn't* try to take orders through the Internet. These days, it seems like every craftsperson has a Web site, as does virtually every company that makes anything. While many still don't accept orders directly through the Internet, most make it easy to find what you're looking for and to call in an order.

There are two other observations at this level. First, the goods received from craftspeople advertising on the Net are of inconsistent quality. You don't know, for example, how good that woman's olive oil will be until you receive your shipment and crack open a can. Second, the goods received directly from manufacturers are generally of a consistent quality, but the price is usually the suggested retail price. Manufacturers have been reluctant to undercut retailers who carry their products. And then you also have to pay shipping and handling.

You can credit Jeff Bezos for starting the second stage by opening Amazon.com, a company that serves as the prototype and predictor for high-volume sales in cyberspace. Amazon understood something very early: that the costs of selling things on the Internet was so low that eventually the only way to make money will be to sell things in high volumes, things of consistent and dependable quality, such as books, CDs, and videotapes. Bezos was so excited about this epiphany that he quit his job as a Wall Street hedge fund manager and risked all by opening Amazon.

It was amusing to me to see all the fuss and bother about Amazon's long-term business model as the mainstream press and many large investors suddenly realized that Amazon would face enormous competition from other large companies selling similar goods. Well, of course, it would. But Amazon has a huge advantage: It isn't saddled with a nationwide chain of brick-and-mortar storefronts. On the downside, it didn't have a nationwide distribution system set up. Building that took a boatload of cash that Bezos raised through a public offering and subsequent high-yield, junk bond sales. (These securities held a "junk" rating because Amazon was still losing money when the bonds were issued. Nonetheless, investors snapped up the bonds given their faith in Amazon's long-term ability to repay the debt.) Amazon's biggest challenges in the future will come on two fronts. First, other virtual bookstores are trying to undercut Amazon's prices, and, second, its own ability to generate and maintain a modest profit during a period of tumultuous growth. This latter consideration eventually will be the nightmare of every company selling almost anything on the Internet.

WHAT SELLS?

As the twenty-first century gets underway, we're seeing other industries starting to wake up to the potential to sell high volumes of online goods of consistent quality. As we note elsewhere, there is heated competition among drugstores, with good reason: a bottle of mouthwash is a bottle of mouthwash. If you can buy it cheaply over the Internet and have it delivered, why wouldn't you?

We've also started seeing many of the mail-order catalog companies shifting their magazines to the Internet. This makes sense given that these companies offer goods of predictable quality and that they already have many of the elements in place to deliver a consumer-pleasing service. They have inventory strategies, fulfillment houses, complaint services, return capabilities, and good relationships with shippers like UPS, FedEx, and the Postal Service. Many of these merchandisers are also used to offering low prices, although the catalog merchants in general have never given the consumers the discounts that are possible when you eliminate a 40 percent retail markup. No specialty mail-order company ever reached the mass needed to undercut competitors in the way Amazon has undercut its brick-and-mortar rivals because the sheer number of catalogs prevented any one of them from taking an early lead.

THE DIRECT MODEL

We're now crossing into one of the most controversial areas of Internet retailing: direct sales. The idea here is for a manufacturer to convince you to buy goods directly from the factory rather than buying a competitor's product through a retailer. This is what we used to call "buying wholesale," except that now the companies trying to do this have been forced to accept additional costs like customer service, administrative functions, and after-market service.

The best example I've seen of the direct model is Dell Computer, which has always sold its PCs directly. Dell initially was set up as a volume supplier to corporations, which buy large numbers of PCs. It did so well in that market that many office workers soon wanted Dells to take home. So Dell started selling directly to consumers, too. While its competitors found themselves in the familiar danger of undercutting their resellers, Dell had no such concerns and offered excellent value to consumers with a quality brand name and a price that often undercut the most aggressive retailers.

Dell was quick to embrace the Internet and has found a big payoff. By mid-1999, Dell was selling $18 million worth of computers a day over the Internet, or $6.5 billion worth a year. Even as cheap, off-brand competition flooded in from Asia, Dell's market share was rising along with its revenue. And by moving first to the Internet, Dell senior vice president Joe Merengi said the company has stretched its lead over rivals. "If we execute [on plan], we believe many competitors will drop further behind over the next two years," he said in a speech I covered for MarketWatch. "We're awaiting the outcome and actually having quite a good time watching it unfold."

Other computer makers have had mixed success with direct sales, largely because they also sell computers through stores. Apple, which saw its retail network nearly evaporate as its market share sank in the late 1990s, has seen enormous growth in online sales. Gateway, which created its own network of retail stores, also has seen good growth. But Compaq hit on hard times, and one reason was its strong presence in the retail arena.

Some people think book publishers will eventually sell books directly, or that drug manufacturers will sell their product directly to consumers. If that happened, it could seriously disrupt the ability of Amazon or PlanetRx to sell books or drugs with even a slight markup. But I seriously doubt it will happen. Manufacturers may be good at making a product, but aren't necessarily good at selling it. Dell had many years of experience in direct sales before moving to the Net; Random House doesn't. Would you even think of buying a CD directly from Sony? Would you buy aspirin from Bayer? This seems like it would be a painful way to shop, and it would eliminate the comparison shopping that many consumers expect today.

Of course, you might buy a car that way, or a Gucci watch, or a shipment of your favorite Texas barbecue sauce. This is where brand name and customer loyalty may make a big difference. Yes, you would buy a Dell computer over the Internet. No, you probably wouldn't buy an off-brand PC over the Internet unless you knew more about the quality.

AT THE MALL

In retailing, we saw traditional specialty stores and direct sales grow. We then saw department stores, the malls, and the superstores. The same thing is happening on the Internet. These types of cyber stores didn't make sense until now because they are based on volume. Now the volume is there.

Although e-tailers take in hundreds of billions of dollars a year, many view the world of cyber shopping as being in its infancy. My favorite quote about the early-stage online retailers comes from IBM chairman Lou Gerstner, who once dismissed them as "fireflies before the storm." While Gerstner accepts that a few of these companies may survive and even prosper, he predicts most will be wiped out as traditional retailers shift their focus to cyberspace. Certainly, the numbers have gotten big enough to pique retailers' interest:

- Sixty-one percent of U.S. shoppers are interested in buying products online, according to IVANS Inc., a technology company. That was up from 50 percent a year earlier.
- Barnesandnoble.com saw a 25 percent rise in sales to $32.3 million during the first quarter of 1999 from the fourth quarter of 1998. It also saw 450,000 new customers at its online site, a crowd the size of Woodstock.
- At AOL, shoppers spent $1.8 billion at its online mall in the first quarter of 1999, spending 75 percent more in March alone than they did six months earlier. Meanwhile, Lycos signed $200 million in commerce agreements with potential mall tenants during the same quarter.
- A survey conducted by Ad:tech and Talk City, a community Web site, found 58 percent of the participants saying the Internet has changed the way they shop. (About 18 percent of the shoppers said privacy remained a big concern.)

With stakes like those, it's certainly time for big retailers like Wal-Mart to take note. These chains that advertise the same wares in thousands of newspapers every Sunday are very likely to offer the same goods online. They control their own stores, which are already geared toward bargain prices; they buy in huge volumes that no new online rivals can touch; and they have vast distribution and fulfillment capabilities.

It's little wonder that Sears' online general manager Alice Peterson told CBS.MarketWatch.com that the company was actively seeking online partners. "We think the Web site will drive traffic to our stores," she said. "The shopper tells us they love to be able to be in control by doing their research on the Web site. If they want to turn the knob and open the doors first, we invite them to go to the stores. They can close the sale there or online."

All this is likely to continue and accelerate over the next few years, but there is another development coming that will cause all hell to break loose: broadband.

THE SUPERHIGHWAY

If e-tailing is growing rapidly now, just imagine what will happen when the bandwidth increases 50-fold or more. It would be equivalent to replace a dirt path to the mall with an eight-lane superhighway. And that's just what will be happening over the next few years.

Broadband Internet service will reach 26 million U.S. households by 2003, according to Forrester Research Inc. AOL rolled out a high-speed DSL service for $40 a month—less than twice the cost of its slow-speed rate—that could reach 41 percent of United States households. In an article for *Barron's*, Michael Dell said broadband "will shift power over to the buyer of goods and services, whether that is an individual consumer or a corporation."

Certainly consumers will have more options, and will have the capacity to do far more comparison shopping very quickly, but the transition of power to the consumer won't be complete for several more years. We can expect to see a tough battle fought in the intervening period by those who have the power now. The battleground will be a very familiar venue: TV.

As noted earlier, the entire U.S. television system is expected to go digital by 2006, at which time all analog broadcasting—the kind we have today—will cease. As we make this transition, interactivity will be blended into programming, so that people can shop through their televisions.

TV is a very powerful medium when it comes to persuading shoppers. How many times have you seen a Pizza Hut or Burger King commercial at dinnertime and found yourself getting hungry. It's not that it's great food (not to knock it, either . . . I'm a big fan of junk food), but TV is selling it to you (see how *weak and powerless you are in the hands of the existing media?*). And then there are the car commercials, clothing ads, grocery ads, and technology commercials.

Folks, it ain't over yet. Imagine you're watching that pizza commercial on your new, super-sharp digital TV, knowing that all you have to do is reach for that remote control and you can have one of those steaming, chewy, cheesy pies delivered to your door in 15 minutes, already paid for by credit card. Tempted?

How will you feel when you can buy just about anything with a click of your TV's remote control? It's coming, soon, to a couch under your potato.

PRODUCT PLACEMENT

Advertisers pay for product placement in TV shows, so your favorite stars on your favorite shows will soon be tempting you to buy the clothes they're wearing, the foods they're eating, the cars they're driving. Manufacturers will pay fortunes to networks for that kind of product placement, and—don't be fooled—that cost will be passed along directly to you.

It won't just be on TV, either. With much of the U.S. online audience belonging to AOL, companies will also place their products there. Popular search engines will be popular targets. Of course, this is already happening, but with narrow-band service, the big spenders don't have that much advantage over their poorer rivals. On broadband, production values will show, and those who can afford the best presentation will gain a huge advantage over those who can't.

You can expect this period of e-tailing to last several years. It will end when Internet users master the new tool we talked about earlier: shopping bots.

What we're going through is something like the original three Star Wars movies. First, the empire suffers a setback as Net consumers get cheaper prices and more choices on the Internet. Then the evil empire strikes back, using digital TV as a powerful death star that deals the consumer a major setback. And finally, the consumers return to power with the help of an R2D2-like piece of software that reestablishes their control over their own destinies.

Bots will act like your servant. Instead of *you* going out and doing comparison shopping, *they* will be shopping for you. For example, you'll tell (really, you'll *tell*) your computer that you'd like to buy a copy of, say, Thomas Pynchon's landmark novel *V*. A short while later, your computer will tell you that the best deal is at the XYZ Book Co. for $8.95 in hardback plus $3 for shipping and it could be here the day after tomorrow. You say "OK," and the deal is done. Your bot has done your comparison shopping for you and you can rest easy knowing you've gotten the best possible deal.

YOUR WISH?

Bots can work for virtually any product. Want to buy a used Miata? The bot can find five in your area code that are available. Want a blue one? The bot will check the ads for you. Maybe you want the names of five restaurants near your house that feature Mexican food entrees for under $10? The bot will have some recommendations.

The bot also will help you with other items. Want to find the best price on a Capt. Zonko doll your kid wants for his birthday? Send the bot. Are you looking for a nearby store that has Calvin Klein jeans in your size at the best price? The bot will track them down.

If you're watching TV and your favorite star is wearing a tee-shirt you just have to have, you won't have to buy it from the show. Your bot will identify it and find the retailer with the best price.

It almost takes the fun out of shopping, doesn't it? Well, it certainly takes the fun out of it for retailers, particularly those who hope you'll pay a little extra for extra service and other frills. In our interview with Chief Yahoo Jerry Yang, he pointed out many retailers and malls may ban bots. Why? Because bots could also be agents for other retailers, snooping around to find out what a competitor is charging for particular items, then undercutting the price. One company could try to put another company out of business that way, he said.

There's a fine line between free competition and predatory pricing, but we have laws to protect merchants against the latter. It's difficult to understand why retailers should be allowed to turn this issue against consumers, and my guess is that any retailer who tries to do so will regret it.

CHAPTER 6

FINANCE
In Your Interest

It's a sad thing that so much of our lives is spent in pursuit of wealth. We all talk about health and happiness. We say the best things in life are free, then we sell our best days to employers, envy the rich, and measure success by the size of our paycheck and what it can buy. Madonna is right: we're living in a material world.

It should come as little surprise then that finance has emerged as a powerful "killer ap" on the Internet, perhaps *the* killer ap, although it's far too early to tell. Yes, the best things in life are free, but everything else will cost you money. And borrowing, lending, saving, investing, accessing, insuring, protecting, and leveraging that money is something that almost everybody needs to do. If the Internet can help to make those things easier, we'll want that, won't we? And anyone doing business with us on the Net is also going to need financial services to complete the transaction. To twist a phrase, the best things on the Net are free, but everything else will require financial services.

Want to buy a house? You need a mortgage. Want to order a book? You need a credit card. Want to buy that stock? You need a broker. Want to deposit your check? You'll need a bank.

Even without the Internet, the financial industry has been undergoing a radical transformation over the past decade. Bank consolidations have wiped out hundreds of thousands of jobs. Congress scrapped most barriers between banks, brokers, and insurers. Retirement savings have shifted from large corporate-directed pension funds to self-directed plans like IRAs and 401(k)s.

While the number of banks and S&Ls continues to drop, our mailboxes are jammed with an increasing number of offers for home equity loans and credit cards. My dog recently received a personally addressed notice that he'd been preapproved for a gold card. He was eligible for a special introductory interest rate of 3.9 percent thanks to his "excellent" credit rating. (The lucky dog has no debt.)

Thanks in part to the Internet and related technology, Americans entered the twenty-first century enjoying the longest sustained economic expansion in their history. But in an era of prosperity, there are also many dark clouds. The personal savings rate hasn't been lower since the Depression. The average personal debt in the country is $8,000. The Social Security system could fail before it can pay back the Baby Boomers for their decades of hard work, leaving millions of Americans on their own in their old age.

Clearly people need to get a better handle on their finances, and it appears millions of them are turning to the Internet for help. According to the Securities and Exchange Commission, 30 percent of trading volume on the New York Stock Exchange and Nasdaq came from the Internet. The Net accounted for 14 percent of the orders. The number of consumers banking online is expected to grow to 24.2 million by 2002, nearly four times the level in 1998 according to Gomez Advisors, a technology research firm. Analysts estimate a quarter of the $1.5 trillion U.S. mortgage market could move to cyberspace by 2003. Interactive tools available on many Web sites are available to help draft budgets, figure loan payments, and estimate the growth in retirement accounts.

The downside is that you now have the power to destroy your financial health with the click of a mouse because the Internet makes it very easy to run up consumer credit bills or to make life-changing investment decisions without adequate counsel from trained professionals.

REAL ESTATE

Georgia Tech reported 42 percent of Web surfers it studied had accessed real estate sites, not surprising since the demographics indicated the average surfer was 35 with a household income of $67,000. By 1995, before the Internet had truly emerged as a mass medium, there were already 4,000 real estate sites on the Web, according to the Fisher Center for Real Estate and Urban Economics at the University of California, Berkeley. Almost all of the houses for sale in the United States are listed on the Internet, making it simple for consumers to look at pictures and compare prices, even when they're far away from the market where they intend to buy.

The Internet greatly enhances the power of a consumer to search for a house because it combines extensive text-based information about different +houses and markets with graphical information like maps and panoramic tours of homes. It also can provide live links to real estate brokers listing homes in a given locale.

Just a few years ago, a couple who wanted to move to San Francisco from, say, St. Louis would have to contact brokers in San Francisco and request such information, or go to the Bay area and drive from town to town until they felt they had enough information to make an informed decision. Whether they picked a reliable broker or not often had more to do with their success in finding the perfect house than the availability of housing in a given market. Quite often, people move to a new city, then move to a different neighborhood a year or so later after discovering a better location.

Now the same person would pick a neighborhood by location and description, check listings in the area, investigate the schools, and then contact a broker to express interest in a given property and to obtain more information. The control here has shifted to the buyer from the broker, enhancing the consumers' chances of getting their dream homes on the first try. It also has led to a more efficient market, expanding the pool of potential buyers in a way that has supported a gradual rise in property values and quicker sales of marketable homes.

There's also increased pressure on brokers to make sure their Web sites are designed for easy use, that their listings are updated, and that their commissions are in line with the competition. Smart real estate sites include regional and local maps, data about local school districts, information about taxes, transit maps, traffic information, crime statistics, and live links to the listing broker, local government agencies, and other parties who can assist a buyer in making a decision.

National real estate chains that can use the same Web site to serve hundreds of communities have a tremendous advantage over local brokers for the same reason that Amazon.com is a threat to local bookstores: the efficiency of scale means a lower cost per transaction. That allows the local agent to provide increased value to the consumer while also providing greater choice and personal service.

What's next in real estate? It has already become much easier to sell your own home over the Net. The challenge here is that the millions of homes in the national inventory of for-sale properties makes for quite a large forest. Finding a particular tree is difficult without the organizational help of a large regional brokerage.

There's extensive information available about real estate at realtor.com, nahb.com (National Association of Home Builders), and fanniemae.com. Home-finding sites like bamboo.com have pioneered the use of sophisticated technologies to tour individual homes from anywhere in the world.

MORTGAGES

Want to buy a home? You'll probably need a big fat mortgage. In the old days, you begged a banker or visited a savings and loan. Then you waited days or weeks. If you were approved, then you could buy that house.

Things changed rapidly in the 1990s. First, the mortgage brokering industry provided an alternative to traditional banking relationships. You'd simply get a broker who found you the best loan available from a long list of lenders and received a commission from the lender. Then came companies like Countrywide that not only would sell you a mortgage, but would package your loan with hundreds of others and sell it on Wall Street as a mortgage-backed security. That enabled Countrywide to lock in your rates immediately. Technological advances and a strong retail presence also helped Countrywide and its rivals to provide quicker loan approval, making it easier to buy your home.

The first impact of the Internet was to consolidate many different possible loans in a single location, to help consumers find the best available loan. A notable site useful in this regard is bankrate.com, which surveys 3,500 lenders and allows consumers to find the lowest rates—sometimes a full percentage point lower than the national average.

Companies like E-loan provide you quick loan approval through the Internet. Loan papers still have to be shipped by overnight mail—often from across the country, but the consumers usually end up with much better deals than they would find at the bank down the street.

BANKS AND S&LS

It wasn't long ago that banks were the center of the average consumer's financial world, and that's still the case for thousands of "community" banks in small towns from coast to coast. In that traditional world, you'd establish an account at a bank, deposit your paychecks there, and apply for a credit card. Then, when the time came, you'd meet with a loan officer who'd go over your history and tell you whether the bank thought you were reliable enough to borrow money for a new car or a home.

That type of banking has been on the wane for many years. The trend has been accelerated by the consolidation of big urban banks, national marketing of credit cards, and by technological advances like ATM cards that you can use from Moscow to Maui.

The Internet is accelerating, although some big money center banks have been more than a little late to recognize it. (Bankers tend to be a conservative bunch, often to their own detriment.) Kudos to Wells Fargo, which aggressively started offering Internet banking services to its customers by the mid-1990s, long before the bank acquired First Interstate or was merged into Norwest. It's interesting, however, to look at the list of the Top 5 Internet banks as reported by Gomez Advisors in the spring of 1999: Security First Network Bank, Wells Fargo, Citibank, Salem 5 Cents Savings Bank, and Bank of America. That's an interesting mix of the huge money-center banks, small regional banks, and Net upstarts, and shows that Internet banking is a wide open arena where consumers will choose their banks by services, not by brand name.

There are two critical factors that are likely to separate the winners from the losers in Internet banking: accuracy and fees.

The technology to ensure accuracy is ubiquitous, yet I often hear comments from friends who bank online that the bank once again failed to issue a payment on schedule. That is unacceptable and, my powerful friends, we're not going to put up with it any more than we'd accept an incorrect balance or delays in depositing our paychecks.

Fees rose throughout banking during the late 1990s as falling interest rates made it difficult for financial institutions to maintain an adequate net interest margin to ensure growing profits. Instead, banks put the squeeze on customers for such outrageous demands as talking to a teller or using their ATM cards at another bank. Well, you shouldn't accept that any more. Most Internet-based banks will charge for using ATMs at other banks, but they more than make up for it by paying higher interest on your deposits than do most brick-and-mortar rivals. And most Net banks also will provide a 24-hour, toll-free number so that you can ask questions about your account at a time convenient to you.

MUTUAL FUNDS

Most Americans—upwards of 60 percent, depending on what survey you look at—own mutual funds, either directly or through a retirement plan. And most don't have a clue how they're doing from day to day. Many people don't even know that their retirement nest egg is dependent on the willy-nilly nature of the market or, worse, fund managers whose personal picks may fall behind broad market averages.

Some companies—like Fidelity, the number one fund merchant—have done a credible job of trying to inform people about how to pick funds. For example, you'll find many calculators on the Web to help you gauge how much risk is recommended for someone in your financial position.

But virtually all fund companies are in the business of selling funds, so consumers should be on guard. People know enough to be wary of a car dealer trying to sell them a car, but they don't apply that same sense of skepticism to a fund broker trying to nudge them into a high-commission mutual fund.

It leads to what I call the Blanche Dubois syndrome: The less we know about a particular subject, the more willing we are to depend on the kindness of strangers. Unfortunately, the Web has yet to come up with an answer. There are many sites on the Web that offer detailed information about mutual funds, notably Morningstar.com. Ultimately, however, it is up to consumers to ferret out the information they need to make informed decisions. Given the thousands of choices of funds now available, that takes hard work. The answers are there, but you have to find them.

ONLINE BROKERS

I've saved the best for last because online brokers are also the most controversial, popular, misunderstood, largest, and fastest-growing of the areas of financial services on the Web. None of this is surprising, given the stunning growth in online investment activity over the past five years. In 1995, nobody traded online. Within five years, more than 7 million Americans placed stock or bond orders through the Internet, accounting for 25 percent of all orders by individual investors.

"In the next few years, the number of online brokerage accounts will roughly equal the combined metropolitan populations of Seattle, San Francisco, Boston, Dallas, Denver, Miami, Atlanta, and Chicago," predicts SEC chairman Arthur Levitt.

Are we ready for this? Two answers: no, and we'd better be. This is one of the rare areas of the Internet where demand is growing more rapidly than the technology can advance. For this reason, there have been uncountable service problems, mostly with people whose trades didn't go through as expected. Almost every major online brokerage has had its share of problems, including Ameritrade, E-Trade, and Schwab. The problems mostly have to do with scalability—the ability of a computer system to provide a consistent level of service as more users are added to it. When the system crashes in the middle of a trading day, investors are understandably upset.

Levitt also questioned if investors understand what they're getting into. He pointed out that many people believe they are actually buying or selling stock through an exchange when they trade online. In reality, they are simply placing an order through a broker, just as they would through a telephone or in person. He also pointed out that online investors face the same sorts of risks that traditional investors have faced, but it isn't always as clear.

For example, most of the major online brokerages advertise on television in a way that is far different from traditional brokers. Remember those Dean Witter commercials where they talked about winning over investors one at a time, or the Smith

Barney commercial where they made money the old-fashioned way (they earned it), or the Dreyfus commercial with the lion prowling Wall Street? They all suggested that investors should invest through those companies because they have seasoned professionals who could guide an individual to riches.

Not so with commercials for online brokers, which stress the ability of the individual to get rich through their own wisdom. One commercial that irked Levitt featured a tow truck driver who'd bought a small island. Another showed two housewives, one who just cleared a quick profit of $1,400 on a biotech stock after shooing her kids away from the family PC. Levitt thinks commercials like that make investing look easy to the masses, something that could lead to a lot of mistakes by small investors.

"Some may argue that we shouldn't tell firms how to sell their products as long as its lawful. I agree," said Levitt. "But selling securities is not like selling soap. Brokers have always had duties to their customers that go beyond simply 'buyer beware.'"

He may have a point. But the fact is, millions of Americans *are* trading online and millions more are on the way, lured by lower commissions, Internet fever, and the feeling that they are now doing something on their own that used to cost them a lot of money. Much of the popularity has been driven by the steady rise in market averages that coincided with the growth of the Internet. When the market heads lower, much of that interest may wane just as quickly as it rose.

In the meantime, even Wall Street's "bulge bracket" firms have taken note of the growing online marketplace and plan to get in on the action after long resisting the move away from their high-commission, full-service approach. The first to fire a shot across the bow of the online upstarts was Merrill Lynch, which cut its online commission to $29.95. While that's low compared with Merrill's traditional fees, it's three to four times as much as online brokers charge.

At a U.S. Bancorp Piper Jaffray conference, Ameritrade chairman Joe Ricketts told money managers that the low commissions "don't matter" because the company made most of its profit lending money to investors on margin at rates roughly 5 percent higher than it paid on investment accounts. That's more like a traditional banking activity, except that there isn't a bank in the United States that has a 5 percent net interest margin on its accounts.

What does it mean to the consumer? It means more power that must be wielded wisely. People who want to be their own brokers in the investment world will save on commissions, but they won't be getting any calls from a loyal broker telling them their portfolio may be heading down the tube. They can compensate for this by setting "alerts" that go off like alarm clocks if elements of their portfolios go beyond parameters they set. But unless they're in jobs where they can respond promptly to those alerts, they had better stay alert themselves.

While the move now among online brokers is away from full service and toward slimmed down service, you should expect to see changes soon. Unless online brokers and their big Wall Street rivals want to lose business, they'll launch a new generation of investment supersites that include free services. Some companies already offer these services like these:

- Free portfolio services with all the bells and whistles to let you know when something is happening with your account.
- News from independent sources to keep account holders abreast of the latest market-moving headlines.
- Strong privacy protections, posted clearly on the front page of the site.
- Easy access to clear explanations of how the market works. And a toll-free telephone backup to speak to a live person at a minimal or no cost.
- Tie-ins to leading sites for mutual fund information.

Remember, you can demand those things now from your site.

CONSOLIDATION

We've taken a good look at where we stand in the financial services industry early in the new century, but everything will be different ten years from now.

With broadband communication, virtually all market activity will move online. With faster computers, there will probably no longer be any questions about whether your trade went through. With better computers, system failures should be ancient history. And with the likelihood of another recession within those ten years, much of the fever we associate with Internet investing these days will likely be a thing of the past.

But the most important change will be in the area of consolidation. With massive change underway in the finance industry, it's very unlikely that most people will have separate relationships with mortgage companies, banks, credit card companies, brokers, and insurers. Why would you if you were able to get all those services in just one place at the lowest possible rates? Finance companies will finally figure this out and offer you this convenience.

The only trouble is, they will have new competitors. Most analysts today expect companies like Intuit and Microsoft to be the financial superstores of tomorrow. Is that likely? The answer will be determined by you, because you're a very powerful person.

CHAPTER 7

POWERFUL MEDICINE
Cyberdocs On Call

About five years ago, my doctor noted I'd joined the 20 percent of the U.S. population with a high cholesterol level. Given that that group includes my 83-year-old mother, I didn't feel an imminent threat. Nonetheless, I decided to look into whether my cholesterol level could be related to my addiction to rich, black French roast coffee.

My doctor hadn't a clue; he just looked at me blankly and suggested I could take medication if it concerned me. The health guide published by my insurance company only told me what I already knew: that you can lower your cholesterol level through diet, exercise, and blah, blah, blah . . . . And even my tattered, 25-year-old copy of Adelle Davis's "Let's Eat Right to Keep Fit" left me without any information on a possible link between coffee and cholesterol, although it showed no mercy in lecturing me on the risks of caffeine. Then I looked on the Internet.

I searched for the subject "coffee AND cholesterol" on Yahoo and with the push of a button found more than a dozen articles on the subject, including several scholarly papers. A scientist in Sweden had found that coffee did indeed represent the potential of raising cholesterol levels when it's brewed through the most common methods, including drip, steam, French press, and the barbaric practice of percolation. However, he noted a curious exception in the case of paper filters. The way I read that, his research seemed to say the coffee made in most coffee houses was dangerous to me while the coffee from my Mr. Coffee machine was OK. But I wanted to make sure.

I noticed the doctor listed an e-mail address, so I sent him a note, asking if my conclusion was correct. Then I started reading a second paper. Suddenly, my e-mail squawked. It was morning in Sweden, and the kindly doctor had replied to me within two minutes, saying, yes, it was quite OK for me to drink coffee from my machine.

I learned two things that evening. First, I might die from too much caffeine or cholesterol, but one probably wouldn't be responsible for the other. Second, the Internet allows anyone anywhere to find out almost anything about medicine at any time—virtually, for free. I was relieved by the first discovery, and awed by the potential of the second.

In the early 1990s, I saw many presentations—by Pacific Telesis Group, then a San Francisco–based Baby Bell, and others—about "distance medicine." The idea was simple: By the late 1990s, any doctor's office could be linked over broadband lines to the best hospitals where the best physicians in any field would be standing by to take the call. There were numerous exhibits showing how this would work. I recall one in which doctors on each end of the line examined the same X-ray and discussed what the little black thing was just beside the lung. The whole thing smacked of snake oil, and much of it was. Pacific Telesis's vaunted $5 billion information superhighway project was never built, the company was sold to Southwestern Bell, and country doctors today still do what country doctors did then: they make up for their lack of expertise with kindly smiles and sympathy.

SOMEDAY SOON

I have no doubt—indeed, I have considerable *hope*—I will live long enough to see distance medicine become a reality. Some elements of it will never come to pass. I doubt, for example, that the world's leading experts in anything are ever going to make themselves broadly available to make consultations for every Tom, Dick, and Mary carrying a PPO card. If they did, their fees would be so astronomical that only the very rich and the very lucky would be able to take advantage of their skills.

It's more likely that rural doctors will get access to regional medical centers where moderately skilled doctors could bring their colleagues up to date or recommend further tests. Rural doctors also could do what I did with my coffee question: they could do research on the Net (something my urban doctor hasn't thought much about to this day, by the way). And the big city doctors could reach out to colleagues from other cities and, perhaps, share databases of symptoms, treatments, and outcomes.

There's also some promise for doctors in third world countries, who in the past few years have gained access to extensive research that may help save lives.

These sorts of practical applications of networked medicine already have taken shape in medical schools, teaching hospitals, government research organizations, disease research groups, and alternative therapy venues, and they are likely coming soon to large health maintenance organizations and insurance companies. But the Internet's broadest and most immediate impact will be on three far more commercial levels:

1. *Health care vendors.* These sites are "virtual doctors," to use an extremely flattering description, who stand ready to help to guide your health care decisions by providing information about symptoms, diseases, causes, and possible treatments. Unlike a doctor, they won't prescribe medicine and most—thanks to our litigious society—ultimately will advise you to see a physician for anything that has even a minor chance of being seri-

ous. Some sites have stirred ethical controversies. A higher level of these vendors is already pitching itself to practicing physicians, offering them cheap consultative services on just about anything that might ail a patient.

2. *Medical suppliers.* This class includes the drug stores, device makers, and other vendors of the things you need to get well, stay healthy, and live happily. Most experts believe it's likely suppliers will sell prescription drugs at a fraction of the price that a local drug store will charge, although their impact will be limited to ongoing health problems rather than acute illnesses. (Americans spend about $150 billion a year on drugs, or about five times what they spend on books. Imagine if one company dominated pharmaceutical sales the way Amazon dominates the Internet book trade!) In addition to pharmaceuticals, these cyberstores offer toiletries, contraceptives, baldness drugs, and other marginally medical ephemera.

3. *Medical infrastructure.* These are the folks who do the billing, recordkeeping, and other administrative functions that go into the delivery of medical care. Many Internet pundits would argue that there's infrastructure in any field and that it's unnecessary to consider the medical infrastructure differently than, say, the information technology behind the auto industry, which also tracks bills, recordkeeping, and other administrative functions. I disagree because solid recordkeeping in medicine is a life-or-death proposition that is critical to providing proper medical care, and it often is lacking in health care today. Indeed, this is, perhaps, the biggest potential growth area for medical care on the Internet with about $300 billion spent annually on medical administration in the United States alone, much of it unnecessarily.

These three categories included more than 1,600 Web sites by 1999, and the number seemed to be increasing faster than bacteria on a petri dish. According to Cyber Dialogue Inc., a research firm, more than 24.8 million adults have sought health information online. Daren Marhula, a financial analyst for U.S. Bancorp Piper Jaffray, estimates 43 percent of Americans on the Internet seek health information, and 81 percent find the information useful. That clearly puts health care on the Web into the "killer ap" category.

"The benefits realized by utilizing the Internet in health care will be rapid and substantial, and the financial rewards from investing early in emerging companies will be significant," Marhula wrote in a white paper on the subject. "The Internet will be the single most important development for the health care industry over the foreseeable future."

A bit later, Marhula added this:

"Not only will these new technologies help streamline the administrative and clinical process of health care, they will also allow the consumer to become more empowered. The empowerment will go much further than the 'content' that is available today on the Internet. Imagine having the ability to track one's health care status from a home PC, analyze one's own EKG, monitor one's pulse and blood pressure, and track these along with standard encounters over one's lifetime—in other words, become an informed consumer or participant in one's own health care."

Hmmm. Sounds good, but let's take a more detailed look at each of these areas and examine some of the early competitors in the Internet.

HEALTH CARE VENDORS

I think the first thing to establish is that your doctor *probably* isn't going to go on the Internet to consult with the world's leading experts for you. Just as my doctor did little to look into my question about coffee and cholesterol, your doctor probably is just going to go on prescribing medicine unless you demand otherwise.

Beyond that, you can find out just about anything about your health over the Internet. The danger here is that other people on the Internet may not be as discreet or as ethical as your family physician. The key, then, is to get the information you need from a source you trust without divulging more about yourself than you dare.

You'll find two primary camps here. The first is the information providers—the groups, foundations, research centers, and individual doctors—who publish vast collections of information about diseases, symptoms, treatments, theories, and such. Generally, these sites are neither interactive nor personalized, but that can be a good thing in medicine. Reading the cold hard facts about disease can help to strip out the emotion that patients tend to bring to researching their own ailments. The objectivity also can help patients recognize something they'd rather not see, and can send patients running to flesh-and-blood physicians for personalized advice and treatment.

A relative passed away in 1998 from a horrid disease called scleroderma. This modern horror is rare. It attacks organs, such as the lungs or skin, destroying cells as it spreads. I knew nothing of this autoimmune disease before it struck my family. In a single evening, however, I was able to read several informative stories about it, find out current theories and therapies, and even share the stories of individuals who'd been struggling with it for years. This was an instance when the Internet's enormous power gave me knowledge and comfort and guidance all at once, and I share the story to show how this type of free medical "service" is already paying immeasurable benefits to those who take the time to look.

But the Internet can do much more than this. It can help to organize consumer health care by keeping family medical records in a single database, reminding patients of drug allergies, and helping to identify medical problems before they become serious. The greatest potential here involves the same sort of question-and-answer diagnostic techniques your doctor has probably used on you during office visits: Does it hurt all the time? Is it a dull ache or a sharp pain? How long has it been there? How's your diet, your sleep?

If people answer enough questions, the answers will usually lead to a proper diagnosis. A doctor can only try to remember such responses and try to ask the right questions in the right order. A computer can do it perfectly, delivering a textbook diagnosis and allowing people to make the very human decision of whether they need a second opinion from a human, or simply two aspirin and a good night's sleep.

Now, are people going to answer all those questions on the Internet without knowing who's on the other end or what they're going to do with your private medical information? I hope not. Consumers will insist on privacy. They'll favor medical sites that publish a clear policy on the handling of medical information, and they'll go somewhere else if they're not comfortable with a site's practices.

One very logical place to go is to a software store where consumers can buy a doc-in-a-box program that will answer questions faster and in total privacy. The problem is these programs are limited in scope, while the Web is not, and they aren't updated continually, while the Web is.

Protecting privacy on the Web is up to the consumer. It's astonishing to me that most folks don't talk about medical problems with their coworkers or friends, but are willing to blab intimate details on public chat boards with total strangers, and then they act shocked about the lack of privacy. I have a rule of thumb about publishing something in a chat room: I never post any message that I wouldn't be willing to shout from my front porch. What's said on a medical site is the consumer's decision, and any expectation of privacy is a gray area.

Selling Information

In one of her columns on CBS.MarketWatch.com, Rebecca Eisenberg ripped into WebMD just after Healtheon Corporation stunned Wall Street by agreeing to pay $10 billion for the money-losing online health care provider. Eisenberg smelled a rat.

"So I spent an afternoon at the WebMD Web site, Web MD.com, where I found the answer. WebMD's true business, according to the 'privacy statement' hidden two levels into this site, is that of collecting demographic information from its information-seeking consumer membership and selling it as market research and targeted advertising to drug manufacturers, medical equipment makers, health insurance companies, government agencies, and private businesses seeking to minimize risk."

This research is exactly what consumers can and should do before giving out any information about themselves that they wouldn't want the whole wide world to know. Intrigued by Eisenberg's research, I spent a couple of evenings going through WebMD and several other popular medical Web sites and every one I visited also said they collected broad demographic information on their consumers and might share it in some way with third parties. Each also said it would never identify individual consumers to third parties without permission. WebMD, for example, said it collects the IP addresses of its users, e-mail addresses, user profiles, and other data. It also pointed out that any information you disclose in a chat room can't be taken back.

Consumers who aren't comfortable with that will find virtually unlimited medical information available for free elsewhere on the Web. If they are comfortable, these medical sites are pretty good at helping to find information. Let's take a look at a few of the leaders—WebMD, healthgate.com, Mediconsult. com, and OnHealth.com—rating them on the criteria we used earlier: choice, usability, personalization, and safety. All were free, so we'll leave that out.

Choice

All of these sites seemed to offer a wide variety of information to choose from. Some sites have busier designs than others, but you can't tell a site from its home page. Some people are dazzled by clutter, some are turned off; this is largely a matter of personal taste. Overall, I'd give all these sites a good grade for choice.

Usability

The first big difference came in the area of service. I decided to ask each to search for "pain in side," which seemed easy enough. Two sites simply told me they had nothing on that while the other two gave me so many choices that I could find no useful information. So I searched for "cholesterol AND coffee." Mediconsult came up with zero; healthgate gave me 24 choices that reminded me of the search I'd done on Yahoo years earlier; OnHealth gave me 26 choices that were all related to my query and were easy to comprehend; and WebMD gave me more than 2,000 choices—a virtual Tower of Babble. So healthgate and OnHealth each got a B+ while I'd give an F to the other sites.

Personalization

I didn't find any individualized services on any of the sites, except the option to e-mail in a question. Some said they had doctors available to answer questions and I later read that Mediconsult would let you consult with a doctor for $195. Aside from chat boards, I didn't see much personalization on my first visits. So they all get a D here.

Safety

All sites carried disclaimers about their advice, and I can't say I blame them. But how safe is it to take free medical advice from strangers who won't take responsibility for what they're saying? And then there's the privacy concern, which none addressed to my satisfaction. Healthgate.com included articles provided by sponsors that seem to have a conflict of interest. For example, an article provided by the California Almond Board poo-pooed the idea there was any health problem in eating nuts. All sites flunked this category.

My conclusion: These sites have huge potential, but a long, long way to go before people should view them as trusted sources of medical information. For the time being, I'd rather get information from a search engine and skip the potential conflicts of interest and safety issues associated with these sites.

DRUG STORES

Let's visit a few of the medical supply sites: Drugstore.com (45 percent owned by Amazon), planetRx, and SOMA (owned by CVS). All had reasonably well-designed interfaces, including easy-to-use search features. All had many choices, and each had the feel of a large, brick-and-mortar drug store.

Price

On price, they all offered different bargains on various items. Overall, I thought the prices were competitive with each other, although I didn't see the kind of bargains I'd expect from online companies with little overhead. This eliminated a major reason to shop at any of them. If I want to pay $7 for some sun screen, I can get it the next time I'm at the store, skip the delivery charge, and maybe find some on sale.

Personalization

All sites offered personalized services, so a passing grade for all of them there. The critical question, which will take some time to answer, is whether all will do a good job at keeping

records on personal prescriptions, potential drug contraindica-
tions, insurance billing, and the other critical pieces of the puzzle.

Safety

Finally, there is safety. These sites also said they would pass
along aggregate data to third parties, something that doesn't
bother me terribly, but might bother some customers. I would
give them all at least the same benefit of the doubt I would give
a brick-and-mortar pharmacy for spotting potentially dangerous drug combinations and such. And I trust my billing would
be accurate and confidential. SOMA loses a point for not putting
a link to its privacy policy on the home page.

One additional note about safety: about the time I was visiting the sector's leaders, some smaller online drug vendors
came under review by regulators in at least three states. Two—
one in Illinois and one in Kansas—got into trouble for selling
Viagra without examining the patient (one customer was a 16-
year-old boy). A third vendor sold Propecia, a hair-loss treatment, without seeing patients. As the competitive field widens,
it may be very difficult to monitor such problems, leaving it to
the consumer to be on guard.

So, in the retail arena, these stores are all OK, but I don't see
why people would shop at them unless it is more convenient
than it would be to go to the store. My guess is that competition
will eventually drive prices sharply lower as these stores trade
off gross margin for volume. You have the power to demand better from these companies, and you should insist that they meet
your expectations.

INFRASTRUCTURE SITES

As for the infrastructure health care sites, these business-
to-business operations don't fit into my five-point evaluation
scheme, but Marhula's white paper did an excellent job of pointing out the reasons that some of these companies should thrive.

He pointed to companies like Abaton.com, Healtheon (which subsequently merged with WebMD), Shared Medical Systems, Cerner Corp., and MedicaLogic. He made a compelling statistical case and I'll pass along my own summary of it:

- It's estimated that more than $250 billion annually, or 25 cents of every health care dollar, is wasted through delivery on unnecessary care, performance of redundant tests and procedures, and excessive administrative costs;
- 11 percent of lab tests are reordered because the results are lost;
- 25 percent of prescriptions are never filled;
- The annual cost of medical recordkeeping in the United States is $200 billion;
- Less than a third of the 5,500 U.S. hospitals are linked electronically with their health care partners;
- Only 6 percent of the health care industry in the United States uses the Internet to manage supplies, outside the health care field, the figure is 25 percent;
- Six out of every 100 hospital admissions result in an adverse drug event (ADE), and 28 percent of these are avoidable. This leads to 140,000 deaths annually, making ADEs the fourth leading cause of death in the United States (yikes!). A patient profile on the Web could help prevent many of those deaths.

On top of all that, the Congressional Budget Office estimates disposable income will grow at a compound annual growth rate of about 1.5 percent through the year 2005 while health care costs rise 7.3 percent. So there is clearly an economic imperative to bring down those costs as the boomer generation ages.

The Internet, my friends, will generate more health care choices, at lower prices, with better service tailored to increasingly powerful consumers, and it may even save a lot of lives. Consumers should demand all of that and more.

CHAPTER 8

THAT'S ENTERTAINMENT
Unlimited Choice

Herb Allen is an investment banker best known for his stakes in the entertainment arena and for his invitation-only Sun Valley conferences, which have taken on the feel of private retreats for the entertainment superstars and corporate kings. It was at one of these conferences where the heads of ABC and Cap Cities got together on merger plans between rafting trips and golf games.

When I attended a recent conference, the buzz focused on one issue: the rapid approach of broadband Internet service and what that means to the entertainment industry. About 200 executives were on hand for the discussion, folks like Michael Ovitz, AT&T's Mike Armstrong, Intel's Andy Grove, Pixar's (and Apple's) Steve Jobs, Microsoft's Bill Gates, Microsoft cofounder and venture capitalist Paul Allen, Liberty Media's John Malone, ABC's Bob Iger, NBC's Bob Wright, CBS's Mel Karmazin, Hollywood's Jack Valenti, and Oprah Winfrey. They schmoozed, they ate, they laughed, and they talked—very seriously and *behind closed doors*—about what broadband means to the entertainment industry.

"This is a really unique blend of the heavy hitters from technology and the entertainment business. What's clear from all of this year's presentations is the big impact the Internet's having," said Paul Allen, whose Vulcan Ventures had wagered heavily on the convergence of cable, wireless, and Internet companies. "I think everyone here is talking about how to take their businesses forward in the Internet area."

Indeed, it seemed they were, and with good reason. If the most widely held expectations about the Internet are true, we are moving to a world that will dramatically transform the way we think of media—whether news, sports, movies, television, or advertising. And if your company's revenue comes from one of those areas, you had better have a pretty good plan for shifting a good portion of that revenue stream to the Internet before broadband cable, digital TV, and superior levels of interactivity bring new choices to your customers.

Take network television, where big careers rise and fall when a network's share of a national audience shifts a percentage point. What will happen when those audience shares slip 5 percent because the audience no longer is content to be spoon-fed reruns of "Dharma and Greg?" What happens when a sports fan in San Francisco wants to watch tonight's Cleveland Indians game instead of the Boston game offered by ESPN? What if you'd rather watch some good drama from England? Or a Beijing Opera from China? Or a travelogue on the city you're visiting next month?

Suddenly, the viewer's choice isn't limited to the three or four networks, or even to a handful of local stations beaming signals over very high and ultra-high frequencies. Instead, viewers are empowered to choose from hundreds, even thousands, of options ranging from crudely built Web sites to the slickest Hollywood productions. A TV commercial for Qwest made this point nicely as a business man checks into a dusty, roadside motel to find out room service includes donuts and coffee, but the in-room cable offers every movie ever made at any hour. And that's just movies.

BEYOND THE SCREEN

Soon you'll be able to watch just about anything you please, providing someone has decided to turn it into a Web cast or at least a Web site.

There are many people who believe that the broadband age will simply usher in a more advanced age of television, blending in interactive elements and enhanced advertising capabilities. When that high-quality video starts showing up, they predict simpler Web sites will be ignored. But that argument doesn't explain why tens of millions of people are currently turning off the boob-tube in favor of sitting in front of a computer filled with those simple Web sites. Remember, while TV gets better, those simple Web sites will also get better, adding full-motion video, higher fidelity sound, and whatever other accommodations enhance their particular presentation.

This must be a terrifying time for those in Hollywood who produce the mindless fare we see at the movies or on TV. Even as films continue to post box office records, the quality of the films themselves is under increasing attack. And the TV audience is shrinking as the Internet and other alternatives siphon off large numbers of viewers. Only the most arrogant executive would believe the trend toward more intelligent programming on the Web could be reversed by the addition to the Web of advanced TV.

To be sure, there will likely be movie palaces and bad TV shows for many years to come. But it won't take much to throw corporate profits into a tailspin, a shift that could lead to rapid cutbacks in expensive production at the major studios. Fewer productions mean smaller audiences. That means still-smaller profits and still-fewer productions and on and on.

If you multiply that effect by the number of different types of media (radio, TV, film, magazines, newspapers, cable networks) and then multiply again by the number of programming areas (drama, comedy, sports, performing arts, news, financial, educational, adult, etc.), you begin to get an idea of the magnitude of change that is possible when broadband networking services become available throughout our society. And when you add in the rapid changes in technology taking place—the Moore's Law factor—it becomes almost impossible for a company to plan on how best to meet consumer tastes just a few years out.

Finally, there is interactivity—a concept best understood by the video game industry at present, but one that I feel will be the defining element in establishing those who will dominate the coming media age.

ON THE CUSP

Sprint chairman William Esrey told me at the Allen conference he believes we're right "on the cusp" of a broadband explosion that already had begun to reach the business communities in major cities and would expand to most residential areas within a few years.

John Malone, the former chairman of Tele-Communications Inc., told reporters he sees cable company services duking it out with the slightly less-robust DSL (digital subscriber lines) offered by telephone companies. However, he said there's clearly a trend of consumers choosing the higher bandwidth option if it means a superior viewing experience.

That's probably true for the crowd that wants to see a trailer for a new "Star Wars" episode, but for many Web surfers, more bandwidth just means faster access to the information they're seeking. These folks are not your typical couch potatoes; they're independent people who've already chosen to turn off their TVs, the medium through which much of this advanced programming will be carried.

There really isn't much in the past to help us forecast this part of the future. This is a quantum leap not only in technical quality, but in programming *and* in the medium itself. Perhaps the birth of the motion picture industry, or of television, would be the closest analogies. Those media took many years to catch on, largely because of physical limitations of setting up movie theaters or broadcast facilities. Today, fiber optic cables already run near 40 percent of U.S. homes and can be brought into the living room as soon as the demand arises. And that demand is expected to surge in the first years of the new millennium.

Let's take a quick leap forward to see how this is likely to affect different areas of media and who is doing what to get ready. Each major entertainment company has so many Internet projects underway that it would be difficult to give more than a hint of what's to come.

HOLLYWOOD

We've already talked about some of the challenges facing the TV, film, and music companies moving forward, so let's take a look at what some of the industry giants are doing to protect their interests. This is reflected through what's known as vertical integration—establishing stakes in enterprises at all levels of the food chain so that you can control everything from the production of the entertainment product to the delivery processes.

Two of the companies that excel in this area are Time Warner and Disney. A quick glance at each will give you an idea of how vertical integration opens up the potential for a few very large companies to promote their own creative content along with services developed with partners.

AOL Time Warner, of course, owns the world's largest ISP —America Online. It also owns both Time Inc. (publisher of Time and Fortune) and the film-TV studio Warner Bros. Other major units include Warner Music Group, Turner Entertainment Networks, CNN, HBO, and Time Warner Cable. The cable unit has the ability to reach 21 million U.S. homes—fertile ground for AOL services. The company also operates a high-speed Internet service called RoadRunner in conjunction with Microsoft, Compaq, MediaOne, and Advance-Newhouse. And AT&T has agreed to pay $15 for each home that purchases telephone service through AT&T over cable.

Disney, in addition to its famous theme parks, owns a cruise line, hotels, Buena Vista Music Group (which includes Walt Disney Records, Hollywood Records, Lyric Street Records, and Mammoth Records), ABC Television, a radio network, radio stations, a cable network, TV stations, Touchstone Films, Miramax Films, the Buena Vista Motion Pictures Group, and ESPN. It also operates Go.com, a venture it built with Infoseek that will be the hub of Disney's activity on the Web including shopping, a search engine, and access to all Disney services.

It isn't hard to imagine how companies like Disney and AOL Time Warner will leverage all their properties over the Internet, and their competitors have similar plans. Sony, for example, has extensive presence in film, music, video games, computers, and consumer electronics. Viacom's CBS division has stakes in several Internet ventures, including Sportsline, Third Age, and MarketWatch. It has talked of combining those holdings in a single unit. Virtually every major player in entertainment has properties and relationships aimed at sustaining its revenue stream in a new medium—the Internet.

Does that mean they'll dominate entertainment in this new medium? It could be, because consumers are used to seeing entertainment products made by these companies and there is a certain comfort in continuity. However, the door is wide open to newcomers and, just as Fox proved that consumers are open to new types of programming on TV, virtually any company with new ideas for entertainment better suited to the Internet will have a splendid opportunity to attract fans. After all, the most popular things on the Web now are not from some mass medium but rather the tens of thousands of different things that people delight in discovering on their own.

I spent one evening touring Web sites with material about the Vietnam War, and I read many things I'd never heard about that conflict. On other nights, you might find me playing a computer game, talking with strangers in a financial chat room, or watching video clips from a just-released film. With the exception of the film clips, I can't do any of that on TV. And with film clips on the Web, I can choose when I want to watch them. That's the essence of interactive entertainment—the ability to do what you want, when you want.

NOT INTERACTIVE

None of the major U.S.–based entertainment companies appears especially astute about interactivity. As a generation of video game players becomes the bulk of the consumer force in America, that will be a critical factor in deciding which entertainment is best suited to the Internet in the twenty-first century, and which was better suited for the more passive, and aging, TV and film audience of the twentieth century.

Mainstream entertainment companies may be good at making TV shows or movies, but the Internet is a medium with its own peculiar characteristics. Just as it took a generation to develop proficiency in films and TV, it will take another 15 to 20 years to develop quality broadband Web programming.

Of course, there will always be schlock. The most important thing to remember is something that has always been true about entertainment in the United States: You can blame the writers and directors for making bad movies; you can blame the corporations for producing them; but don't forget to blame yourselves for demanding them. In the end, if consumers want to point fingers at the people responsible for the violent, vulgar, and shallow entertainment they see, they should point those fingers at themselves for watching.

SPORTS

Since ninth grade, my best friend has been a fellow named Charley, who for many years was a devout fan of the Washington Redskins. The only problem was, we grew up on Long Island and unless the 'Skins happened to be playing the Giants, you couldn't watch them on TV. One season, he discovered that when conditions were right, he could faintly pick up an AM station from somewhere in Pennsylvania that broadcast the Redskins games, but it was a painful way to follow his team. He went on to college at Northwestern in Evanston, Illinois, at a time its Wildcats football team was . . . well . . . horrible. After college, Charley suffered many more years trying to find out what happened to the 'Cats.

It's little wonder that sports programming has become one of the most popular features of the Internet, and the only thing that surprises me is that it hasn't become far more popular much faster. There are, very conservatively, about 10 million Americans who have a rabid interest in at least one team or one sport. Those folks just aren't happy unless they can quickly find out the results of their favorite contests—be it a pro basketball game, the Tour de France, or tennis at Wimbledon.

Imagine how many of them would be trapped in their homes if they could watch virtually any contest they want. Colleges have already found out the Internet is an excellent way to keep in touch with alumni, who can now get the latest news of their teams on university Web sites, and frequently can listen to radio broadcasts of the games, or even watch live Web casts. This is the tip of the sports iceberg. How long will it be before every professional team, every major golf or tennis tourney, and every major college offers Web casts to fans around the world?

Just imagine how much advertising revenue a university would generate if a quarter-million of its former graduates—college educated young adults—tuned in to watch the weekly football contest. But it won't be just a great thing for the colleges and the pro teams . . . it will be great for my friend Charley and the millions of Americans like him who simply must have their fix of their favorite team.

By the way, Charley's moved on to soccer these days . . . yet another sport that is difficult to follow from most major U.S. cities. But he can get all the results he needs over the Internet.

SMUT

Frankly, I don't believe the statistics I've seen about pornography on the Internet. For example, I don't believe that 35 million individuals—roughly one in three U.S. Internet consumers—regularly visits adult-oriented sites to gawk at pictures of naked people engaged in sex acts, but that's a number I read on sextracker.com, a site that purportedly keeps track of such statistics.

I do believe that we are sexual by nature and that a large number of Internet users will turn sex into a big business on the Internet, just as they have done with 976 numbers, adult movie houses, videos that lurk on the back shelves of video stores, nudie magazines on newsstands everywhere, and the pulp papers that litter nearly every street corner of tourist districts.

Whether you call it pornography or smut or adult entertainment, what we're seeing on the Internet is hardly anything new. The difference is that the Internet allows any idiot with a video camera and a couple of hundred bucks worth of equipment to become a porn producer. But it can't turn society into a bunch of smut-addicted sheep, unless, of course, a lot of people choose to graze in that pasture. If they do, well, it's a free society.

As for the risk to children, there's plenty of software out there that can help parents guard their offspring from the offensive. Get it and use it if you like, but attempts to regulate Internet content should and will fail. First, regulation is impractical because much of the content originates in other countries. Second, restricting free speech is a dangerous action that, in the long run, could cause far more harm than it eliminates.

PERFORMING ARTS

In the late 1980s, when the San Francisco Ballet had soared to world-class status, I had an extraordinary opportunity to compare it with the Bolshoi, the Kirov, the New York City Ballet, and the American Ballet Theatre within a three-week period. At the time, I was writing some ballet reviews for The Associated

Press and all five companies happened to pass through San Francisco. It was a remarkable windfall of culture that I shall never forget. But I won't say I'll never see anything like it again.

One of the things that I most look forward to in the next several years is the ability to watch a symphony performing in London, a play being staged in Dublin, a ballet company dancing in Paris, the Beijing opera from China, and folk dances in South America.

For many years, I've bemoaned the decline in public television and the near total lack of cultural programming on the commercial airwaves. Still, I regularly attend sold-out performances of the symphony, the ballet, the stage, and the opera. These shows are filled with audiences that constitute an extraordinarily high demographic—one that is highly appealing to the corporate sponsors of such events. And, trust me, prime orchestra seats at the ballet (you *just have* to sit close enough to see the faces) will easily cost you as much as a the best box seat at the ballpark. Alas, even with these factors, it apparently is not commercially viable to air great performances over a television network.

We're entering an era where the culturally starved will feast at a banquet of plenty. Imagine being able to check a culture guide and choose between a dozen great symphonies, ballets, or plays on a single evening. Imagine being able to read about the artists through an interactive program guide. Imagine participating in interactive discussions with the performers and their directors, with an author or a conductor.

Culture has, for too long, belonged to the rich. Soon, it will belong to the powerful—to the consumer. And while my friend Charley catches the latest soccer game from Buenos Aires, I'll be catching the *Symphony Fantastique* by Berlioz from the old Florence Opera House.

ADVERTISING

Clap if you're sick of banner ads. Shout if you're tired of pop-up ads. And scream if you're sick of finding out a previously trustworthy Web site just convinced you to click on a page generated by one of its advertisers, excuse me, "commerce partners."

Like it or not, most Web sites are there to make money. And if they aren't selling something directly, chances are they make their money through advertising.

Is that necessarily a bad thing? No. Advertising has supported major newspapers and television networks for decades. It supports most of the "content" we receive through traditional media, including—especially—special interest magazines. Without those ads, those media would cost many times what we pay for them, or they simply wouldn't exist at all.

Are there ways to provide entertainment over the Web without advertising? Yes. Sites *can* charge admission. In fact, most professional sporting events will charge admission. But those admission costs will be lower if there's also advertising on the site, just as the cost of a baseball ticket is incrementally lower because there are billboards out by the bleachers. We *could* have government subsidies, but we've seen how unreliable those are as the funding for public television and the National Endowment for the Arts has been whittled down over the past 20 years.

Companies sell stuff to make money. For example, we can watch a movie while people try to sell us a poster or the soundtrack. For the near future, expect to see a lot of boring banner ads because that is the state of the art. As bandwidth increases, Web site ads will only become more dominant and more closely integrated with content. For example, on WebTV, viewers can already flip between a program and a window offering additional information, along with a goodly number of ads. On ExciteAtHome's broadband service, you can call up "rich media" commercial areas that provide video and extensive information on particular products. (And ExciteAtHome says people tend to spend several minutes in such areas once they enter, suggesting consumers find this an attractive option.)

Some retail sites are currently trying to sell goods below cost while making a profit by selling ads. Can that work? Well, commercial television has been giving away programming by getting us to watch commercials, so there's reason to believe it can.

We could just get more of same in the years ahead, but can expect advertisers to get a whole lot more sneaky than that. If you watch a movie, and you like that blouse Julia Roberts is wearing, you can click on it and find out if it comes in your size. That's advertising. If you watch Bonnie Chastain rip off her shirt at the end of the World Cup to reveal her Nike sports bra, you can click and find out which colors and sizes are available.

Deeper along the negative end, your kid will watch cartoons, knowing he can order toys at the push of a button (hopefully with your permission). The famished will no longer have to lift a phone to order pizza—just click the remote. Are you watching a sexy movie? Well, would you like to chat with a "hot young teen"? Somebody will figure out how to make that happen.

This may not sound like a better world until you stop and consider that we'll be able to block virtually any kind of ad. In fact, there are already software programs available that will block large ads on existing Web sites. Not only can consumers choose to bar advertisers from sending data, but the sites will download more quickly without all those graphic-intensive images.

CHAPTER 9

JOURNALISM VÉRITÉ
The Global Newsroom

To be "free," to have choice, you must have reliable information. Without reliable information, choice is an illusion. The mission of journalists in a "free" society is to provide reliable information. It is an inherently noble mission, and one that, frankly, is nearly impossible to achieve.

We're embarking on a new age in journalism, one that both excites and terrifies me as someone who has spent the past quarter century in that profession. As noted earlier, my professional fascination with "real-time" journalism began 20 years ago with The Associated Press (AP). My obsession with interactive journalism began in 1992, while watching children play video games. My experience with multimedia journalism blossomed at Bloomberg News. My focus on Web journalism led me to the tiny DBC newsroom, where we created CBS.MarketWatch. After all this time, I feel like I'm only witnessing the birth of "journalism vérité," a form of news that puts the choice of stories and sources into the hands of the consumer. This will fundamentally change the flow of information in society and, with it, our ability to make choices.

Journalists have done a remarkably good job in the twentieth century, but the information they serve to the masses is never entirely trustworthy because it takes a special type of people to be journalists. On one hand, they are determined, altruistic souls willing to work long hours at meager pay in service to society. On the other, as public opinion polls often tell us, they tend to be arrogant, condescending, and paternalistic. We journalists present ourselves as guardians of "the truth," often forgetting our perspective isn't necessarily the same as everyone else's. We think we need to educate people, often failing to recognize the inherent intelligence of the consumer. We consider ourselves as having more rights than fellow citizens, often forgetting we are all in this together.

The perspective that good journalists bring to stories is important. Without perspective, it is difficult to ferret out the important facts of a story from the marginal. However, a growing minority of Americans think journalists go too far. According to a poll conducted in mid-1999 by Gannett's *USA Weekend*, only 65 percent of Americans still support freedom of the press as we know it. That may seem like a solid majority, but it suggests a third of Americans are ready to rewrite the First Amendment.

There's little doubt some journalists have abused the public's trust by invading the privacy of celebrities, sensationalizing horrid crimes for the sake of ratings, or dishing out official government viewpoints without acknowledging their inability to corroborate the facts. And, like all people, journalists tend to fall victim to their own prejudices, whether political, racial, religious, sexual, or national.

Now, the Internet is transferring the power of the press to all of us. We're entering a phase where the contents of the news will be largely determined by the consumer and the sources rather than by a news organization. The individual may choose to read a particular news story from a particular news organization, or to ignore it entirely. People may choose a subject that interests them from a source *they* personally find trustworthy—be it a political extremist, a sitting president, or a corporate spokesperson.

This will change the nature of journalism more dramatically than the invention of the telegraph, wire services, radio, and television all together. This is what I refer to as "journalism vérité," and many of my colleagues would question whether it's journalism at all.

READER'S CHOICE

Journalism vérité is when people are able to obtain information *that they consider reliable.* It recognizes that everyone is unique and, therefore, requires a unique set of information. It recognizes that information can at times be more accurate without being colored by reporters or media corporations. It recognizes that everyone is capable of asking questions and of demanding satisfactory answers. And it accepts that what is really important to society should be determined by society, not media corporations.

In the past, journalists decided what went onto page one. Now, increasingly, individuals will be in control.

The great danger is that we all tend to be a bit myopic, meaning we may fail to identify stories that are important to society as a whole. It isn't hard to imagine, for example, that someone might choose to see all the news about their local schools, the environment, rock music, business, and sports, but won't look for news about Congress, crime, Asia, or Africa. As a result, they may never learn about a famine that killed tens of thousands of people, of corruption in government, of Chinese protests, or of a murder spree in their own town.

Another danger: Unless people understand the different sources of news stories, they will be unable to tell a reliable story from a biased report written by someone with a special interest. The good news is that many of us have learned to be skeptical. The bad news is many of us put too much faith in the honesty of strangers.

As Mike Bloomberg pointed out in our discussion, Hitler started out by speaking on street corners in Germany, but at least you could see who was speaking. On the Internet, you really don't know.

The old-age journalist in me wonders if the public can handle this, if society will be taken over by propagandists, if anyone will protect us from manipulators, if consumers have the horse sense to spot the next Hitler. The new-age journalist in me respects the intelligence of the consumer to choose the stories, to pick trustworthy sources, and to drink in knowledge according to their own thirst. There is substantial evidence that thirst is nearly limitless, and that journalism is alive and well under the control of its new owner-consumers.

HAVE FAITH

In any case, consumers on the Net choose their news, and the early signs are they are choosing wisely. Mainstream news organizations are finding huge new audiences through the Internet. *The New York Times,* for example, has far more readers online than it has in print. And tens of millions of Americans say they use the Internet largely to get news. As we move forward, news organizations will find ways to blend what they do best with the personal tastes of readers, and consumers seem to be welcoming a helping hand from news pros.

According to Media Metrix, an Internet research group, there was a 70 percent increase in usage at online news sites like AP.org when the massacre occurred at Columbine High School and the United States led attacks on Yugoslavia. That says that people wanted to get more information about particular events that they thought were important to their lives, and they went out to find it on their own at high-quality news sites—all reassuring signs.

When I was at Bloomberg News, the most popular story had nothing to do with Wall Street. It was the acquittal of O.J. Simpson. That's because the sea of money managers sitting behind Bloomberg terminals elected with near unanimity to make that the most important piece of information. Normally, their interests would be scattered among hundreds of other stories.

Scores of Web sites were strained or crashed when the grand jury testimony of Monica Lewinsky was released. Surely millions just wanted to see the sensational details, but millions also realized that those words would help determine if Clinton should be impeached.

These are all examples of masses of people determining what constitutes an important event, and certainly, the media served up heaping helpings of Simpson and Monica. But the media didn't do it on their own. It was the public's demand for such stories that made them into epic events.

While these kinds of mass media stories tend to be the most talked about, most people are interested in news more relevant to themselves. At Bloomberg, for example, tens of thousands of money managers seek information to make informed investment decisions. At MarketWatch, it's the fact that hundreds of thousands of different types of information are requested each day by consumers who pick and choose what they each want. And in other Web-based media, there's an almost endless array of news stories, opinion columns, press releases, graphics, and data available in almost every language on the planet.

INFORMED READERS

Quite simply, we are moving to a world where journalism is closer to accomplishing its mission: to pass along reliable information to people who need that information to make informed decisions, or, in effect, to be free. The irony is that the media is now largely in a passive role, serving the demands of the newly empowered consumers.

NEWS QUALITIES

There are four key factors that will keep journalism alive, and will keep the Internet from evolving into a Tower of Babble:

(1) immediacy, (2) reliability, (3) editorial judgment, and (4) inter-activity. Let's look at them one by one.

Immediacy

We've talked about "real-time" news before, but what does that mean? You might as well ask why "news" is called "news." The news business involves "new" information, facts that have a value in current time. Consider two items: one tiny and one enormous. Item one: There's a 65 percent chance it will rain in your town today. Item two: A tornado is spinning toward your town.

Fact one might be important to you because you want to stay dry, because you'll remember to take your umbrella, and because your lawn is looking a little dry. Will the information have value tomorrow? Well, it won't matter any more in terms of staying dry. You won't care about the umbrella. And your lawn either got some water or it didn't—not necessarily critical. So the news value is mostly gone.

Fact two has obvious importance that could make the difference between life and death if you act on it immediately. Tomorrow, you'll only be interested in the aftermath.

The lesson here is that no matter how important or trivial the information is, it has a useful life. And the more important it is, the more urgent it tends to be. In truth, most information falls between these types of extremes, and its importance tends to vary depending on your proximity—physical or relative—to the news.

For example, your local newspaper may have a story about a fatal car crash on page one. On page seven, you might find a short story about a crash in another state that killed six people. On page 32, you might see a one-paragraph item about a train wreck that killed 23 in India. Your interest in these stories might be very different if you happened to be Indian, or if you were visiting from the state where the other car crash took place.

If ZZZ Corporation said it won't meet earnings estimates this quarter, you probably won't care at all unless you happen to own a large stake in the company. In that case, you'll be eager to get the information before other shareholders drive the stock's price lower.

If a murder occurs in a downtown bar, you may have a morbid curiosity in hearing something about the value of life in the city where you live. But it probably won't generate a lasting impact on your life unless the murderer's still on the loose and headed your way, or you knew the victim.

The Internet makes the world smaller and infinitely more immediate. When there is a school shooting, or a plane crash, or a killer tornado, the whole world can know details of those events as quickly as they become available—providing immediacy that enhances the value of the news and allowing for variations in the proximity of the event to the consumer. Hence, consumers can get the information most relevant to them when they need it.

Reliability

Does Matt Drudge, the king of cyber-muckraking, have as much credibility as *The New York Times?* No. Is he credible? That's a very different question.

Traditionally, journalists have had to decide the credibility of sources before reporting them. A supermarket tabloid clearly has different standards for its sources than, say, the AP. The tabloid might run a story about the desperate last days of an aging film star with attribution to an unidentified close friend who supposedly confided intimate details. The AP trains its staff to attribute virtually any piece of information to recognized authorities in the area covered by the story, and to name those sources whenever humanly possible. That's why you'll often see AP stories that repeat the phrase "police said" a half-dozen times in as many paragraphs.

You don't have to have an inquiring mind to see the difference. If the AP announces that Martians have landed in the nation's capital, you might run to a phone to call your loved ones. If the tabloid reports it, you'll probably chuckle and finish checking out your groceries.

But the Internet places the perception of the reliability of sources largely in the eyes of the reader. For example, if you read on a university's Web site that there was scientific evidence that Martians landed on Earth one million years ago, would you believe it? What if you saw a press release from Exxon announcing it had completely cleaned up all the oil from a tanker spill? What if the governor of your state told you his opponent had embezzled funds from a local school board?

In addition to common sense, it takes training and experience to sort out reliable sources from unreliable sources. Most people don't have that. They may have high intelligence, but two equally intelligent people might disagree as to the veracity of a piece of information. They have always left that up to a medium they trust.

Editorial Judgment

Remember NAFTA—the North American Free Trade Agreement? It made quite a stir in the 1992 presidential campaign when George Bush hailed it, Bill Clinton defended it, and H. Ross Perot derided it, saying it would result in "a great sucking sound" of American jobs heading to Mexico.

Why was NAFTA front-page news? Sure, the economy was big news, given that tens of thousands of Americans had lost jobs in the just-concluded recession. Still, Clinton successfully focused his campaign on less esoteric economic issues. My guess is that most Americans and the two major candidates would have gladly ignored NAFTA if it hadn't been for the news media, which seemed bent on boring us all to tears with front-page stories about how important it was to the U.S. economy.

This is a good example of editorial judgment, which is probably the most important element of journalism, aside from accuracy and timeliness. While many Americans might be mostly interested in entertainment news, newspaper editors and TV producers have taken it upon themselves to determine what they think is important and to put that on page one.

That sort of judgment is being replaced by the new choices of the Internet. Aside from special interest groups like union members or economics, would the public take it upon itself to read about NAFTA? Will the public at large choose to read about poverty, discrimination, and violent crime? I have my doubts.

Interactivity

Imagine for a second that you're reading a story about President Clinton, and it refers to Monica Lewinsky, and you think to yourself: "Who was her friend? Ah, yes, Linda Tripp. Now, what group was Tripp associated with? And didn't that group receive funding from conservatives?"

None of those questions may be answered in the story you're reading, but it's natural for the human mind to want to ask questions while reading down a news column in a news-paper or watching a report on a passive medium like TV. In the Internet, each consumer has the opportunity to ask questions all the time, and to get immediate answers. With broadband, they'll also have the opportunity to arrange their own replays of video clips and audio recordings to help provide substance to the news.

Probably the greatest change in journalism vérité is that the consumer's ability to choose the subject will extend into every sentence. This is also an enormous change for journalists, who must build the potential for interactivity into every story. It may be possible, however, to incorporate a search engine that allows readers to search for related stories on any term in the story.

We are just at the dawn of interactive journalism, and it appears to me it will be a decade or two before journalists figure out how to make the most of this new medium, just as it took 15 or 20 years to master radio or TV news production. With the Internet, one problem is that veteran journalists and editors, who tend to put out the nation's best known news products, know very little about interactivity because their generation grew up reading newspapers and watching TV. Young journalists, who grew up playing video games and working on personal computers, tend to understand—even expect—interactivity, but don't yet have much experience in journalism.

As one generation replaces the other, and as technology advances the opportunity to build interactivity into news, there will be a dramatic shift. Consumers, at that point, will have the power not only to define which subjects they want to read about, but what they want to read about those subjects.

This may seem alarming to a journalist who is used to the public sitting still and accepting the story as the journalist wants to tell it. It would be as if the consumers constantly were interrupting the journalist's story with questions.

Love it or hate it, this is the way news will be delivered in the future. While I have concerns, I think it's generally a good thing because it amplifies the news-gathering experience for the consumer. If an investor reads a quote about the economy from Alan Greenspan and is concerned about the specific context, the reader can click and read the entire speech. And if she's concerned about Mr. Greenspan's tone at the moment he spoke, she can click again to watch a video.

We're already building interactivity into every story at MarketWatch. A typical story there is linked to a half-dozen related stories, to other top stories of the day, to charts for stocks mentioned in the story, to press releases about the story, and to other types of data that support or amplify statements in the story. Major stories link to "multimedia" reports—TV clips of an interview, or an audio report about the subject. It's not uncommon for a 300-word story to include as many as 30 or 40 live links, not counting the navigational aids present on every page.

This gives readers a traditional news story along with the ability to investigate further on their own. They also can investigate our sources to check our reliability according to their own filters. If they find a problem, they can click on our names to send us a quick e-mail, or go on our discussion boards to talk about the story.

PART TWO

INTRODUCTION
Planning for the Future

Is there one correct vision of what the World Wide Web will become? No. If there were, it would be easy to run an Internet company, to invest in an Internet stock, and to predict how the Web will change our world. Perhaps the most exciting thing about the Internet is that no one person can be certain where all this will lead.

The conversations that follow—all of which took place prior to my recent move to infoUSA.com—reflect some of the best thinking about the future of technology and our society. I'm very grateful to the ten men and women who agreed to share their private and professional viewpoints. In selecting them, I imagined I was assembling a "dream team" board of directors for an Internet company. Each has a working knowledge of the Internet and business, but each also has expertise in a specific area: Trip Hawkins, interactivity; Andy Grove, data processing; Paul Erdman, economics; Barry Diller, entertainment; Paul Saffo, forecasting; Rebecca Eisenberg, law; Jerry Brown, society; Ann Winblad, entrepreneurism; Jerry Yang, content; and Mike Bloomberg, finance. I also intentionally chose this diverse group of people because they lead interesting lives *off*-line.

My hope is that their words, particularly their views about their individual areas of expertise, will expand ideas about the Web Rules for the Information Age.

ANN WINBLAD

Cofounder of Hummer-Winblad Venture Partners

Behind every great Web entrepreneur, there's a smart venture capitalist who put up the money. Quite often, it's Ann Winblad, cofounder of Hummer-Winblad Venture Partners, who started off as an entrepreneur.

In 1976, as Steve Jobs and Bill Gates were just getting started, Winblad took a $500 investment and cofounded Open Systems Software, which produced one of the first successful accounting software programs. She sold the company six years later for $15 million.

After consulting for such companies as IBM, Price Waterhouse, and Microsoft, she cofounded her venture firm with former NBA star John Hummer in 1989. The firm was unique in that it only funded software ventures. It gave birth to such companies as PowerSoft, Scopus Technology, Hyperion Solutions, Wind River Systems, T/Maker, and many others. At least 18 Hummer-Winblad companies have been acquired, and 7 have gone public. Its 20 Net companies run the range from Pets.com and HomeGrocer.com to Liquid Audio and AdForce.

Winblad holds bachelor's degrees in math and science, and master's degrees in education and international economics, from the University of St. Thomas in St. Paul, where she now serves on the board. Her father was a high school sports coach and her sister teaches high school Spanish, leaving her with strong personal feelings about education.

Winblad, who also serves on six corporate boards, has a reputation for taking an active role in day-to-day operations. *Business Week* called her one of Silicon Valley's Top 25 power brokers and, for three straight years, *Upside Magazine* named her one of the 100 most influential people of the digital age. Her management style bespeaks the simple values acquired during her upbringing in rural Minnesota: a warm personality, a strong sense of teamwork, and an unquestioned dedication to hard work.

What do you personally use the Internet for?

I'm a product of the software industry, so I was actually on the Internet a long time as an e-mail user. Now that everyone is an e-mail user, my primary use of the Internet is as a platform for worldwide communication. And I think as more and more consumers become e-mail users, it will become the dominant activity on the Internet as the preeminent communications platform. I can anticipate that I'll have my voice mail and e-mail interface there and that telephony will take on a new shape. So e-mail is my dashboard.

I am a consumer. I tend to be a little different a consumer now than when I was an up-and-coming entrepreneur in Minnesota in that I tend to be operating in a time-famine. I tend to know what I want. And when I want it, I want it now. I'm not as price sensitive as I am 'this is something I need to do my job, to make my life easier.' So I'll go to selected sites for shopping. I'm really Ann.com. Whenever I can use the digital interface, I use it. I prefer to use my analog time in a place like a movie theater or on a bicycle or playing tennis or on a hike versus bricks-and-mortar shopping.

You're beyond the early adopter. You're a functioning consumer who's made the Internet a part of your life. As a successful businesswoman, though, you don't really have to search for bargains on the Internet.

I make a healthy income, so I'm not a value shopper. I don't use some of the tools for comparison shopping, like shopping bots, bargain dogs, whatever they are. But I use some other tricks because I was a computer programmer. I installed the little utility from a company Amazon bought called Alexa that shows me if I go to a site, what other sites people came from. It's really great for me to see that this is the vortex of sites that you belong to. If you look up CBS.MarketWatch.com, you can see where users aggregated that are typically going to your site as well. It does make me aware of other sites that I might not otherwise think of that are so closely associated by traffic in the domain area to that site.

So you can follow the crowd from store to store?

Exactly, exactly. So I sort of like some of the secret sauce stuff. And I'm always out there telling people what they could have as far as a consumer experience. I'm on the board of a little company called the Knot.com, like tie-the-knot in weddings. So every time I hear of someone getting married, I tell them to go to the Knot and sign up for the registry. I'm on the board of Liquid Audio, so I've become much more of a digital music user.

I think it's going to be really interesting to see how willing the TV networks are to embrace new technology. As you well know, it's not just a matter of moving TV to the Internet, it's a matter of taking advantage of the elements of the Internet and creating a new vision.

I grew up one of five daughters and one brother of a high school basketball and football coach, so we were very attuned to sports. I still love watching the playoffs. I thought the women's soccer game [the World Cup in July 1999] was unbelievably interesting, and sort of an American experience. At the same time, I find my attention span wanes. I want them to show the score more often. I want them to show the stats of the players. I just want more. Television feels very thin to me where the Internet feels thicker. I guess that's the sense a consumer would get be-tween interactive and noninteractive — this feeling of dimension.

Today there seems to be an increasing overlap of the people who have a computer near their television and who are watch-ing and surfing on two different devices. If I go down to one of the [TV] studios today and do two minutes on 'how's the world today,' by the time I drive back eight blocks, I'll have a lot of e-mail here. And I know they're not touching the screen to key it in, and they're not on Web TV, so the consumer is trying to com-press the two even as we're keeping them apart.

You and I have seen some interesting attempts to put rabbit ears on PCs or to use the video blanking interval. Unfortunately, we could never get enough critical mass behind any of that stuff. So now we're just seeing digital cable boxes and Web TV. But I think the more important thing is watching the consumers have a television here and dragging the PC closer to it, so if their syn-apses are not being absorbed enough by the TV experience, they can just go right there to their PC. So consumers tell you what to do, and they're saying these two belong together.

One of the things that got me into interactive journalism was seeing this generation of kids playing video games and saying 'Hey, this is a medium and these kids aren't going to grow up to read broadsheet newspapers.' Some of them will, but they'll also want to interact with the news.

My nephew is 17. He's going to be a senior this year and he wants a career in broadcast journalism. He goes to a public high school in Minnesota. They don't have school papers anymore. They have closed-circuit TV and he's the TV news anchor at his public school. So he's going from college to college to college. One of the colleges he went to produced Ted Koppel and all sorts of people who make a lot of money on air. And he rejected that school because he said the equipment they had was a generation older than what he has in a Minnesota public school. Now kids are so facile with all pieces of technology, they just accept it as part of the fabric of their lives.

**Let's talk about venture capital.
It seems to me there's just a flood of venture money.**

There really is. It went from being a desert to having Hoover Dam burst. We started our fund in 1990 and it took us a year and a half of excruciating time to raise $35 million because it was targeted all to software. That was considered so outrageous, that you'd give all of a fund to software. We took our first company public at an $80 million market cap in 1991 and people thought it was a stellar success. Of course, Wind River has a more than $1 billion market cap today, so that's not bad.

That *year* $250 million was invested [by venture capitalists] in software; there was no Internet. This last *quarter* [Q2 1999] it was $2.5 billion. And last year it was something like $7.5 billion in software and Internet. At the beginning of 1990, there was $25 billion in the hands of venture capitalists and $250 million got spent each year, accelerating over the next two years to a whopping half-billion. But now there's $50 billion unspent in the hands of venture capitalists, plus the majority of that, the largest hunk, which is probably over 30 percent, is being spent on software and Internet companies.

It's wonderful for entrepreneurs. As a result, people no longer have to be convinced to be entrepreneurs. Quit your job and work for a startup. That's all the silver lining. The dark side of the cloud for us is that it's a huge polluted pond.

When we invested in Pets.com, we did the first pets thing. In 102 days, there were six other pet companies. Hundreds of millions of dollars got invested in them. There was petopia, there was everything. There was probably petophile. And articles were being written with titles like 'Let the fur fly' and 'Dog eat dog' and 'Venture capital goes to the dogs.'

Lots more venture capital, lots more competition— what does this do to price margins?

What it does is drive up the number of entrants in the pond. There's ten canoes and somebody says, 'I've got to build myself up into a yacht so that the canoes look really small.' You can't just beat each other off with a paddle. The risk-reduction path used to be 'Let's hire a couple of people, let's get something going, let's see if it plays in Peoria, and then we'll put some rocket fuel in it.' Now it's 'You're a rocket day one. We're going to put in enough fuel to put you in orbit and make sure you go faster and higher than other pop bottle rockets.' It means the risk is compressed and that over time you're going to see some great successes and also some wonderful 'POWS!'

You see PointCast spend $20 to $30 million and sell the company back to the founder for $1. You see a PowerAgent spend, what, $20 to $30 million, and you don't see the sensational 'Hey, we don't have lift-off here' unless a journalist writes about it, because there's so many more positive stories. But we are really forced to put all the fuel in the rocket on day one.

Pets.com's story is a very good one. Pets.com, on April 22 [1999], decided to launch the Pets rocket. We hired Julie Wainwright as CEO, we agreed to put $10 million in the company and we told Julie that if she wanted us to split that with a strategic partner, we would. Immediately when we did that, Julie and I went to my computer on my desk and wrote a press release saying 'Pets.com: Julie Wainwright signs as CEO, Hummer-Winblad funds. Now dominating the $30 billion pets and supply market.'

Within hours, we had almost every venture capitalist calling Julie, begging to be in on the deal. Also, Amazon called and said, 'Can we do the deal instead?' so we split the deal with Amazon, putting $10 million of fuel in the rocket. By June 20, less than 60 days later, we had raised another $54 million. Julie had found 20,0000 square feet of space at Fifth and Brannan in San Francisco, and within two weeks she had hired 30 people. By July 22, Julie had more than 60 people, she's operating out of a 50,000 square-foot warehouse, she's got $60 million in the bank, and she's got relationships with all the major suppliers of dog food. People were beating the doors down.

It stirs up the hornets' nest, doesn't it? And there are big brick-and-mortar companies out there that start thinking they better get their acts together and get on the Internet by acquiring one of those companies or starting their own very fast. There's a lot of competition there and that's good for the consumer.

Well, it is. It's good for the consumers in a number of ways. Companies have already learned that the major reason we as entrepreneurs have an advantage over everyone else is that we have surrendered to the consumer. We said 'We know if you don't like us, we're out of business.' We know if this experience doesn't play in Peoria, then $60 million and a rocket is not interesting.

We're letting the consumer touch us, tell us what to do, drive these sites. We know we can't just get someone to build it on spec and hope we built the right thing. We are no longer packaging a product and seducing consumers into the product. We are saying 'OK, on the other side of this site is dog food, dog leashes, veterinarians, whatever. . . . You start telling us what you want. Oh, you don't want this? It's off the site. You want more dog food? It's on page one. You want the pet of the day on the upper right corner? Then that's where we'll put it because that's where people are clicking. We even let them post what they like and don't like on message boards. We let them chat with each other—they can say 'I hate this' or 'I love this.' And that is really standing naked in front of a mirror.

That's exactly the kind of interactivity that people expect. They want to be involved in these things. My sense is, also, that if you disappoint them, they're going to leave fast. What do you think is happening with brand loyalty?

There's a term used now—customer relationship management—that I think is more a corporate term. What we're saying is there is a customer relationship and relationships take work. It requires attention, even if you're madly in love. Customers can change. C4onsumers have different needs and wants, which brings us to lesson two of the Internet, which is we can treat you differently than we treat someone else. We do have the facility to say you have different likes and dislikes than someone else. We don't have to put you in a box where you have to say 'I don't want to see that stupid dog in the corner anymore, I want to be on there to talk to the vet.' You sign on as someone who just wants the vet.

I think this seems obvious to us here, but it's really subtle to people who think 'We're going to market something to you. We're going to convince you that sugar-coated peanuts are cool,' even though I've never heard anyone say they taste good. We're going to convince you that burgers with horseradish and bacon on top are way cooler than anything else.' And we're saying, 'Look, if there's anything wrong, we'll fix it.' Now we have to be in the target area to get to play. We have to be pretty correct in understanding you in the beginning, because our core marketing is getting you to tell someone else. The customers are driving our business.

I think of it as Sim City (see Chapter 4).

I love Sim City!

And, to your earlier point, in Sim City, all the sims are the same. On the Internet, every sim is different and every one has unique likes and dislikes, so it becomes a very three-dimensional game of Sim City.

Clearly, customer service is not about fixing the problems, but really finding a way for the customers to tell us what they want instead. The other great thing about the technology community—because we're always moving on some plane on the bleeding edge, is to see the glass is half full versus half empty. This is really core for a venture capitalist, because it's never full. It's at best half full. And if you look at it too long, it starts looking half empty. In many ways, people don't really want to see that much change. They're really not comfortable about moving into the future versus building on the past. They will immediately look at that glass and see that it's half empty. And that's an enormous competitive advantage that we have in this young technology industry.

Let's talk about price. Service is enormously important. Customers recognize good service and they're willing to pay a little more for it. But when you get to the point that a book is 30 percent off here and 60 percent off there, well, the heck with the service, I'm going to take the 60 percent discount. How do you manage price margins on the Net?

I think you have several types of consumers and rationales for buying. The early Internet consumers were driven by convenience. It was the number one reason, not economics. And they represented a higher income class, a higher educated demographic living in wired cities. That has pretty much changed.

In 1998, according to Ernst & Young, 40 percent of all commerce was conducted by people who lived in cities with fewer than 50,000 people—on the margin of whether they'd even have a Wal-Mart or any superstore. So there you expanded into availability, things you couldn't get unless you went onto the Net. But you also started moving into a broader demographic of income and education. And there will be something for everyone here. I'm not going to price-shop for things. I'm not going to key in all those shipping addresses I have at Amazon anywhere else. Amazon would really have to screw up to lose me as a customer.

On the other hand, for people who are working on budgets, the Internet is a wonderful thing. They can see price wars happen. I don't think everyone will surrender to every single price war. Not everyone has 'name the price and we'll find the ticket for you.' Not everyone has the free PC and 'We'll flog you with advertising if you agree to be flogged but you'll get a PC.'

Let's look at a commodity like a book. I know the title of the book. It's the same book wherever I buy it. Why wouldn't I use a shop bot to go out and find it at the lowest price and place the order?

Well, because I'd have to key in the ship-to address, my credit card number, and for me, that's going to take three or four minutes. I'm going to have to dig in my purse for my credit card. I'm going to have to give information to one more site—where I'm not so sure of the privacy policy—my home address. I want it shipped to my home. Let's say I want two copies, and I want one shipped to my mom or my dad, I have to key in their ship-to address. I probably have to confirm through e-mail that, yes, that was me and, yes, I really did want it. And to me, time is money. We probably just described 15 minutes of time. A woman digging in her purse is a very time-consuming process.

You once told me about how you regularly read the encyclopedia when you were a little girl, and the effect that had on you in rural-suburban Minnesota. You were talking about the effect of software on kids and how edutainment software was such a great breakthrough.

Let's bring that up to date. What kind of
social effects do you think the Net can have?

I think what really has made a bigger dent on the social implication of computing is Moore's Law, the price drop in PCs with more performance, and the ability to buy used and reconditioned PCs at even lower prices. Second is the competition in ISPs so that people can get free Internet access. What I've seen is not really what happens inside the school walls. . . .

But I think we have to be kidding ourselves to say that computers alone will change our educational system. Again as we see the Internet economy, as we described, bringing journalists into very important roles in stock-driven companies, I don't know any teacher who gets stock options. At last count, they were actually getting paid less than journalists. We're asking people to be educating our children as if they joined the Peace Corps.

That's a good question for a venture capitalist.
Why don't we see Internet schools being funded?

Because we have state regulations about academic standards about what kids read, even *how* they learn to read, which is very controversial here in California, even which languages they're allowed to speak or not speak in the school. And what we've gravitated toward on the Internet are the unregulated marketplaces, the marketplaces where we're free to not follow rules, but really to set new rules for the new economy. Unfortunately, education is a regulated industry, and the regulations make no sense; they're controlled state by state.

We can put educational tools in the hands of parents for the first time, and they can really help direct and use the Internet as a tool to have access to better than most small- or mid-sized town school libraries. So I think the responsibility does rest in how you use these tools.

I know my parents scraped together a lot of money to buy those Collier encyclopedias for us and it was our Internet. It was our view to all knowledge. To buy a PC and have Internet access would have been much cheaper for my parents, given the percentage of their disposable income compared with what they spent on those encyclopedias.

Let's look at another industry, like medicine.
It's extremely regulated. I've read one-quarter of every
dollar spent on medicine is spent on administration.

Right, and we spend more than any country on Earth on medicine, but our rates of infant mortality are not the lowest. We're spending more and getting less.

There's an awful lot of interest in doing medicine on the
Web. There's a lot of liability issues, but there's a lot of
diagnosing what's wrong with you, or researching it,
or getting a clue of what's wrong with you. There's
strong interest in selling prescription drugs.
And it makes a lot of sense in a lot of ways.

Well, all that stuff is happening, too, in the education system. Textbooks and other expensive things. You have Big Words right over here in the park [San Francisco's South Park, a center for multimedia companies]. At Twenty-First Century Internet, you have Follett, which is doing textbooks. I remember trying to get my textbooks. In fact, I started an accounting software company and 'The Fundamentals of Accounting Principles,' which is where we wrote our software from, I was the third person to own that textbook. I would never have been able to buy that textbook new and I had to hope I could get a used one. Now you can get new and used textbooks through the Internet.

As a student, I can also get services at a better price, because they're being sold to me as the college market. I can find jobs better because recruiting sites are tied to the campuses. It is a better life for the student. But that's all college. And so much is happening at the college level. K–12 is another story.

We've talked about competition. We've talked about the potential for some social change, if not a lot. We've talked about all the money flooding into this. Do you see a shaking out?

Both of us have been in the industry long enough to know it's volatile. The thing that really is a little frightening here is that we're in an industry where we know it's a roller coaster. The highs are high, the way up is exciting, and the way down is really fast. You don't know what hit you. It may not be in your control.

I think there are new entrants here who don't believe that the roller coaster goes down. They believe this is stability. It is now, but people lose trust. Some of the stuff just doesn't work. The market panics through world crisis. Interest rates have remained pretty unchanged here and we've averted being sucked into global disaster.

We have no control over that, despite the fact that our industry is contributing to the national product and is driving the economy, we don't control the world economy and all the variables that control our stock prices. All the masked men out here are not necessarily Zorro. It will take less than kryptonite to kill some of these companies. That will be interesting and it will be new for the new economy. For those of us who've been around, it will be an old behavior.

TRIP HAWKINS

Founder and Chairman of 3DO Company

During a remarkable career, Trip Hawkins has inspired hundreds—if not thousands—of software designers, technologists, and business managers with his often provocative views of interactive technology.

He founded his first company while a freshman at Harvard University, developing a board game that taught football strategy. He earned a degree of his own design: strategy and applied game theory. Hawkins was the sixty-eighth employee at Apple Computer and its first business marketing manager. He co-founded Electronic Arts in 1982 and led its rise to become the world's largest independent video game maker.

In 1992, he founded 3DO Company in a brash attempt to "shoot the moon" by setting technical standards for interactive communications on the information superhighway. Although it attracted major investments from AT&T, Matsushita, Time Warner, and Electronic Arts, the technology was never widely accepted. The company raised $60 million in an IPO before unveiling a single product, and subsequently rose to a market value of $1.2 billion. But the cancellation of superhighway projects and other miscues left it unable to meet its lofty goals. Today, 3DO makes video games based on other standards.

Was Hawkins wrong about 3DO's early goals? Absolutely. He admits humbly he was naïve in thinking he could pull off such a feat. But many of the notions he described in 1993 are either on the Web today or will be there tomorrow. And his theories about interactive entertainment apply equally to education, shopping, journalism, and other areas of our lives.

What do you personally use the Web for?

I would say the most obvious personal use is that I've been in a baseball fantasy league for more than 20 years. So, I regularly use the Web to get information about baseball players, including anecdotal information about how serious a guy's injury is, if he's pitching poorly because he's tipping his curve ball—things like that. But I also get up-to-date statistics and statistics broken down into more categories than you'd be able to find in a print publication, and information that's more timely.

And on the professional side?

One of the nice things is that you can go out and check on a stock quote or look for a particular news item on a competitor (or yourself for that matter), if you're trying to figure out how something is being covered. I'm looking at what information people are picking up and how certain things are being characterized.

It seems like there's a generation coming up that's interacting with a medium as if it were a video game. And these people will grow up to be adults who probably won't be content to get news from a static newspaper.

Absolutely. Something about the human species is that we are fundamentally social and interactive. Other mammals are interactive, but they're not really as social as we are. We have tremendous capacity for imagination and creativity. A cow may be content to sit in a field all day chewing grass, but that would be a horrible life for a human being. We instinctively know that, and it's resulted in the success of a lot of entertainment products, and also in the success and the popularity of media in general. A lot of our fascination with media is how it plays to our creative and imaginative side. If you look at what things get covered in ostensibly 'news journalism,' there's definitely a hungering for news that will create an emotional reaction from a human being.

That's interesting. I have a slightly different take, and we can talk about that, but tell me what you mean by that.

Our species has a blood lust. So there's a tendency of Hollywood to exploit that. There's also a tendency of the news media to exploit that. One of the ways you might see that is the countless number of times you saw an image of the blood stains where the bodies of Mrs. Simpson and Ron Goldman had been, and the excessive coverage of the Columbine High School tragedy. I don't mean that the coverage itself is bad, but the kind of coverage that is aimed at evoking a gut-level emotional response. The human being is a predatory carnivore, so part of us is an animal that has a visceral response to it.

Now when those predatory readers go to the Web for news, do you think they'll choose mostly the bloody stories?

I think they already do. Certainly, the world's population— if you divide it into the Web users of today and the non-Web users—you can certainly imagine that anyone who watches television today will use the Web within 20 years. But, today, the people using the Web are better educated and more affluent. They're probably more likely to be the kind of people who have enough social training that they'd be better at suppressing their blood lust and other behavior that would be considered socially unacceptable. On the other hand, there's plenty of popularity of sexually explicit material on the Web, and—not that I've gone out to ascertain this—I'm sure there's a lot of violent information as well. 'We have met the enemy and he is us.'

I assume we'll always have both groups of readers and more readers in the future. Do you think there will always be choice for all those people?

Yes. Society will adapt and learn to filter and censor things based on social values. You have to differentiate between what's in our nature and social values because our society isn't based on what we do naturally. It's based on what we're able to learn and our ability to transfer that knowledge to the next generation. That's one of the reasons why when you have a calamity, such as the rise and fall of the Roman Empire, you have to go through a dark age to reestablish all the things that were lost.

But going back to my central theme, we have all this capacity for imagination and interaction, and we instinctively know we're that way. In the past 30 years, two things that have happened are very exciting to me. There's a brain scientist at Berkeley, Dr. Marion Diamond [professor of integrative technology], who for more than 30 years now has been doing research primarily focused on laboratory rats. She's proven very convincingly in a number of studies that you can make a dramatic difference in the level of intelligence of a mammal by getting it to interact more through both play interaction and social interaction. Of course, you can't take human beings and cut up their brains and study them. What she would do is to cut up the rats and study their brains. She found thickening of the cerebral cortex and she could measure a significant increase in the number of neural connections, synapses, and so forth—all very scientifically precise. Meanwhile, in just the past five years, and I don't recall who conducted the study, but I recall reading articles where there were longitudinal studies over a period of 15 years where they'd studied infants less than one year old and concluded that if you significantly increase the degree of interaction in an infant, you would increase its IQ by 30 to 40 percent.

So interaction really relates to who we are. Of course, we don't always know what we're doing. One example of that is that your stomach uses different kinds of enzymes to digest different kinds of food. If you combine protein with sugar, the enzymes require completely different environments in your stomach— one alkaline and one very acidic. So the foods completely neutralize each other.

I think that's what happened with interaction. We are fundamentally interactive, but we developed the medium of television before we developed the medium of computers. Television is fundamentally passive. And there are a lot of studies now that show television is a problem because it's *so* passive. It's sedating. People frequently feel worse after watching television. People feel guilty because they're wasting so much time watching television. We are clearly now in the midst of this revolution that will be going on the rest of our lives, a transition from where television is the dominant medium to network computers as the dominant medium. Television will be relegated to a minor role as the technology you want to use when you want to see a live broadcast like the Super Bowl or an election.

There are some people, maybe they're cynics, who think that as the Internet develops, television will move to the Web, that the masses will demand the same kind of entertainment that they like—that they like passive entertainment.

They'll get it. They'll get plenty of it. I just believe that within 20 or 30 years, it will be integrated seamlessly into a digital environment, so it will just be part of the digital system. You'll have a digital system, and you'll have more children growing up in a digital world. It's in our nature to play, it's in our nature to interact, and the studies have shown that. Today's children are different. They have had the opportunity to grow up doing things that are better suited to their social and creative natures, fueling their imaginations in a more profound and natural way. They're just not prone to care about television the same way as people who grew up with no alternative to television.

One of the things that made me want to go into interactive journalism was that when you go down a news story, your mind says 'Oh, here's Monica Lewinsky. Who was that woman she talked to? Oh, yeah, Linda Tripp. And wasn't Tripp associated with some group?' You ask those questions as you go through a news story, and a good journalist tries to anticipate them. But you can't anticipate them all. So the best thing to do is to make that an interactive story, so that the reader can take left turns or right turns at will by following links.

Exactly. We're talking about turning control of your experience back to you instead of having somebody else in control of it. Obviously, if I write a story, it's not going to be as good a story as a fictional story written by a genius fiction writer. And therefore, there will always be a market for the genius fiction writers, because they will do a better job at bringing out emotion in me, and bringing out a sense of wonder in me. They're professionally qualified to do that. But at the same time, a lot of the exploration and imagination that people go through is stuff they come up with on their own.

So, as you were pointing out, I can be reading the newspaper, but I want control of that experience. And I'm the only person who knows where my imagination wants to go with whatever questions I have about a particular story. And you're right, there's no way a journalist could perfectly anticipate the directions that various readers want to follow.

We talked a little about TV. Do you think that same theory would hold for television, that people will want to take left turns and right turns?

There are a lot of times when all you want to do is relax. But if you look into the future, people who have grown up with interactivity don't consider it to be work. If you take someone who's grown up with passive media, try to force them—say at the age of 40 or 50—to learn to use an interactive tool like a computer, it feels like work and it will always feel like work. A kid who is facile with video games from an early age doesn't think of interactivity as work.

In fact, they almost expect it.

Yes. I'm a little bit of a technology luddite. I'm not the kind of person who uses a Palm Pilot. I'm not the kind of person who carries a cell phone. I view a telephone as an annoyance; I don't want to be that reachable. Whereas you get younger people for whom it's indispensable. They really want the ability to be reached and to reach out. I don't want that as much. Why is that? It probably has to do with the environment where I grew up and being in my own head as opposed to being networked with a bunch of other heads.

It's all a question of what you're comfortable with. It's a form of literacy and, again, it's something that's been studied. You can take a film of two people having a conversation that includes camera cuts from different angles. If you show that to a tribesman in a remote region of New Guinea, he won't have any idea of what's going on because he can't understand the context of the camera movement. It's the same thing with which TV programming evolved. It started out like radio, with the camera focused on a newscaster. Then you look at how it's changed as we got to MTV. The design style of MTV started to influence sports programming, TV advertising, Web design—

there's a chaos to visual literacy today that's understood effort-lessly by people who've grown up with it.

They're not intimidated, it's not work for them, it's perfectly relaxing and comfortable. They can handle these multiple stimuli firing at all times, and they can pick out from that stream of information the things that have meaning for them. This obviously affects user-interface design and a lot of other things, even how movies are presented. So interactivity branches out from there because it's allowing me to go in and do what I want to do instead of sitting back and just having this information washing over me.

When you started 3DO and you were doing a lot of speaking about the 3DO platform, you gave several speeches that I saw on what interactive entertainment would be like. As I recall, you talked about watching a show, and liking a sweater and having a little video image of you trying on that sweater to see how it looks on you, and in other colors and can I order it today?

I foresaw the coming of Amazon.com and a whole lot of other things. I was talking a good seven or eight years ago how it would be really advantageous for people to be able to buy books over a network. So it's been fascinating to me to see how the Internet has allowed a lot of these things to come to fruition as quickly as they have.

**Are you surprised by any of it?
Do you think the speed's a little slower?**

Everybody was taken a little bit by surprise, and I think the reason for that is, going back six or seven years, the Internet already existed and it was viewed as being a little too much of a dinosaur to be at a point where you could invest. There was a lot of talk about leap-frogging technologies that would do more than PCs from a processing standpoint, networks that would have a lot more bandwidth, interactive TV, and other buzzwords of the time. What happened was there was a recognition that to make that kind of leap involved a huge amount of capital. Rather than betting the farm that way—there's that expression: 'life will find a way'—the concept found a way by using the Internet as existing infrastructure where incrementalism could add things to it.

The Web was a pretty ingenious invention because the Internet was already there; e-mail was already there. This very simple technical idea of the Web page and HTML—that was a work of genius, no question. Simplicity is elegance. That was something simple there that was very powerful and ignited the whole process to where we are now.

Relative to where we were seven or eight years ago, I think there's a sense of disappointment because some of the great ideas still haven't happened. On the other hand, the Internet has turned out to be a great foundation for evolving to the point where all of those things will happen. So when you add it all up, it's probably happening about as fast as I expected it to happen.

If you want to focus on what is really happening right now, I think the whole Internet revolution compares very favorably in historical significance to what happened in the nineteenth century where we completed the exploration of America and created an information infrastructure that included railroads, automobiles—which had to get invented along with roads for them to drive on—the telegraph, and the telephone. When you look at all the instant billionaires who are being created right now, it's a period of time that will be looked at in the history books as very much like the robber-baron phenomenon of the nineteenth century.

Do you think it will stay that way? One of the ideas I'm exploring is that, instead of having giant corporations seizing control and dominating consumers as they have over the past few decades, we're moving into an era where

consumers have more and more choices and, perhaps, some better bargains. For companies to compete, they're going to have to compete on price, on service, and on interactivity.

Yes, although consumers also are limited to a 24-hour day and are probably busier now than they ever have been. And they're also a little bit lazy, so once they understand there's a way of solving a problem, they're going to be less likely to hunt and study and find other ways of solving that problem. That's where the power of brand recognition comes in and in creating a visible connection. Of course, networks are all about connections.

So if I go into a search engine, and I do a search for a fairly common topic, it's somewhat arbitrary what will happen next, and for some reason, that's for sale. If I go to a search engine and type the word "book," are they going to turn me over to Amazon.com? Or is some other company going to pay more money than Amazon.com [to be that link]? And how much money will I get when they turn them over to me?

Clearly there are some battle grounds where the fighting will be very much like the fighting in the previous paradigm where it will feel like there are distribution pipelines and distribution bottlenecks. It'll feel like it's hard to get your brand to register with the consumer. You'll have some of the same issues getting people to your site that you'd have in getting them to your brick-and-mortar store.

But the other thing is that it is the proverbial paradigm shift. The guys that are from the old paradigm are extremely vulnerable because they tend not to understand how fast things can change. They continue to do things the way they've always done them because they've had so much success with it. . . .

Obviously, investors believe that a lot of new companies that are more innovative, that are more agile, can be successful. The part of that that's bunk is that you can't have five brand new toy Web sites that are each worth more than Toys'R'Us. You can't arbitrarily decide that for each trillion dollars in the GDP there's now $10 trillion of value in these Web companies. That's just not realistic. Even if there's going to be overall growth in the economy, it's really going to be more of a competition for market share between the old paradigm and the new. And clearly, there's a tremendous irrationality to investor behavior right now, and that has to do with supply and demand. If I put water through a hose, and I constrict the opening, it's going to go flying out of the hose, but it's still going to go up in the air and come back down to the ground.

That's kind of how IPOs work. They're designed to be a constricted form of distribution that guarantees profit to the investment bank, and guarantees profit to the elite customer base in the institutions that the bank wants to please over and over again. Then, after the elite institutions bail out, and after the rocket has reached the peak of its trajectory, it's up to the day traders and the less-informed mom-and-pop investors who think 'Gee, if it went from 20 to 70 yesterday, then it will be at 150 tomorrow.'

It's kind of tragic in a way. There's going to be a lot of people hurt by the way this will go during the next few years.

You're probably better positioned than most people to understand what you're talking about. 3DO really came out of the chute fast. It was a huge IPO. I really think too many investors expected too much too soon, and that you were being moderate, trying to temper their expectations a little. But my sense was that it came out so fast, and was followed by a wave of disappointment, that it took you a long while to get the company regrouped and back on track.

Yes. If you look at it in a broader sense, it started in biotech. They were the ones who invented the model of going out and getting people to invest in a company that had never made any money. 3DO was the first high-tech company to do it, and there were a lot of comparisons at the time, saying this was like a biotech deal. One of the ironies is that one of the biggest critics of the 3DO offering was Jim Clark, who in one article called it a betrayal of the public trust, that a high-tech company could go public without an earnings history. And of course, he's become the poster child for Web offerings since then, so he's changed his tune, much to his success.

I've read articles recently about how the biotech industry is having a hard time raising money. They're further into that cycle. In 3DO's case, we were trying to hit a home run with 37 men on base. It became clear to us that there was fundamental instability to how we were trying to do things. To do what we were trying to do required that you'd have about $1 billion in capital, and we didn't have anywhere near that. Secondly, you had to have control over all the business elements—the hardware, the software, the marketing. And we didn't really have control over anything but the technology. The guys in the video game industry who had been successful had control over all the elements.

By the time we realized that we had the wrong structure, investors had figured out that the rocket wasn't going to go to the moon. So we had exactly that trajectory. I was fortunate enough to sell the hardware business and generate enough capital through the sale to start a nice little software business. So our revenue last year [1998] was up more than 400 percent—we did about $50 million in revenue. We just had a profitable quarter and we can fuel our growth through our own working capital.

So we managed to survive because we figured out quickly enough that our initial idea wasn't going to pan out.

How does this apply to the Web companies?

Some of them are going to be very successful. Some of them are going to grow into the big shoes investors have bought for them. A lot of them won't, and I think right now investors and entrepreneurs aren't being very discriminating, though they think they are.

From my own experience, you go through a period where everyone tells you you're terrific, you're wonderful, and you're going to take over the world. And some of that is going to go to your head. As a result, you're going to end up making some strategic mistakes and spending your money too fast because, if it's too easy to raise capital, you'll spend it less wisely than if you had to generate it through operations.

Also, companies are spending their stock as a currency and they're buying things they'll later have to support with real dollars.

That's true, too. Although, there's some sense to that, if you have stock as a currency and you're smart enough to know that, it's a little of an illusion.

When you're building an operating business, it really helps your discipline if you have to plan your growth from working capital generated from your operations. When you're not doing that—in other words, when you're just able to raise a heck of a lot of capital—the fact you can raise money easily tempts you into spending a lot of money. On top of that, if you look at some of these companies like Amazon.com, they have a stated policy of trying to outspend their competitors. The belief is that by doing that they can build up a barrier to entry. I don't really think that's going to turn out to be valid in many cases. It might be true in this case (and Yahoo! and America Online), because they're real standouts. There are not a lot of companies that have the visibility they have. A lot of other companies will try to use the same strategy, but they don't have as much capital and won't have as much of a chance of overcoming their fundamental disadvantages.

A lot of companies are getting investment money now even though their business model is fundamentally unsound. Again, you can look at the experience I had with 3DO, where we thought we had a viable business model, where we were able to get funding, and then found out from experience that growth wasn't as easy as we thought it would be.

One of the things that's interesting about the Amazon model—and that is a standout—is it's become a kind of prototype for a lot of companies. They've spent a lot of money, they've developed a lot of real estate on the Web, but it seems like they're very vulnerable to a price war.

Yes, I think that's accurate. And that certainly happens in other commodity product categories. You can look at Dell and realize that perhaps it anticipated the PC was becoming a commodity and, by going with direct mail and an 800 number distribution model, were able to eliminate some overhead expenses and recapture some margin they might have given up if they'd been relying on the retail channel.

The other thing that's happened in the PC industry is that in the early days, a lot of the manufacturing was done domestically with higher labor costs and overhead, and the fact that it was going to become a commodity forced them to become incredibly disciplined about manufacturing. So the gross margin for a PC manufacturer is something like 12 percent today when they started out at over 50 percent. Yet there are PC manufacturers today who are so disciplined that they know how to make money on those margins. So there'll be guys out there selling books on low margin that are still able to make money.

Here's where I see the real problem—and let me know if you agree with this—I think there are two dominant business models on the Web, and this may be overly simplistic. First, there are portals trying to sell products (or) information. And when they try to sell information, they're just charging you a fee like a subscriber, or they're supporting the site through advertising and that allows them to create the impression they're giving the information away. The second model, which is less direct, is when the search engines get a kickback. If I go to Yahoo and go to Amazon and buy a book, Amazon kicks back some money to Yahoo.

If you look at those two models, they both have a serious flaw. The guy trying to sell things runs the risk of low barriers to entry, drawing them into a price war by competitors selling the same products. With the guy trying to sell information, the fundamental flaw there is that consumers are resistant to spending money for information. And I don't think the advertising model works in a lot of cases. I think the guy reading a trade magazine views advertising as editorial. But with a guy who plays video games, he goes onto a site that's free, because he doesn't want to spend any money, and they try to get him to read a few ads, but he's not really reading any ads when he's playing a video game.

So here's my big idea. The better model for the Web is to combine the information and the product in the following fashion. Position yourself as an expert on a topic and build your information base to convincingly become the expert. And when someone comes to your site, they get all the information they need about a topic, but you have chosen a topic such that you know people spend a lot of money consuming products around that topic. They're at your site, they're getting all this free information, and they're starting to like you and trust you because you're such a font of wisdom. And then, lo and behold, you've helped them so much that they're now willing to trust you and buy those products.

There are two schools of thought on connecting information and product promotion. The first is that it's becoming widespread. If you go to a lot of the financial news sites that compete with MarketWatch, you see a lot of advertorial kind of stuff where one minute you're reading a news story and the next, you're being led into an advertisement. The other model you see is a newspaper approach where the news columns are over here and the ad columns are over there, and there's a clear delineation of each. I think right now the public is so used to that model that they're going to resent it if they feel they're being sold a bill of goods. And I think the public is hip to those kinds of things.

You have to be selective. There are some categories where it works and others where it doesn't work. Take me as an example. I told you I like information about baseball players? I can get all the information I want for free and I can get it without reading any ads. So I avoid all the sites that want to sell me information or sell me a product.

You've designed an awful lot of good interactive entertainment. What do you think lies beyond video games? Where do you see this going as far as entertainment goes? There's an awful lot of interest from Hollywood over the past decade.

One of the things we discovered is there's not a tremendous amount of synergy between Hollywood and video games. In fact, the production disciplines are pretty different. And the product itself and the end experience are pretty different. There's much more synergy between a book, a record album, a tape, a film, and a TV show. Video games are really off on their own. What they all share is that they're all forms of entertainment.

What we're ultimately trying to go for is an emotional reaction and emotional meaning. I think you could even make the case that once you get past the bare necessities of survival, like eating and sleeping and having a roof over your head, we're all in a similar position in that there's a limit to how much we can consume. However, there's no limit to how emotionally rich our inner lives can be. And that's really what you're going for. You look at the last Star Wars movie. There's tremendous emotional meaning to people in the fantasy world of Star Wars, and that's why there's so much interest in that movie.

I remember where I was and what I was doing when I saw the first Star Wars movie, and that was a long time ago, so it brings back my personal history. And now I'm introducing my children to Star Wars and it's exciting to me to know in the future I can talk to them about how we first experienced it together. I think, ultimately, that's what the reward and the excitement of human life is all about—the emotional context. Eventually, I think a lot of the value we'll get out of computer networking will come out of that.

**How do you think that will manifest itself on the Web?
I go to a lot of Web sites today and say to myself,
'Boy, this is a boring Web site.'**

Yeah, one of the things that's hit me about video games today is that the development of the fantasy world represented by the game is now more important than the gameplay. You still have to have good gameplay. But having good gameplay by itself can be boring.

So you have to have kind of a culture behind it?

Yes. Another way of describing it is that you can play chess, which is an abstract game with abstract pieces, or you can have a game where the pieces are represented by Luke Skywalker and Darth Vader, and that's a lot more interesting because there's something really weird in the father-son relationship there and— you know what?—every man has something weird in his father-son relationship. So there's something deeply personal. And you think, fine, if I get to hear a story and play a game, that's fine; it keeps me off the street. But what you're really going to take away in terms of meaning is perhaps how getting immersed in that relationship makes you feel about yourself and your family relationships. One of the things I know George Lucas feels very strongly about is family connections. Star Wars is ultimately a story about redemption, it's a story about good and evil, it's about the redemption of the wayward father. And that's really powerful stuff. That has an emotional impact on people.

You can look at the evolution of television the same way. MTV is about feel. It's not so much about information content. Even things like sports broadcasting and the way news is presented on TV, it's a lot more entertaining. Barbara Walters is not going for news. She pretends she's going for news, but what she's really going for is feeling. So you take all those trends and you apply it to the Web and you're going to see a lot of the same methods emerge.

**In the video game world kids—and adults—have a
tremendous choice of programming. If they like a game,
they will like that manufacturer for at least a little bit. But if
another good game comes out from another manufacturer,
they'll be fickle and they'll switch. I'm wondering if loyalty
will work the same way on the Web, that people might
expect a few good things from this manufacturer or that
one, but they'll be willing to switch to another site as
soon as they hear there's something hot over there?**

Yes, I think that's right. I think, as with other forms of
media, whoever you identify as having delivered something of
meaning, that's who you're going to be loyal to. If it's Sting sing-
ing to me, I'm going to be loyal to Sting even if he quits The
Police and starts his own band. And I'm not even going to
remember that A&M produced The Police record album.

**People talk about books selling over the Internet and ask:
Why can't the publisher just sell them directly?
I think there's a problem with that myself.
With video games, most aren't sold directly.**

A Web site can be about anything people are extremely
interested in. If I make a Web site that's all about Star Wars, you'll
go there because you're interested in Star Wars. But I could have
a separate site that's all about science fiction, and Star Wars could
be included there, but probably not to the same degree or depth.
I also could have a site dedicated to the works of Isaac Asimov.
In my case, I'd be more likely to go to the Isaac Asimov Web site
and the Star Wars Web site, because those are two particular categories in science fiction that I know I care about. And I don't
have the time to read about every science fiction fantasy world.
And once you read about some of these fantasy worlds, you
become loyal to that ongoing story and you really don't have
time to learn about all the other ones.

I'll give you another example. You could have a site where you go for help to build a deck in your back yard. You say: 'Here's my yard, here's the dimensions, here's the grade of lumber I want to use,' and the site could kick back to you a purchase order with all the parts you need.

There was a company that did that on CD-ROM— Books That Work.

It's a lot more powerful if you can then follow through with the materials and the expertise being shipped directly to your door. I think you can have many, many cases where the topic is extremely focused. It all comes down to a focus on what problems the consumer's trying to solve and what topics are of emotional interest to them. And those topics could be divided in many ways. There are people out there that would be generally interested in science fiction and would go to a fiction site because they want to know about the latest happening.

So, ultimately, you're saying whoever is doing whatever on the Web, they'd better pay attention to what the consumer wants because that's what it's all about?

Absolutely. And what the consumer wants is either the answer to a problem, some very practical problem like they've got to get a deck built, or they've got to fix their washing machine, or they're trying to buy a dog. Whatever. That's problem solving. The site that does the best job at giving them that information and does it in a way that makes them feel good, that's going to be the most popular site.

Meanwhile the other category is the site that's relevant to emotional meaning, whether it's video games, or books, or whatever. Now you're talking about what it is that's emotionally meaningful. In the emotional realm, I think you can slice it and dice it in a lot of ways. That way, some guys can be big, some guys can be small. They can all pick different ways to approach it.

JERRY YANG

Cofounder of Yahoo!

Born in Taiwan in 1967, Chih-Yuan "Jerry" Yang arrived in the United States at age two. His interest in the Internet began in 1994 when he posted his own Web page in Chinese with such self-centered factoids as his recent golf scores and his favorite Net sites.

Later that year, working with his friend David Filo, he cofounded Yahoo! as a directory of rapidly proliferating Web sites.

Today, Yang and Filo serve as co-Chief Yahoos of the company, providing the creative elements that complement the managerial expertise of CEO Tim Koogle. Together, they've helped to establish the company as the world's most popular portal.

Humble, friendly, and funny, it's easy to forget that Yang is one of the world's richest men with a wildly fluctuating paper wealth measured in the billions of dollars. His candid views on everything from corporate politics to the direction of technology mirror the many great uncertainties facing even the biggest Internet companies because of the role individuals play in deciding how the Web will affect our world.

You're an advanced user of the Web, and I think a lot of our readers would be curious about how you use it.

What *don't* I use the Web for? I'm probably getting more traditional, more mainstream as time goes on. I spend most of my time on e-mail and I use a Web-based e-mail rather than a client-based e-mail. My Yahoo! Instant Messenger is on whenever I'm on, and sometimes when I'm not there. I use the Web for keeping track of news, stock quotes, finance, and portfolio. My 'My Yahoo!' list of companies I track is probably a couple of hundred, so I use that religiously. I do a fair amount of shopping on it now. I'm in the process of trying to buy a car through the Net. So it's gone from trying to buy tiny, little things to big things.

What else do I do? I do a lot of research on companies we're looking into and new technologies. That's about it. A little bit of entertainment—looking into my sports teams. I'm a big baseball fan. I'm a big football fan, too. And college sports. You have to keep up on these things. Sometimes you can't do it at home, and I travel a lot. That's it.

That's a lot.
Roughly how many hours a week are you on the Net?

If I'm not traveling, I'd guess 50 to 60 hours a week.

You saw some of this coming and formed Yahoo!.
Still, I have a feeling a lot of this is different from what you expected then. What's different about it?

I think the biggest difference is that things happened a lot faster than any of us expected. I remember we had just sort of started putting a directory together that eventually became Yahoo! and we said, 'Look, putting together a Web site's kind of fun, but you're never going to have really massive collections of quality content.' I think the speed in which it all happened was pretty amazing. At that time, you never even thought about having a market-driven mechanism, like taking it to the IPO market and the post-market. You never thought about how much capital that you guys [at MarketWatch] and we might generate, about that financially motivated machine to create more and more content. So the amount of content that's been generated has been incredible.

I didn't think it would get commercialized this fast. 'Commercialized' doesn't necessarily mean a bad thing. From 1994—where arguably it was kind of an academic, interesting, noncommercial thing—to 1999, that five years to where there is now hundreds of billions in the value, it's just incredible it happened.

Just before that we had the whole information superhighway movement, which didn't pan out.

Yeah, it didn't pay off. It was policy driven. There was the NII by Gore, and the telephone companies tried to create their own walled-off interactive TV and cables and whatever. And the whole time you had this Internet thing sitting in the background, getting more infrastructure built, getting more users. Then, in 1994, Netscape became a company and in 1995 Netscape went public. Then, boom! You had the rest of the world. That's when AOL took off.

I think the other difference is we always thought it would be international, but I'm surprised how long it's taking the rest of the world to catch up. In Europe and Asia, they're still fairly far behind in terms of adopting this as a business tool and a consumer tool. The U.S. didn't have any proprietary advantage other than entrepreneurism and market-driven businesses.

**One difference I see is the phone rates
people pay in Europe and Japan.**

That's exactly it. When you look back and see deregulation, if you go back as far as that, one of the ultimate rewards is really the Internet. The fact that phone rates are not time-based has been an incredible boon to the Internet.

**I have to make a toll call to my ISP from my home
up the coast, so I have a sense of what it's
like to pay $5 an hour to use the Net.**

Oh, yeah. It isn't affordable after a certain point. It's very price sensitive, especially for schools, especially for the public sector, and especially for the poor. This has to be more like a utility over time.

**Let's talk about that—the social aspect of the Net
and whether this is another haves and have-nots thing.
Will we see some publicly supported aspects to this,
or at least some affordable aspects?**

I think public and affordable are two different things. You could argue through public policy you could make it affordable. Or you could argue through commercialization you could make it affordable. I happen to think it needs to continue to be a three-way partnership between the public sector, the private sector, and consumers. A lot of time, people say that if the industry's working with the government then the whole thing will be solved. But in this interactive world, where consumers have such a big say, whether you look at haves and have-nots issues or policy issues like privacy and censorship, I think this is one area where, if we don't include consumers in the dialogue—and it's hard to know exactly who the consumer is—we can go make all the policy we want, but they'll just go somewhere else and click on some other Web site.

We've kind of grown up with that reality. It's one thing to say we're going to protect the consumers, but if you try to cheat them or do something they're not comfortable with, they'll just go somewhere else. There's enough competition out there that a lot of the policies don't address all the issues.

Here in California, one of the ironies is that we have all these riches, yet the schools are ranked 47th out of 50 states for spending per student.

When you talk about the haves and have-nots, I think a lot of the public effort has to be focused on building schools. And just giving them computers and data lines doesn't give them better education. I think [we need] a whole sea change in terms of curriculum, in terms of having the teacher feel comfortable [with technology].

My wife is involved in wiring schools and a lot of times she'll go in and ask 'How long have you had that computer?' and they'll say six months. But in the first week, the teachers were so uncomfortable with it, the kids started running circles around them. So they turned it off and they don't use it anymore. I certainly believe that there's enough people in this industry— whether people like us or hardware manufacturers—that they're going to be incentivized to populate the schools with hardware. Then it becomes a content question.

Yes, and then you have to ask: Can there be a school in a box, or is it just there to help look for random information?

That's the right question to ask. I think there you do need some sort of government initiative. It ties into the whole question of what happens to schools. But to me, without changing the way schools operate, it's still a local, state, and federal initiative to drive better software and changes in technology into schools.

I'm pretty optimistic about the potential to do something like that. It's a part of the Internet that really fascinates me. In fact, if I ever change careers, I'd be very tempted to go into the public sector and work with schools.

That's why Kiko, my wife, spends a lot of time in it. It's such a worthy cause. It's one of these areas where you could get caught up in bureaucracy, but you can also change quite a bit if you put your heart into it.

How confident are you that we could see a sea change in terms of a quality education for kids?

To me, unfortunately, I think the Internet and the content of the Internet is only one component of the overall quality. I think schools need to become more competitive, whether it's standards-driven or free-market driven, or schools competing with each other for kids or whatever. To me, California has fallen so far behind in public sector educating at a K–12 level that I don't have a lot of confidence. I think it's a larger question than a lot of technologists can address. But can we solve a more targeted issue that will contribute to quality? Yes, I do believe *that's* going to happen.

What do you mean?

For example, if we go in and say, 'How do we make the Net more effective?' there ought to be a Net initiative distributed through all the schools where teachers can start to get educated. Whether that would raise all the test scores, I don't know. But that's the kind of thing you can do.

Let me ask you about politics. There's been a lot of talk about Internet polls of the public, and whether they'd be scientific, or too limited in scope. I've also heard a lot of people express confidence that someday we'll probably all be voting over the Net or some other network like it, and doing other things that will bring a lot more people into the electoral process. What do you think about that?

I'm a bigger believer in that the Internet could be a better forum to certainly create awareness of specific issues, whether it's propositions, or candidates' positions, or whatever, and potentially encouraging a certain sort of dialogue. So essentially, it's an easy way to reach people who share a common view, without marketing hype and what have you. And I think getting people interested might transfer to a higher voting population. Would that ever convert into a national election where voting's done online? Yeah, it's going to happen, but it's going to take a while, knowing how little incentive there is to do that today. Having more people vote doesn't do the electoral commission any good. They're set up so they don't have to do much work.

I do think that in some election, sometime in the future, a close election will be decided by how a candidate went out to reach his or her constituency on the Internet. That, in my mind, may happen this year, it may happen next year.

In California, it can make a big difference. If you're talking about one of the San Francisco Bay area counties, these guys would be crazy not to use the Net as a way of reaching out to their constituencies. It's targeted; you don't have to pay the same rates as on TV. It's the same dialogue. If they want, [they can] create a club, or a community, or a chat, or whatever. You could even have that town hall meeting, like they do on TV.

And in addition to a town hall meeting, you can also have that really wonderful individual, interactive experience of researching a candidate's positions.

And some people—myself included—would really like to know what the real issue is. I read the ballot measures and I don't understand anything, and there's really no outlet to understand some minutia of the schools bonds measure. You just don't understand that kind of stuff unless you're involved in it. But I think a lot of people would really love to understand it, and I think candidates or organizations with some interest in promoting these things could create a dialogue.

Let's go back to that question about the consumers. One of the things I'm pointing out in the book is that it's really easy for a consumer to go from one site to another. What does that do to brand recognition?

I think it makes brands and brand choice that much more important. Consumer choice is what makes this a level playing field for young companies like us. In other mediums I think it's much tougher to create that choice. It's never been so easy to create a Web site. And if it's a good Web site, you can create a great brand. And it's still happening today. There are tiny little Web sites that nobody heard about three months ago, and now they're getting a million visitors a day, and the venture capitalists are crawling around on them. I think the Net is unique in that sense, and I think the Net is powerful in that respect—that you can't take consumers for granted.

We've been on both sides of that. We came out of nowhere. People liked us and chose us, but now we run the same risk that you're talking about where somebody may come out with something better. I think people need to [do more than] create a brand that is well-known. Rather than create brand awareness, we want to build brand relationships and make sure there is a trust.

There needs to be brand attributes that translate into a relationship that people want to do things with us.

**I agree with what you're saying.
There are companies—Amazon, I think is the classic
example—that do an extremely good job with this.**

Yes, and that's why they have 60 to 70 percent repeat buyers. To be successful in an environment where consumers are fickle, I think there's even higher value for those brands. For brands that can stand the test of time and also the test of the marketplace where people can always go someplace else, I think those are more valuable than a very protected brand where you're the only thing on the shelf. To me that's not a brand, that's a forced choice.

Like the big store in the mall.

Right.

**You guys have an interesting perspective, as the managers
of the mall, of seeing what your retailers are going through.
What's happening with margins? Are we heading to a world
where there'll be razor-thin margins on commodity goods?**

It's a great question. I don't know which way the pendulum is going to swing. Most people who are in the retail commodity goods area think about branding and think, 'How can we build brand so that we can withstand some of the pricing chops?' At the same time, they have to be aware that they can't give away too many customers at a time that they're building market share. So Amazon's probably sitting there thinking, 'If we need to hold our price, we can because people come to our site for the relationship and service. Yet, should I be giving away customers who are a little more price sensitive?' So they do this pendulum thing and think we can move it here and get more customers.

I do believe it's going to settle somewhere. It's going to be a game of scale. So people who end up having—in two, three, five more years—more customers, can do more with price because, even if it's a lower margin, they have more dollars to play with. But I do believe it's going to settle into where 5 cents, 10 cents, 50 cents on a book isn't going to make you go from one to the other, if the merchant can create an incentive for you to stay, whether it's a rewards programs, whether it's frequent shopper, whether it's preregistered service, or maybe it's just a return policy. If you go to Yahoo! shopping, you'll start seeing us include other things beside the price. Do they ship free? Do they have votes? Have other people said this is a good place to buy? Do they have availability right now? A lot of people will quote you, then they go and try to buy the damn thing without having inventory.

All these other attributes, even on commodity price stuff, is going to start counting a lot. People will say 'I'm not even going to consider buying from a place where they don't ship it overnight' or 'I'm not going to consider a place that doesn't have a rewards program.' It's like airlines. Would you fly something that doesn't have a rewards program? If you fly as much as I do, you might as well fly on an airline where you can get rewards. So I do think that people can add a set of attributes that translate to a set of services that makes the price less of an issue, the question is how do you do that and get scale really, really fast?

One of those things that people talk about is how bots will go out and do your shopping for you so you don't have to cruise all these malls, so you don't have to worry about not getting a good bargain.

There've been a few efforts that have been similar. Amazon bought Junglee, which is a shopping bot. And we have a shopping bot. And everyone has their standard list of crawling things that go out to retailers and try to be your agent. The interesting thing is how much you let your agent do for you, both as a filter and as an alert mechanism?

Let's say I'm looking for a particular bottle of wine. And it may appear in auctions. It may appear in one of 400 Yahoo! merchants. And it could be outside of Yahoo!, on eBay or somewhere. And I'm going to write an alert that says to alert me when something happens. And I think those things will be very effective, but the question is what's the business model behind those things? Do you charge the merchants for doing that? Do you charge the consumer? You're serving the intermediary role, but the merchants hate that because they get even more commoditized. They don't even get the option or opportunity to pitch the buyer. They're a faceless merchant, and no merchant wants to be faceless. They all want to be the person at the counter, shaking your hand, saying 'How can I serve you today?'

And so I think the question is how do you build the relationship with the customer? [Bots represent] the kind of thing where you can buy this, but the merchant never knows you. There's always models around this where [the bot says] I can find it for you [the merchant] and let you meet the customer, but I think that tension has always limited it from being really successful. Technology-wise, I think it's the right thing to do. It's the perfect filter.

You're looking at that, appropriately, from the commerce end of it. If you look at it from the consumer point of view, you'd probably say this is going to be a wonderful day. I can get bots to go out and do this shopping for me, and I'm going to be much more powerful because of it.

Oh, I think from a consumer standpoint, there's no question. That's why these things will exist. The problem has always been that if you're just a small intermediate bot player and you can't get merchants to go out and cooperate with you, then you're always going to be challenged from a consumer standpoint: Are you the most comprehensive? Can you go out there and search everywhere where this bottle of wine might exist, or is your database limited? Once your database is limited, then you have multiple bots and it becomes unwieldy. I think one of Junglee's challenges after being purchased by Amazon was [retailers saying] 'I'm a merchant. Why should I let a Junglee robot come to my Web site? It's owned by Amazon.'

Let's follow that up. I'd say you should allow it because you want to sell your stuff.

You should, but what if it says, 'Tom, you're selling this book for eight bucks. And before I go back, I'm going to automatically decrease Amazon's price to $7.50.' To me, they could certainly do that. The technology is there.

Well, they slit their own throats by doing that.

But they may say 'I want to kill Tom's bookstore today.' They could do it methodically, by going around figuring out what their competitors are doing.

It's like robot war on the Web.

It is! That's what it is! It's this whole notion of whether you really reflect consumer choice or are you using it to undermine other merchants.

And, yet, if you ban any particular bots, the consumers probably aren't going to take that kindly.

**Or they'll buy something from someone else
because that's where they found it.**

They may. That's right, but nobody today has so much volume that you can't say no. And that's the chicken and the egg thing. I don't know if this is true, but The Gap, for example, might say they don't want any bots because they don't want to be compared to Levi's. 'It's never been part of our strategy, because when you're buying our jeans, you're buying Gap.' With a bot, you don't have a category for Gap; you have a category for jeans. And they say, 'Don't search me, I don't care. In fact, if you search me, I'm going to sue you.' That might be an example. And maybe the consumer wants to buy Gap because *they* don't think of it as jeans. So I think there may be a place where brands, where merchants, build relationships. Things may not get commoditized as easily as some people in technology think it will.

We've been down both sides. We work with the biggest brands, and we work with bots. We see the plus and minus of both.

**So as we start to move toward broadband, all the TV
networks are pumping up content to deliver interactive
TV-quality images—and I don't know how realistic that is.
I have to wonder what Yahoo! would look like at that point.**

We really think that for part of what we've built, and we can't claim credit for all of this, but for the part we've built, we allow people to do things that they couldn't do before. We say you can create a relationship with a bunch of servers over in the Internet world. So as long as I can get to a terminal that's hooked up to the Internet, I can access my personal information—my calendar, my address book, my e-mail, right? This could work for your shopping list or your travel itinerary. You think about all the stuff you used to have to carry around. You could start having a server relationship that's personalized, that's you, that's really a server-in-the-sky kind of thing.

So what does that mean? It means it's crazy for us to constrain you to only view it on a device that looks like a PC. You ought to be able to look at it on your watch—if I could connect the thing to the Internet, on your TV, on your refrigerator, on your microwave, on your cell phone, on your PDA. It sounds kind of fantastic, but it's possible and it's affordable.

So one of the things we've been doing, with an acquisition we made [of Online Anywhere], is to say consciously, 'We're going to have to make sure Yahoo!'s content is viewed on multiple devices over multiple bandwidths.' Part of Online Anywhere's strength is the technology allows us to take an existing Yahoo! service, define a device, and, say, a cell phone is the device, create a Yahoo! experience that matches that device. So it's a low-bandwidth device with a small screen factor. So it's a Nokia 7320, so it looks good on my Nokia. To have Yahoo! go on there is very different from having Yahoo! up on a big screen. So Online Anywhere is going to help us get started to do that. Ultimately, you ought to have a consistent personal relationship with maybe a brand, maybe a Web portal, but clearly you want to access everything you can access on the Web today, but from wherever you are, however you want to do it.

So that's what I meant not only with the bandwidth, but also the devices. We're still a long way from being there. But it's going to start.

Maybe you're not very far along on this path, and it's understandable. But the idea of a TV-based Yahoo! is something I can't quite imagine. Does it have video? Does it have bigger print?

Let me put it this way. If we took Web TV as the service, and we wanted to create a Yahoo! experience for Web TV, it would be an NTSC (National Television Systems Committee) compliant-looking thing, but it would still be primarily textual because it's a low-bandwidth device.

OK, now think of TV, NTSC, but with a big fat pipe going into it. Cable or satellite or whatever. Well, that thing would look a little more multimedia, but will it look like TV? No. Yahoo! isn't TV. I have no incentive to re-create Yahoo! and make it look like a TV experience. The incentive I have is to show the people what they want to see using the preference files I have on that person.

Hopefully, if you, Tom, define that you want Yahoo! at home to be your family device, then you'll primarily see activities you do with your family: photo albums, e-mail, your kid's area, whatever. That may be the interface. Whether we put graphics or streaming video, that's a secondary question. But to me that interface—you've defined it and that's what we want to show you.

But you come to work, or you're on your PDA, that's your personal information space. To me, being able to make sure that we can really provide an experience where it's obvious what it's for, and to interact with it and change it—that's first and foremost. Then we take advantage of the bandwidth. Do we have any sports clips so when you get home at 11 o'clock at night and you missed all the TV we can say, 'OK, here's the top five sports clips from your favorite cable stations'? We can definitely blast that through your cable modem. And you can definitely get the sports scores on your cell phone. But to me it's defining first what information we want to push to you, and then defining the media types of how to deliver it to you.

Does that make sense? It's very Yahoo!.

It really does, and I don't think you should try to turn Yahoo! into a TV network just because you have a bigger pipe. Yahoo! has loyal customers for what you are. But I think one of the temptations for companies like yours or America Online or even some nontraditional companies, is to try to turn into a TV network. And the TV networks are

**trying to figure out how to be Web companies.
And I don't think either side is really good at the other.**

That's for sure. I know what I'm good at and what I'm not good at.

**Let's talk a little about regulation and competition.
You had a beef with AOL over instant messaging [in 1999]
and AOL had a separate, simultaneous beef in San Francisco
in which it teamed up with Pacific Bell against AT&T and
AtHome. It seems like we're getting into some issues where
there are times you want to work with PacBell and AT&T
and AOL, and there are other times where different
companies will get into protracted, even legal feuds.
This is a strange world we're moving into, and I see a
potential for gridlock somewhere down the road if we get
too restrictive about who can work with whom on what.**

That's a good observation. I guess if the regulators are overly aggressive in their jobs in regulating the Internet, I think that's the more likely scenario of creating gridlock. Once you have laws in place, or hints of laws in place, you get a chilling effect on the marketplace. One way or the other, it's tremendous.

Putting that aside, putting regulatory gridlock aside, certainly there's a possibility for alliances to form, but the fundamental driving growth engine for the Internet today is still open platform and technologies that people can really develop for. Anybody can put up a Web server. Anyone can create an e-commerce engine. To me, as long as that's in place—and you have people fighting over certain versions of Java, certain versions of a browser, certain versions of HTML, certain versions of instant messaging—and as long as a market mechanism is in place, then there's going to be an incentive for people to talk to each other.

So, I guess the short answer is I trust the market mechanism a lot more than I trust the regulators, and I trust the market mechanism to always create a place where people can grow their share, and a bad alliance—one that doesn't allow you to grow your share—never works. You end up trying to find ways around it. When it's the law, you don't find your way around it.

I'm also interested in hearing your view of the things you see happening over the next five years or so.

I don't know. If you asked me five years ago where I saw the Net going, I probably would have missed by so much I would have looked foolish. But I feel the same kind of feeling for the next five years or ten years, that there are so many little moving pieces that I haven't even comprehended, so many pieces of our lives: the devices we talked about, and the ability for users to be independent of what device they use is really incredible.

Certainly, internationally, when you look outside the U.S., the wireless markets are way out ahead of the U.S. People are sending SMS messages in Europe by the millions a day and they're difficult to do. I don't quite understand how you do them, but those are instant messages. They're no different from the ones you and I send today on our pagers. That growth, and that ability to communicate wirelessly, is going to be something we're all very used to in five years' time, whether the Internet's part of that or Yahoo!'s part of that, or whatever.

I think we have to make the Internet a lot easier. We have a huge population like my parents who are still freaked out by the computer. They don't understand it. They don't know how to use it. They don't really want to know how to use it. We have a large population that doesn't understand keyboards. These things look so daunting to them in areas where they don't speak English that they've really been a deterrent, a retardant to Internet growth. I don't know how you fix that. There might be technologies, there might be interfaces.

Voice translators?

Yeah, voice translators. It's not surprising, but the voice technology in Asia has really gotten a lot of research because they don't have an easy way to input and handwriting recognition doesn't work. So I do think there will be an ease-of-use push. I think you'll see very specific Internet devices. So instead of general purpose PCs of the 1980s, you'll see very cheap e-mail devices.

Almost like the network computers that Oracle chairman Larry Ellison and Sun Microsystems chairman Scott McNealy talk about?

Yeah, exactly, but you may only have an instant message. Pagers may become instant message machines. They'll come preloaded with your buddy list and you'll say something into them and it gets translated. But these things will become more specific, because more and more functionality is being put on the servers. So you end up having very specific devices for the Internet, which is, again, kind of a cyclic thing where you have general purpose people who created software. Now you have this ultimate service software thing called the Internet that's going to drive the hardware. I think that's going to be pretty exciting.

I think commerce is going to be huge. I think that the Internet five years from now may be totally unrecognizable by you and me. It will be maybe totally embedded in most things. Maybe I'll have a flat panel on my fridge that will tell me what things I need to go buy and will tell me 'Jerry, please eat more calcium.' This is all stuff you can do.

I take it you believe this will be a much better world in terms of choices and prices and consumer power?

I'm a big believer in the upside. Every day we sit here and say there's a lot of negative things happening, too. And we have to make sure we do our best to make sure bad things don't happen. On the whole, we have to make sure we're moving in the positive direction. The net benefits have to far outweigh the potential for negatives.

The Internet is always going to be a place where if you don't have a good mechanism to be aware of and to potentially penalize and prosecute criminals, a lot of bad things could happen: child pornography and drugs and hate groups. They have their rights, as long as they're legal. If they're not legal, we have to make sure we do what we can do to find them, penalize them, and do what we need to do to make sure this is a good place to grow.

REBECCA EISENBERG

Vice President for New Markets at Ecastinc.com

Rebecca Eisenberg isn't a CEO, doesn't sit on any corporate boards, and, at last check, remains a long way from making her first million on the Internet. Yet she's one of the most successful people I've come across in the Web's wide world.

After graduating phi beta kappa from Stanford with a degree in psychology and decision sciences (Jerry Yang was a freshman dorm mate), she graduated cum laude in 1993 from Harvard Law School. Eisenberg spent the next two and a half years helping to write legal decisions that often involved copyrights, patents, business, and personal freedom.

Fascinated with the emerging technology of the Internet, she stopped practicing law, although she remains a member of the federal and California bars. She's Vice President for New Markets at Ecastinc.com and also writes about the Internet for CBS.MarketWatch and other publications. She's been named one of the Top 25 Women on the Web by the San Francisco group, Women on the Web.

Eisenberg's gift rests in her ability to blend her expertise in evolving legal standards with an unerring judgment of emerging technologies and a hair-trigger readiness to challenge the status quo.

What do you personally use the Net for?

Everything. I rely on it as my primary means of communication with friends and with people with whom I have business relations, and with family. Basically, there's hardly a person with whom I don't use the Net as my primary form of communication. It's also my primary means of research, at least in the beginning stages of anything. I find out great company information and news, and there's so many different sources. However, I never really trust any news sources. So it's helpful to compare MarketWatch versus *The Wall Street Journal* versus press releases versus Hoover's take on the company versus etc., etc. So research and communication are my two big things.

How many hours a day, or a week, would you say you spend online?

I'm always online. I have a connection that is always up, so I'm continually downloading e-mail.

I mean, when you're sitting in front of the computer.

Oh, that's how many hours I work . . . 90? It's however many hours there are in a week minus 8 a day! I really think I'm in front of my computer about 100 hours a week.

You're a Harvard-trained lawyer. Why are you doing what you're doing now?

Well, I loved the first two years of the practice of law because I was in court with people. It was exciting and it was interesting, and a lot of the issues I dealt with were novel. A lot of IP (intellectual property) stuff; a lot of patent and trademark stuff. But the third year, I was doing appellate work. When I realized I wasn't enjoying what I was doing as a lawyer, I knew I had to work in the Internet space because that was my creative outlet and my hobby, and it was what I was so sure was going to be a big thing.

So writing on the Web was a natural outlet there?

I was math and science my entire life before I got to law school, where I was forced to write. I would write up psychology reports of my experiments, but it was all statistics. I was told I was a good writer, but for me it was more of a burden. But putting up a Web site was what I ended up doing. I really put up the Web site when I moved to Houston. To me, having a Web site was the ultimate act of being part of the Internet community—this was before it was so commercial. You contribute to the Web and you take from the Web. That way, you're part of the network. And that was the best way for me to get out to people what I was doing, what I was thinking. They were all freaked out that I was quitting, etc.

My first job after lawyering was not writing at all. I was a systems administrator and a manager of information services for a small business is Houston. I moved out here to put up a Web site for an Internet project that ultimately failed. I only got into writing because I was posting things up on the Web. I noticed I was acting like a writer, but I wasn't very good at it. Also, that was what it was easiest to market myself as, as a woman. It was too difficult to say 'Look, I have this training in law and business. I can do consulting in technology.' If you're female, it's easier to be a writer.

As it happens, a lot of the people I went to college with are now working on the Internet. Some good friends of mine from my freshman dorm were working on this really interesting company, Ecast, which would distribute music, games, and services to public places like restaurants and bars. They asked me to help develop their business plan. They were impressed with my work, I was impressed with me, and they made a position for me as a vice president with the company. I'm identifying new markets for their products and services.

Let's talk about the right to privacy from the corporate side, which doesn't get much coverage in the press. What right does a corporation have to collect data on an individual, to distribute that information, or to sell that information? Do they have an inherent right to do that?

Well, if the consumer agrees, yes. These rights are governed by contract, at least as far as I'm aware. This sounds so 'free market,' but companies compete in the marketplace on all sorts of levels: on goods, on prices, on services, etc., etc. And one of these services is what kind of privacy protection they offer. If the market is working, the consumer will choose the company that offers the best protection, by contract, by agreement, by warranty, and by disclaimers on their site.

Yes, but if I just go on a Web site, unless I adjust my browser to reject cookies, I don't even know that stuff is going on. It's basically just being collected.

Cookies aren't a collection of information. There's this whole misconception of cookies. Cookies are a way of storing information on *your* computer, rather than them taking information *from you*. If people really understood how cookies worked, they'd be far less nervous about them. Cookies are a convenience, and you don't have to agree to a cookie. You can set your preferences every time.

But that cookie does give information back to the company.

Well, it gives information about your preferences that you gave to the company because you wanted your experience to be more convenient.

OK. We talked about the rights of corporations, but what about the rights of individuals. What rights does an individual have coming to the Web, in terms of privacy? Say I have a fondness for something I shouldn't have a fondness for—I'm left-wing or right-wing or I'm looking at sexually explicit materials.

I think it's important for individual users to actively seek out the privacy policies of any Web site they visit. Most Web sites have privacy policies, and they can click there.

How do you do that without going to the Web site?

It goes without saying that being on the Web means Web system administrators and Internet companies are going to know what domain you've logged in from. So that's either your ISP or your employer. And it's tough luck, because you are accessing this information for free. In exchange, they get to know where you're coming from. It's just like you attend a conference or a porn show, like PeeWee Herman, they're going to know you're there.

The difference between that and this is PeeWee Herman was in a public theater. You're in the den of your house.

That's a big misconception of people on the Net. The Web *is* public. Just because you're accessing the Web from the den in your home doesn't mean the Web is also in your den in your home. You are going out into public from your den. The Web is a public space. You are leaving your home. It's important for people to realize, if this is a concern of theirs, what kind of tracks they leave. The Internet would not be able to function without the domain system that goes on numerically. Every Internet address has an IP number, a unique number, and without those numbers, the traffic would never be routed. You'd never get to a site you're aiming for.

Let's say Mary Smith shares a computer with her son and she decides to go to a lesbian lifestyle board.

These types of concerns are addressed in very good ways in the free market. If you don't want the Web site you're visiting to know where you're from for any reason, you can log in there through an anonymous proxy site. Yeah, you're going to have to take the extra step to go research those companies. A lot of the Web sites out there for organizations like GLAD and anti-discrimination groups provide those resources, understanding that sometimes there are very real risks. So if you have a reason to want to protect that information—for example, even though it may be illegal, site visitors might lose their jobs if their employers found out they were gay—you should turn to these resources, and many of them are free. And that's really good because one of the biggest benefits of the Web is that people go out to meet with other people who are like themselves. So the same thing that helps these gay teenagers who are being discriminated against in school, and that brings them together so they can meet other kids and discuss their issues, is the same thing that also causes some very difficult problems that they then have to protect themselves against—the Web.

There's one more thing I want to say about privacy. Offline, people very often don't have very good protection. The privacy online is actually much better than the privacy offline. When you subscribe to a magazine, the magazines always sell your address. Offline, they actually get a lot more information on you than they do online. Compare your computer address to your postal address. Which do you want the psycho stalker to get ahold of?

The other thing I want to say is that companies are getting better about being explicit about their privacy policies because of the global nature of the information marketplace. Europe has very different societal standards about privacy. In Europe, governments go out of their way to keep personal information private because of the history of privacy violations in the past; for example, [pre-WWII] Germany, where if the government found out you'd been involved in organized labor, had a Jewish family member, or had a retarded family member, you'd be killed.

So Europe has very different standards and they're not willing to trade with U.S. companies unless the U.S. companies demonstrate similar attitudes about privacy. This is a huge, huge issue. It's a big deal.

Let's talk about liability. If an auction site sells a gun, is it liable for how that gun is used? Is it like a traditional store?

That's a case that's still being tested and until it goes to the Supreme Court, it's not clear. There always are disputes over what kind of responsibility the auction site had to do due diligence. What the auction site will do is provide a disclaimer: 'We're not responsible for harm that occurs. Do you agree to this disclaimer? If so, you can use this service.' Of course, people who are not subject to that disclaimer, like your neighbor who gets shot by the little kid who ended up with the gun, were never privy to that contract, so never gave away her right.

So that's something you think will have to
be worked out in court?

I think it will have to be. And I think it will be analyzed similarly to a store and, even more so, to a newspaper classified section.

It's like a mail order situation, isn't it, because you don't have
the personal contact? Even with a newspaper classified,
you're likely to go out, meet the seller, and buy the gun.

Well, from what I hear, very often weapons and illegal goods are exchanged not by postings on the Web sites themselves, but in the e-mail conversations that follow. They'll advertise flowerpots, and really that might be a symbol for heroin or whatever.

And the privacy issue is very relevant here because one of the reasons companies want to collect information about you is to protect themselves in cases just like this. If they have information about the person selling the gun or the illegal good, they then can track it down and go after the perpetrator.

Are they then responsible to go do that?
Do they have an affirmative obligation?

Do they have a duty to find them out? They'll try to disclaim it, and either that disclaimer will be held up or not held up in court.

You mentioned ISP slander cases?

Right, AOL had a whole bunch of them. Matt Drudge was involved in one. And the question is—and these still haven't been tried in court—is the ISP responsible for publishing what people say on the site? And the answer is, it depends.

If the ISP is acting like an editor, like MarketWatch does with my column, then a certain sort of duty applies. I thought the AOL case should have gone the other way, because what happened in the AOL case was they were found nonliable. What AOL does is they disallow certain swear words and such. They try to be an editor of what is published on their site. The flip side is the more you edit, the more you say no. The trouble is some people call that censorship. It's never censorship when you're a private party—give me a break. They're an editor, they have rules and the more rules they have, the more likely they will be, and should be, found liable.

I think to the extent that consumers are shareholders in companies, what we're seeing a lot of is shareholder liability suits. If companies have irresponsible and bad privacy rules, then that could be a breach of fiduciary responsibility. And also, just as with any company that tanks and then you always see shareholder liability suits, to the extent that a company doesn't make appropriate use of user information—in marketing purposes, for selling ads, that sort of thing—they are also breaching their duty to their shareholders. I always ask people to look at it from the company's point of view. They have a duty to make money, but they have a duty to make money in a responsible way.

What about brokers? Let's say a broker has a computer breakdown and the consumer can't sell the stock when he wants to. I suppose most of these sites have a telephone back up, but I wonder how many are set up to handle that amount of traffic? I should add the SEC is currently looking into this.

The SEC is the most anal-retentive government agency ever. And many of the anal-retentive policies are terrible. They're so interested in protecting investors from ordinary information. I hate that.

What online brokers say is that they make it very clear consumers are getting $9.95 service for their $9.95 trades, then the consumer who loses money due to time delays has no complaint because they saw the warning. It's a fact of life: You get what you pay for.

**So when you sign up for a service,
you'd better read the fine print?**

Supposedly, companies that can't deliver even $9.95 worth of service soon won't be used by consumers.

**And that's an example of consumer power.
If the broker doesn't meet their needs, they'll just
go to another broker because there's a lot of choices.**

Right. More than anywhere else, consumers have power on the Net. That's what I always try to tell people in my column, too: Vote with your money. Don't have accounts at these banks. And decide which of these banks is good and which is bad before you decide where you're going to put your nest egg.

**Do you think American corporations are used to having
customers that fickle? It used to be if you lived in a town,
you kind of had to go to the big stores in that town.
If there were three bakeries, you had that much choice,
but no more. On the Web you have a lot more choices.
You can go to a lot of brokers just by flicking a few buttons.**

They say the barriers to entry on the Web are zero. But, of course, the barriers to entry on the Web are who has the good customer information and who doesn't. If you have the best customer data, you can deliver the best services.

The customer does have power on the Web unlike anywhere else. Of course, the ironic twist I want to go back to is that people say one of the bad things about our society is all the anonymity. You go to your Wal-Mart and nobody knows you. But you go to your corner store and they know your name, they know what you want to buy, and they know when the last time was you bought diapers for your kid or Tide detergent for your laundry. And that makes you feel good. I think that's one of the goals of the Internet companies: to make consumers feel like they're at their corner store, which they can get to even though the corner store is located in Israel or Australia or the Bahamas or whatever.

In content, copyright has been a difficult issue for the software industry for a long time. When you had something printed in a book, it was a lot easier to enforce copyright. But when it's lines of code in a software program, it gets more difficult, especially when those lines can be taken surreptitiously and hidden in the middle of millions of other lines of code in another program. On the Net, it's kind of a cross between the two. It's so easy to get content from somewhere, lift it out, and put it somewhere else.

I want to start by separating out the line of code in a program because software programs are usually dealt with . . . under patent. There's currently a huge debate now in the patent bar because patent doesn't protect it and neither does copyright.

That aside, I think there's two different things here. One is HTML, which *is* publicly accessible, unlike actual software code, because HTML is just a mark-up language, it's not a coding language. And yeah, HTML can be stolen easily and the copyright violated. The flip side is the thieves can be caught more easily, too. That's one of the great things about the Web: What users do—and again, there's a lot of user power that they have here—is do a search. It's what you should do if you run a small business, or if you engage in anything having to do with intellectual property for a living. Do a search on your content.

I always check Lexus-Nexus regularly to see if things I wrote appear there even though I didn't give them rights. I often search for my name on the Web to see which of my stories were reprinted somewhere without my permission, which happens often. And then you should make a decision on whether you want to pursue it. Very often, a firm but friendly e-mail will get them to stop. And you can resort to your local lawyer. So that's the HTML issue: Yes, it can be stolen more easily. Also, it can be found more easily.

Actual writing is a big thing among people like yourself and myself who actually write for a living and it's easy to steal what we write.

The interesting thing there is recourse. I mean, what can you do if you see your book translated into another language. What are you going to do? Go over to another country and sue?

That can happen offline as well. And again, you're far less likely to catch it in the offline world. You have to go through your same old means of recourse, but tracking down the perpetrator is much easier because of the Web. And again, I'd advise the readers to keep abreast of what's out there. I've had my content stolen in the past, both my HTML—my HTML sucks anyway—and my [writing] content, and I've often found that by a friendly letter—'Listen, I see you'—they will stop.

What you're saying here, again, is that the power of the individual is enhanced by the Web. If you're the writer, it's easier to track down a copyright violation as an individual. Corporations always had the power to do this one way or the

other. But now an individual freelancer can track this and pursue a remedy and, at least, have a better starting point.

Yes, and you can get your resources through a free Web site. There's a legal publisher in Texas that was just sued for the illegal practice of law. They're a great resource. There are so many legal resources found on the Web that the individual is far more empowered as an individual and the individual is empowered as a group. You can meet with people who have similar problems. You're being underpaid because at work you're a contractor instead of an employee, and you want to be an employee. You can meet with people like that. You can join unions, or you can fight unions.

There are even Web sites right now that are using the power of the individual consumers to join up—do you know about PopularDemand.com? That's a great idea.

The Web also gives people mobility. Yes, maybe that's why their salaries are deflated, but it lets them look for the best job fit. Monster.com has an auction site for individuals auctioning off certain services, whether it be programming, writing, consulting, or what-not. This could be an example of bidding for the most attractive employees. Of course, it could also result in people undercutting each other and wages going down. But if that's the case, they don't have to engage.

So that's what so thrilling about the Web. With eBay and Monster.com, there's so much opportunity out there, which I have to keep reminding myself all the damn time. There's so many options out there because of the Web. I never would have been able to quit being a lawyer and go into business for myself, either as a writer or a geek, without the Web. I learned everything on the Web. I learned HTML on the Web. The resources are there.

ANDY GROVE

Cofounder and Chairman of Intel Corporation

It's difficult to think of anyone who's had a greater impact on computer technology over a longer period of time than Andy Grove, the chairman of Intel Corporation.

After earning his PhD from the University of California, Berkeley, in 1963, the native Hungarian joined Fairchild Semiconductor. In 1968, he was a cofounder of Intel Corporation and became its president eight years later. Intel named him CEO in 1987 and he became chairman a decade after that, turning over the CEO duties to Craig Barrett in 1998.

He's taught at Berkeley for six years and still teaches a course at Stanford University. He's authored 40 technical papers, holds several patents, and has authored four books, most recently the best-seller *Only the Paranoid Survive.* He's also written for several publications, including *The Wall Street Journal, The New York Times, Fortune,* and *Working Woman* magazine.

His many honors include the Medal of Achievement from the American Electronics Association, CEO of the Year from *CEO* magazine, Technology Leader of the Year by *Industry Week,* and Man of the Year by *Time* magazine.

Despite his position at the pinnacle of the technological world, Grove has retained the disarmingly humble persona of a great teacher, ready and willing to discuss any question and always conscious of the impact of technology on the world around us.

I think a lot of people would be interested in how, as an advanced user of technology, you personally use the Web.

Oh, I don't think I'm an advanced user of technology. I'm a lazy technologist and I think my usage is probably closer to low-brow mainstream usage than advanced technical use. I'm not doing anything very spectacular. I shop on it. I get a lot of news from it. Every once in a while, I browse a little and look at this and that. I'm fairly involved in prostate cancer research. I use the Web to look at advances in that. I use the Internet for correspondence; my communications are almost exclusively e-mail. I do some interviews.

Are you conducting any video conferences at this point?

Not anymore. For a while, I was very excited about the potential for video conferencing—pre-Web. And over time, it didn't take off in the sense I liked using it. The community I liked doing it with didn't grow. Then a funny thing happened. The emergence of e-mail virtually obviated the video conferencing usage. A strange development, really. It was the store-and-forward nature of e-mail and the ability to send attachments with e-mail, which our video conferencing solution had also. At the time, you could send attachments with video conferencing so you could see material as well as video conference. That was 1992–93, so it was before the Web, or before attachments could be e-mailed in a common manner.

I recall seeing you demonstrate that. It was an interesting technology. Maybe it just hasn't hit its time yet.

You know, one of my most embarrassing undertakings was the amount of effort we—and I, in particular—pumped into video conferencing. And I don't know why it hasn't taken off. And I'm not sure it will, because I have a hunch it goes against the grain of the direction communication is heading.

Communication is heading more alpha-numeric. Look at the take-off of online messaging, instant messaging. It's keyboard-based. It's contemporaneous. It's real time. The billion e-mail messages that get sent around are nonreal time, asynchronous. But both of them are keyboard-based. About ten years ago, actually before I got enthused about video conferencing, I thought e-mail annotated with video messages would be a big deal, because you could attach small video files appropriate for a voice mail message. Nobody uses it, and it can be done pretty easily today. Such a minority use it that it's almost nobody.

I think it has a lot to do with the fact that most people are still on narrow bandwidth and it takes a long time to download a file like that, or even to set up video conferencing.

If that is the case, I think by the time that broadband and a stable infrastructure—where you don't have crashes and driver problems and plug-in problems—become ubiquitous, people's communications habits may have gone so far away from video-based communications that it may just miss its window.

You're probably right. Let me ask about something else. We're at a fascinating moment in history, as you're well aware, and I see it as a very transitional time where leadership of certain technologies could shift, or where new

technologies can come in strongly and change the structure of some of the things we've seen. Do you think this is true?

Yeah, yeah, I think it's true, but with a bit of a 'but.' It's probably not as true as the proponents of that point of view think it is. It's a little caveat. Some of the leadership will change, but not all of the leadership will change. Perhaps it's that the late 1990s come after a terrible '80s for American corporations, and a lot of these corporations still have the same management that was in charge when their corporations almost died in the 1980s. They're not going to let themselves be swept away.

So there's going to be a lot of the current leaders who'll reinvent themselves and emerge in a leadership position also.

We've seen a great example of [change] with Amazon coming out of nowhere in this new dynamic and becoming very big in e-commerce very quickly, and Barnes & Noble taking its time to get used to the new technology and slowly making a transition, and dragging with it some of its investment in the brick-and-mortar world. Do you think that's an example of the kind of transitions we're going to see?

Yes it is. A more successful example is what Schwab has done. You know, Schwab is combining their electronic infrastructure and their brick-and-mortar infrastructure more efficiently. I'm more familiar with what's happened there because I've been teaching a case on them at Stanford.

Chuck Schwab is a great technologist. He really believes in it.

That's what I mean. Those people have lived by technology before. Not Web-based technology, but telephone-based technology. They understood the remote customer, the connected customer. They revamped their operational style. They revamped their pricing, and they soared back after an initial decline. I think you're going to see examples like that.

That's a good one. People don't often mention it, but it's an excellent example of a traditional company that's made the transition of competing head-to-head with new Web startups and doing very well.

So, yes, there's a potential for reordering. But for reordering to happen, the incumbents have to fall asleep at the switch. Some will try to evolve and fail, and some will try and succeed by not falling asleep at the switch.

Let me ask about the productivity gains we've seen, both with technology on the broad level and with the Net, more specifically. Thanks largely to your efforts at Intel, we've seen an astonishing yet predictable growth in technological power over the past many years, and yet the fast growth of the Net over the past few years has really caught a lot of people by surprise. What was different there? Why was one expected and the other not so expected?

I'm a chemical engineer by background, so the thing that comes to mind is a catalytic reaction where you put two compounds in a reactor and stir them and they are in proximity with each other and you heat them and nothing happens. And you introduce a third agent, which is a catalyst, and all of the sudden a chemical reaction starts galloping.

What do you think the catalyst is in this reaction?

The Internet protocols. The two reagents that have been going on for a long time in a predictable past and a predictable fashion, but not in an explosive fashion, are the deployment of digital computing—PCs, basically—and corporate networking. Without Internet protocol allowing the Internet to become as ubiquitous as it's become, those islands would have communicated through a proprietary protocol with each other, some using this protocol, some using other protocols. Instead, a lingua franca of productivity has burst on the scene and allowed all of that investment that has taken place for a decade and a half to be interconnectable. I view that as the catalyst.

Do you think this can continue for several more years?

Yes, and the exciting part of this is that the United States is getting pretty wired and in a few more years we're going to start seeing the S curve appear. You're going to be looking at a lesser and lesser part of the population, particularly in business, that is not wired. And there's still going to be action with the wiring, and I mean wiring generically, where it will get replaced and upgraded and made more robust. But the U.S. is a small fraction of the world environment. And the same development that's taken place in the U.S. in the past five or six years, is barely starting outside of the U.S. So even if the U.S. stopped today, there is a decade worth of development taking place outside of the United States. And it has to happen, because its *not* happening would condemn the rest of the world to a 1 percent productivity penalty in domestic product that it cannot tolerate.

You mean their growth would be 1 percent less?

Yes. [Fed chairman Alan] Greenspan called this a 1 percent effect. And in the absence of anything else, it's as good a number as any. For an economy that is reasonably wired and has this 1 percent accelerator, versus the rest of the economies—with monetary policy, people training, and all other things being equal—there's a horrendous national advantage for the U.S. So 1 percent compounded year after year is going to cause a major divergence. And I think the technology is available, so you'll see a growing investment internationally catching up with the United States in this fashion.

A few years ago, some people were talking to me about the telephony in China and predicted China would skip over the hard-wired stage of telephony and go straight to wireless. And now I hear people talking about parts of the world jumping to IP telephony. Do you think that's a realistic leap?

I don't see any evidence of that. And even with the wireless part, even if you see a lot of wireless local access, you still have to build the switching infrastructure and the billing systems and all that stuff, which is a much bigger deal than stringing up a few antennas to the population for the last mile.

I guess the argument is you have to build an infrastructure anyway, so why not build one gauged toward IP?

Theoretically, they may make that argument. But practically, nobody has demonstrated the big scale viability of IP telephony going into place. China is building a U.S.-style RBOC [regional Bell operating company] per year. So that's what's happening and it's been happening for years.

That's amazing.

Well, it's a huge country. And [going] back into the same thing I was talking about with the S-curve phenomenon, they're well into the S curve, so their population grows, in spite of everything they do, 20 or 30 million a year.

**Recently in a speech, you said all companies will be
Internet companies in five years or they will be dead.
I was wondering if that was a slight exaggeration.
Do you mean that they'd have an Internet presence,
or that they will become Internet companies?**

This goes back to your earlier question. The distinction between a Schwab and an E-Trade is going to be absolutely academic. I think for companies to prosper in the five-year to ten-year horizon, they will have to make Schwab-like conversions or else they will be reordered to the back of the line.

So they won't really be dead in that time frame, but they will lose position, lose market power, and lose profitability to those who have made the adjustment. And once these companies have made the adjustment, the distinction between them and the people who were 'born on the Web' will be increasingly lower. You get to that stage where your company either has taken a physical infrastructure and is adopting Internet commerce for intercompany and company-to-consumer transaction, or you can build the infrastructure for the transactions and then go and back-fill the physical facilities that you need to transact business.

In the long run, the overwhelming majority of the world's business is going to be physical goods, no matter how advanced networks are going to be. So you will see a billion-dollar undertaking by Amazon.com or a billion-dollar undertaking by Webvan, building their network of warehouses, and you will see billion-dollar enterprises by Wal-Mart and Safeway building their transactional capabilities. They all end up looking more or less similar.

**An interesting concept you raised was in talking about
the 'cloud' of the Internet, and I love that metaphor.
I always think about how complicated it is to do
television right, and yet it seems so simple to most
people—they just go and turn it on and it works. The**

Internet is really a very complicated system, too, but people like you understand it and people like me really don't. Would you talk about where Intel might fit in and what other kinds of companies would be in there with you?

I think there's going to be three types of actions in all of this. There'll be hundreds of millions of access points of different kinds, but primarily kinds of PCs—PCs streamlined for their predominant use being Internet access. There'll be enormous amounts of communication control functions, shaping and storing of digital signals from the client to some other client after having progressed through that cloud. And in between all the transactions—the data mining, the customer records, the plain serving of Web pages—all of that is going to be done on servers. Actually, the computational load on them is more than linearly growing with the number of accesses. The complexity of the transactions grows as well.

And our chips are used, or are aimed at being used, in all these areas. As getting on the Internet becomes a necessity, the questions of killer applications and arguments of why one should have a personal computer at every place where one lives—at work, at home, and in between—become nonstarters as questions. The predominance of the servers today are built around Intel chips, and we have a major set of developments that are targeted for that. Through our own internal developments and through a half-dozen or more acquisitions, we have acquired and are honing the same kind of expertise to develop network processors, if you wish. They're versions of microprocessors oriented toward communications functions.

You can't go anywhere on the Internet without microprocessors, or devices that may be called differently, but they are still microprocessors, doing their jobs. Our developments need to be shaped so that they are more responsive to the needs of Internet computing than they were some time ago.

With the processors in that cloud, would some of those be gathered in—I hate to oversimplify here—but in a kind of Intel server farm that would be a processing center?

Yes, absolutely. I think that's actually a very good way of looking at it. We're figuring out exactly how we're going to brand them, but we're going to brand them as some sort of Intel service. Our first statement, that all companies will be Internet companies, includes small companies as well. And the same way a lot of small companies farm out their conventional data processing to outside companies because they can't afford to have their own IT organizations, they will do the same for Internet applications as well. We think we will be able to sell our technology in service form to companies that choose to go that route. Nobody knows what portion of the use is going to be bought as service as opposed to bought as product, but we want to be neutral to the possible shapes in that development.

I heard you say a few years ago that even if there were a need for network computers, there would probably still be a demand for PCs in the den, where people want to keep their personal records and that sort of thing. Do you still think that, or do you think we're moving to more of a network computing architecture?

I think we're moving more and more to network computing, and that is where we should be moving. But I think there are going to be bumps in the road because the opportunity for the misuse of peoples' records will skyrocket as more and more records are kept on the network.

I have to admit that, although most of my personal records are on a computer network here or there, I somehow would be a little uneasy about having all my personal files in a single, company-owned database somewhere.

So am I. And it won't take too many horror stories plastered on the front pages of newspapers to enhance that negative feeling that you just described, that you and I both have, whereas it's going to take a whole lot of time in the absence of any such stories to build up our comfort. How many issues of the newspaper without such stories will we need before we forget one bad story where somebody was harmed by this?

If you look at it from a standpoint of computer engineering and efficiencies, the proper use of networks and centralized data should take place as rapidly as the reliability of the networks and the broadband capabilities of the network get there. But I think there are more issues there and consequently it's going to be a struggle. And data that is close to your heart, you're going to continue to keep on your hard disk. And your hard disk will contain protection software, because your hard disk is accessible, too. So this is not going to be a smooth phenomenon. It's just that there are such compelling advantages that you've got to move in that direction over time, but there'll be a lot of bumps.

The government is working on its own records and is getting into this complicated project that they described with different government agencies getting involved in protecting the government's own networks. And the civil libertarians are up in arms over this 'big brother' computer system. So that's just one example of it.

That's a good example, too. I want to ask you about some of the social implications, both positive and negative— some of which you've talked about already. Positively, it seems like consumers are gaining an enormous amount of power here with many more choices, at lower prices. We're seeing enormous competition on price and with

services. People are getting much better service now than they can get from the store down the block because they can go on the Web and choose from 15 or 20 different stores. Do you think those are all accurate trends?

Yes, they are. I think the buyer is going to be king in this new world. I liken it to what the emergence of Japanese competition did to manufacturers in the 1980s. That's the kind of power this shift to the buyers is going to bring. It's going to be a much tougher life for corporations as suppliers, and a much easier life for corporations or consumers as buyers.

Intel's blessed with having a pretty good and unique product in microprocessors, and one that requires a lot of expertise and has a lot of barriers to entry. But if you're selling books on the Web, or some other rather standard commodity, it seems like there would be almost zero price margins for most of that. What do you think is going to happen with price margins in the long term? Do you think they'll erode for those kind of commodity items?

In brief, yes. I'm equally puzzled over how companies will make money, like eBay and Priceline and yet-to-be-invented variations of them, that are basically using price to gather customers in the hope of making it up as time goes on by servicing those customers and getting a revenue stream out of them. The barriers to entry to doing the same thing by other people are not that hard. These are standard technologies. People are trying to patent business models, but it remains to be seen if that can be any kind of barrier. But this is going to be a tough living for old or new participants in this world. We'll live, but I'm not euphoric about the business prospects associated with it. Everyone [says they're] going to make it up with advertising, and I'm getting increasingly skeptical of that as a source of revenue, as a source of profit, that makes up the difference.

But the bottom line is this is going to be a sort of golden age for people in terms of power and individual choice and consumerism?

I think that is correct. My skeptical outlook is from the standpoint of the supplier. From the buyer's standpoint, it is going to be an absolutely wonderful development. And that normally is good for the economy as a whole. It drives the suppliers and intermediaries to be much more competitive. It shakes nonvalued activities out of the chain of events. It's going to be good for the economy.

MIKE BLOOMBERG

Founder and Chairman of Bloomberg LP,
and Chairman of Johns Hopkins University

Internet entrepreneurs looking for a role model would have a hard time finding a better one than Mike Bloomberg, founder and chairman of financial news and data provider Bloomberg LP, and chairman of Johns Hopkins University.

Bloomberg, who studied engineering at Johns Hopkins and graduated from Harvard Business School in 1966, built his multi-billion-dollar company on the belief he could provide a superior product and better customer service for the financial industry, which is always willing to pay a premium for both.

Running against the popular tech philosophy of the 1990s, Bloomberg long insisted on delivering his service over a private network using proprietary hardware, commonly referred to as "the Bloomberg." Since then, he's discovered the value of the Internet as a communications medium, but continues to doubt many of today's widely held beliefs about e-commerce.

I know you use the Bloomberg to get information. Do you use the Internet?

Bloomberg's involvement with the Internet is that we use the Internet as an information service provider more than any other company. All of our customers who dial up around the world come to us over the Internet. A lot of our customers who come to us over our private network use the Internet as backup. If our network line goes down, they come to us over the Internet. There are parts of the world where we no longer or never did provide our own network just because the economics don't make any sense. There is Internet access, and people come to us over the Internet. And I think if you look down the road, my expectation is that a year or two from now, the Internet will get reliable enough and sophisticated enough that we can push all our customers to come to our mainframes only over the Internet.

It would save this company $90 to $100 million a year if everybody came to us over the Internet—if we didn't have to have 500 locations to which we run high-speed lines, if we didn't have to have the service people and the air-conditioning and the power backup, the insurance, the maintenance, the cleaning facilities, and all that kind of stuff.

How do you personally use the Internet?

Well, my terminal goes to our mainframe over the Internet. So if you're just talking about the Internet as communications— I want to separate these things—I use it all the time. But I don't think that's what you mean.

Are there things beyond the Bloomberg for which you use it?

Well, let's switch the focus from using the Internet as a physical communications device, or a logical communications device, to what you mean: Do I use the Web and go to different sites around the world? That *goes* over the Internet, but that's a separate thing.

Do I use it as a source of entertainment? No. I don't spend time 'surfing,' if you will, whatever that means. I don't do that. Generally, it's interesting, but get a life. If that's how you're spending three hours a night, I think you better go to shrink.com.

Do I do e-commerce on the Web? No. I still tend, when I want a book, to stop at the corner. There's a Borders a block away. The books I want are the ones I read a review about in the *New York Times* book review section, and they're right out front. I don't need the enormous list of books in print that an Amazon would have, and Amazon doesn't solve my basic interest in the bookstore, in that I want instant gratification. Amazon is a great way to order books, but it has a lousy way to deliver them.

I would argue in the long run that the corner bookstore survives. It may survive in big chains, not individually owned. But I still think bookstores have a long happy road ahead and that, in fact, the online bookstores—and not all commerce works this way, but a lot of it does—have a problem with delivery.

Whether it's a grocery store delivering groceries or a bookstore delivering your books, they have an advantage over an Internet site where they have a handful of warehouses to deliver the groceries, and a handful of warehouses to deliver the books. In fact, it's a lot cheaper for your local bookstore and your local supermarket to create a Web site to order your books or groceries—and they'll deliver it—than it is for the guys who have the Web sites to build the physical infrastructure to store groceries, deliver them, and know how to take care of groceries so they don't sour or whatever.

So I don't surf the Web for entertainment. I don't do e-commerce on the Web. I *do* use the Web for information. If I want a map to go from here to there, I go to, say, MapQuest. What Bloomberg does is we'll take you to the Web, and we'll bring up MapQuest's Web site on the Bloomberg terminal, connecting to the Web through our computer room in New York or Princeton, using our network to deliver their data out to the desk. So, if you go over there and up comes 'MAP,' that's not the same as giving you a browser and letting you go anyplace. We do the indexing and vet sites in advance. Our customers generally do not want our users to spend their time with a browser, spend their time trading stocks, spend their time buying books, or going to sex sites—pornography's a very big problem for the commercial world. So on one hand you have all these people saying isn't it wonderful that everybody can go everyplace and, yet, the people who are paying for it don't want you to go everyplace. They frown on you sitting at your desk reading a newspaper, they frown on you sitting at your desk having a television on to MSNBC or CNN, and they frown on you going with their PC onto the Web and going everyplace.

Another thing you should get in your book is that we, the providers, think technology's great because we can get more ads to the public. The public thinks technology's great because they can get *fewer* ads. And there's a lot of that, when you read: 'We want to bring all information to everybody for free.' Yeah, good, except if you're an author, you don't want that. And there are a lot of those things. 'We want to make capitalism frictionless.' Not if you're a middleman, you don't. So, the press writes about one side, but there are two sides.

That's an interesting thing. I'm looking at price margins for the e-commerce sites, and they're quickly going down to 3, 2, and 1 percent. Some sites sell at cost and try to make a profit in ads.

Yeah, there was a guy a long time ago—Milo Minderbinder in *Catch 22*—who did that with eggs, if you remember. Joseph Heller was way ahead of these guys!

Exactly! So can these companies succeed?

I would argue there are three things that people always confuse. One is technology. 'Technology is great. We're going to use more and more of it everyplace. And it will keep getting better and better.'

Second is a company using technology to make money, and we're going to talk about that. It's much more difficult.

Third thing is the stocks. And the connection between those three things is tenuous, and between points two and three, it's probably zero.

The business model for most Internet companies doesn't work. And the reason it doesn't work is because they don't have anything that's unique. They have the same thing everybody else has, and they tend not to have things that you have to have. Which means you have big supply/low demand, and as that old Scottish economist Adam Smith said, prices are low.

Why can Bloomberg and Reuters charge for data—and we charge $1,225 a month, and we're growing at 30 percent a year—when everybody else can't sell data for anything? The answer, I think, is that Bloomberg and Reuters, to some extent, have something that nobody else has: unique content—small supply; and it's something people need to do their jobs—big demand. They're addicted to three meals a day, so they really do need this stuff. So you can see, when there's small supply and big demand, prices are high; and when there's big supply, small demand, prices are low.

The basic business model of the Internet has difficulty because the reason the Internet is so attractive to start a business is because of the ease of access. The reason it's so problematic is because of the ease of access. If I want to compete with the Borders store at 57th and Park, I've got to find big, visible, easy-to-access space, with people walking by, in the neighborhood. In case you haven't noticed, I don't see any storefronts in this neighborhood that are available. So Borders has a lock on the market. That's their marketing cost. The brick-and-mortar and people that Amazon-like companies make fun of are their great strength. They're going to beat them in delivery, and their marketing costs may be high, but they're fixed.

The trouble with Amazon and those kinds of companies is that you've got to spend to get people to come to you because they can just as easily go elsewhere.

And you've got to have a business model long term that others will have trouble duplicating. For example, with Bloomberg, I would argue that MarketWatch can come in and try to compete with us and you can do some things just as well as we can, and you can get up to speed very quickly. On the other hand, there are a lot of things we do that have taken years, almost two decades in our case, that you would not be able to replicate. Particularly because we're a moving target and established and have a brand name that is worth something, there is some barrier to entry to your competing in our business. Some of our customers won't feel that way, but most—at least I hope and my kids hope—will. It's what Warren Buffett calls building a moat around the company. The bigger the moat, the harder it is to cross. I understand the moat around Bloomberg. I understand the moat around Reuters, because we've been competing with them, trying to cross that moat, and we've been working at it 18 years and they still have a lot of business. They're still double our size, remember. We can't knock them out.

On the other hand, I don't see why you can't compete with Amazon.com. You might say, 'Well, they're there first and have a great name.' Great name, but if all of the sudden AOL has somebody else's button on the front page, you're not going to go Amazon, you're going to go somewhere else. And that ease of access that first let Amazon get out there is, in the end, its great Achilles' heel.

This is a really good point. And they can compete on price, and we talked a little about that. But one of the things you've done very successfully at Bloomberg is

your customer service. That's a big part of your moat. Nobody does customer service like you guys.

But keep in mind that customer service doesn't fit the Internet business model. Customer service is that old brick-and-mortar. When somebody says an advertising-supported Web site is going to compete with us, well, maybe they will, but we do have 1,200 people collecting data. We have 1,000 people answering the phones, explaining how to use a function, sending out a new piece of equipment, getting it installed. Not everybody needs those things, and if you don't need them, then we can't compete. But to the extent you need the services we provide, a competitor is not going to be able to provide those same services for materially less.

You may be a better manager than I am, and you may be able to do it slightly better, but you just aren't going to be able to provide for $100 a month that for which we charge $1,200 a month.

When I sit here and I agonize about whether we're going to be in business tomorrow, I really don't worry so much about somebody coming along and providing the same product because it would be a very daunting task. I don't see anyone doing it. I don't even see Reuters doing it. My great fear is that the market doesn't need what we provide, that the market can do with a less-sophisticated, accurate, reliable, quick-response product. That's my fear. Most companies have both fears. We're at the point now where I'm reasonably confident that not only do we have the best product, but it's getting better and our competition . . . not only are they less good, but they're getting worse. Both of those things are true, so that's not our fear.

Our fear is not everybody needs the level of sophistication, not everybody needs news from 100 different countries, not everybody needs data for every bond and stock in the world. If what you want is open, high, low, close for a stock on the New York Stock Exchange, and a couple of stories once a day about the big companies, then go to MarketWatch.com, an advertiser-supported site, they'll do a fine job. People ask, 'Will the Internet put you out of business?' We never could sell to the person that MarketWatch sells to. They were never going to spend $1,200 a month.

I think that's true. If you did try to serve those customers, you'd be cannibalizing your core business.

Keep in mind Christianson [Clayton Christianson, author of *The Innovator's Dilemma*] would argue is that that's what keeps the established giants immobilized—the fear of cannibalization. It's a good book and he's got some good ideas, but there are plenty of companies that are big companies and innovate. Consumer companies like Sony and Philip Morris and, I hope, Bloomberg, do it all the time. But cannibalization is a *real* issue. If you take a look at Bloomberg.com, which gets 150 to 160 million page views a month, it's agood Web site. Having said that, there's no recorded evidence of anyone ever taking out a Bloomberg terminal and saying, 'I'm just going to go to Bloomberg's Web site.'

I had a young programmer come to me yesterday. He'd printed out a whole bunch of screens (available on the Bloomberg terminal) and he said 'We should put these on the Bloomberg Web site. It would make the Web site much better.' Yeah, unfortunately he couldn't eat because I couldn't pay him anymore, but short of that minor problem. . . .

How do you view the Bloomberg terminal versus Bloomberg.com? Obviously, there's a limitation on how good you want Bloomberg.com to be, but you could make it the best financial site on the Web overnight.

People come to us over the Internet, so you *could* have the whole thing. It's just that would be giving it away for nothing, and I don't have a big interest in doing that, nor do you.

Let me ask you about a couple of themes I've heard you talk about over the years. One is about empowering people with information. One of the things the Bloomberg does is it gets information out to a lot of people and they all have the same information, and that really makes for a more democratic and more efficient market. In a way, a much smaller way right now, the Internet is doing this, too. It brings a lot more information out to a lot of people.

The fundamental change in the securities industry since I joined in 1966 and today is that in 1966, the sell side had all the information, all the power. And all the compensation was on the sell side. The buy side was a bunch of clerks working at the Morgan bank who just were told to invest, and what they did was they called the broker and they said, 'I got a million dollars. What do I do with it?' And the reason they called that guy was because, maybe, they were being taken to the hoops and the pucks and to dinner, and it was a social-relationship business. The broker who had all the information made all the money. Over the years, that has changed. If you take a look, you can make as much money, maybe more, on the buy side as a venture capitalist, as a portfolio manager, as a buy side analyst, or even as a buy side trader than you can [make] on the sell side.

That shift in compensation is a function of the shift in power, and that's a result of, not just us, but systems like ours that have leveled the playing field. Remember, only 50 percent of the world wants a level playing field.

It is also true there is a lot more information available to the public today than there ever was before. Whether that really changes a power relationship, I'd be much more skeptical. Number one: Not a lot of people invest directly in stocks; most of them do it through mutual funds. In fact, you could make a case that an individual should always do it through mutual funds for the diversity and the professional management. And if you do it through a mutual fund, then all this information is worth zero. And there's some indication the public really doesn't care.

The circulation of arguably the greatest business newspaper (*The Wall Street Journal*) has gone from 2.2 million to 1.8 million during the greatest bull market in history. Yet the FT (*Financial Times*) has gone from 40,000 to 80,000 circulation in the United States. My recollection is they also cut their price from $2.50 to $1.00. If you cut it from $2.50 to $1 and you double circulation, it does seem to me you're still a little bit behind, and that assumes a 100 percent profit margin, so you're probably way behind. And *Investors Daily* exists today, but they have 250,000 subscribers and it's stayed that way and it's costing them a lot of money to hold their ground.

I honestly believe the Net has a lot to do with this. This is retail information. Look at a MarketWatch or Street.com or some of the other competitors and they're picking up readers. MarketWatch has 3.8 million unique readers a month. That's a big number.

But if you tried to charge them, what would you have?

I'm not sure we need to charge unless they want special services.

There's no question there is a demand for news. Whether it helps investors get better returns or not, I don't know. Whether it lets the investors better compete with their brokers, I don't know. On the institutional side, clearly it let the buy side better compete with the sell side. Whether it does that on the retail side is a much harder case to make.

You're very interested in education, I know. And one of the things I hope is a potential for the Internet is providing some common context for education. Maybe it can't serve every need at every school, but perhaps it

could provide some basic teaching plans to reduce operating expenses. Do you see a potential there?

At Johns Hopkins, where I'm chairman of the board, we're experimenting with a lot of things, and we happen to be very big in elementary education. Teaching isn't just getting the best teacher, who may or may not be a Nobel Prize winner—in fact, generally isn't. It could be teaching assistants, but nobody wants teaching assistants even though they may be the ones who teach the kids the most. If all it was was getting the best one, you'd video tape the teacher and play the tape everywhere. We have the technology to do this, and then maybe you have an assistant to answer questions locally. That would be very efficient. That's not caught on, and I'm not sure why.

I'm thinking more about the Net as an alternative to textbooks. That sort of thing.

It's not just education, but in everything. We have more electronic information transmittal, retrieval, and search devices in this company. That does not mean the managers should spend less time with the people they supervise, or that our people spend less time with the customers. Quite the contrary. We're taking away some of the drudgery or the mechanical part and they should spend more time managing, interacting, or whatever.

A lot of the business models—whether for education or society or information distribution or commerce—think that automating the mechanics is a substitute for what really takes place. Most people buy from a human being. Most people look at the context rather than the facts. Most people get sold rather than buy. They feel comfort in dealing with human beings. There's no evidence I know of that says we're really going to move all commerce over to the Internet.

It's like a pill for food. If someone invented a pill you could take and you no longer had to have a meal, I don't know how many people would really like that. Maybe long term, society really would change. You eventually do adopt some of these things. But overnight, all restaurants wouldn't close . . . no restaurant would close. And I think that's the same thing in education. As a delivery device for facts, it's fine. The question is: Are you going to sit in your room and interact with the device, or are you going to go to the classroom and have the big screen and the professor at the keyboard.

I hope it's really neither of those. I'd hope you'd go to a school and there's a teacher in the room and they use this as an interactive tool to get kids involved.

You would hope that. I think, unfortunately, the reality is some of this technology is misused. It is a great idea to have the Internet able to provide a six-year-old or seven-year-old with information in second grade. They can sit there; a professional can decide how to steer them through. Hopefully, we can teach evolution instead of creationism. But the real world is the kids are going to get dumped in front of that computer, the teacher is going to teach less, the teacher's salary is going to get cut because somebody will have to pay for the technology, and they'll also argue the technology is doing it, so we don't need as good a teacher.

Where do you think the Internet will be five years from now? Most of the people I've spoken to believe it will be very, very pervasive. I've heard knowledgeable people talking about having your refrigerator and your coffeepot hooked to the Net. Do you think we'll go that far, or does it come back to what you were just saying about limiting technology?

The trouble with the Internet is we confuse the physical with how to use it. I think it's true that five years from now every telephone will be an Internet terminal. You'll get data and text in graphic form as well as in audio form, and, also, we'll get it in video form. That's coming five years from now, that's probably a reasonable time frame.

Tying in all appliances? Yeah, there'll probably be a lot more of that. Whether you bother with the coffeepot and the refrigerator, I don't know. You do have the problem with people who really aren't very good at specifying what they want. If I ask you 'When do you want the coffee?' and you respond 'in the morning.' Well, today that might mean 6 but yesterday it meant 7. And I have all these separate remote controls and that's a problem. Take a look at peoples' audio-video systems—they can't handle it.

The great improvement that everyone's working on is to provide infinitely more internal complexity to give you external simplicity. So you walk into the kitchen and say to a device the size of a coffee cup 'Weather. Cleveland. Tomorrow.' And up comes this weather map and there's a fat guy pointing to the screen showing you. It's giving you that. You could go onto the Internet right now and get tomorrow's weather. It's just that it's hard to do. And there are lots of those kinds of things.

The argument that we need our kids to become computer scientists is absolutely fallacious. You'll need less 'computery,' technological kinds of stuff in the future. But because of all the technology, their world will be much more open, much more egalitarian, and much more competitive.

Clearly there's no argument about openness. You hear about it and it's there. Egalitarianism: It's pretty clear that as these technologies get accepted and the volume increases, the prices come down. Creating haves and have-nots is not something we've done in our society. In fact, the smarter the machine, the less you need knowledge and skills to use it, so it's available to more people. So somebody who's a farmer can still be a farmer, it's just that the computer decides how much fertilizer to put out as the tractor goes around the corner. He or she doesn't need to know it. So it really is a very enabling technology. And statistics do seem to show that we've taken a lot of people off the welfare roles with all this technology.

The third thing, the bad thing that all this technology does, and it's computer speed as well as bandwidth, is it makes the world much more competitive. As we said before, only half the people like that. The quality of your writing is going to matter more in the future, not less. Why? Because more people can get your book than ever before, but they can also get more books than ever before. So the good news is if you're better than average, you'll be able to sell more books and make more money. The bad news is if you're less than average, the customer has a lot more books to select from, and you will not be selected.

The thing I would worry about with my kids is that they have better reading skills, better writing skills, better mathematical skills—not being able to add, but being able to understand when you add versus when you subtract—and better presentation skills. People say those old-fashioned things don't matter. Bullshit. I'm going to be able, when I talk to you on the phone, to *see* you. So how you dress, how you present yourself, how you look me in the eye when you talk to me, will be *more* important, not less important.

We aren't going to go and work from home. The Internet is an academic's equivalent of standing around a water cooler. It ain't and it isn't gonna be. You still need the communications. There's no evidence, as a matter of fact, that more people are working at home. I haven't seen a study in a long time, and I haven't heard anybody in a long time, predict that we're going to use all this technology to work from home, and they used to do that.

I haven't read in the past few years of anyone predicting we're going to close all offices and work from home. Today they write we're going to close all stores. Those same people used to write we're going to close all offices.

I think the great use of technology is as a tool, not as a substitute. The problem is that the pundits have to write these grandiose things about change; otherwise, nobody reads what they write. But I don't see that taking place.

If you look at how mobile phones have taken off, they've become pervasive. But people still go to the office. They use the mobile phone not as a replacement, but as an adjunct, if you will.

The Internet will be around a long time, but what the press writes about is stocks, and they write about the technology, but that middle piece of how you use the technology to make money is a very different thing. And it's just hard to see this bubble from being any different from the CB radio bubble, the PC manufacturing bubble, the biotech bubble. There have been all these things, and out of every one of them there have been a handful of stocks that succeeded and what they developed got integrated into the next generation and maybe they made some contributions. And maybe some people got their money out, and some didn't. But it's hard to see this being any different in the stock market.

In terms of whether the technology of the Web is something enormously different in changing the paradigm, if you were to write a history of the world, I guess I would argue that because writing began back in the Egyptian days, the modern day telephone really changed the way we do business for the first time. Maybe the telegraph for a few days. But the telephone really let you start doing business. You could live anyplace and still stay in touch.

It was the first interactive real-time medium.

Exactly right. And the Internet you can think of as being something that you type in and read instead of speak in and hear. The addressing is somewhat simpler, arguably simpler, although if I want to get to the right person at General Motors and it has 50,000 employees, I don't know I'd go on their Web site to use General Motors phone book. It would be a useful thing to have it mechanically delivered, but I would argue the telephone probably made a bigger change in terms of how we were able to run our businesses and live in different places

I think the thing the Net adds is the potential to be a mass medium at the same time, so you're no longer limited to one-to-one interaction, which is a very limiting factor.

You can use e-mail that way too, but we don't send messages that way. They tend to be one-on-one. You could use a telephone instead of most e-mail, but you say it's easier just to click and send an e-mail rather than dial.

The big difference the Internet provides us is that individuals can get their messages out to the masses. In the past, you couldn't do that. In the past, only the wealthy and the powerful could control that. It takes a lot of money to own a printing plant and books and paper and ink. It takes a lot of money and political connections to have a radio or television license. And the telephone, as you point out, is a one-on-one thing.

And if Adolf Hitler, if you think about it, was just standing on a street corner able to get a big chunk of the world to follow him and to cause some pretty serious destruction, what will happen on the Internet? At least in the olden days, I could look up there and I knew that was Adolf Hitler speaking. The trouble with the Net is there's no audit trail, and I don't know who's really talking to me.

There's a study I saw the other day: 40 percent of all the medical advice offered on the Internet is from people with no qualifications to give it. After all this talk about security and secrecy and privacy, I'm not so sure down the road we aren't going to go and insist on an audit trail. The libel laws and those sorts of things really require that.

JERRY BROWN

Former California Governor and Mayor of Oakland, California

One of the most enigmatic and influential leaders of our time, Jerry Brown has been on the bleeding edge of social change for more than three decades. It seemed only appropriate to find out how Brown, now mayor of Oakland, California, views the Internet and its potential to affect education, politics, and society.

In 1974, at the age of 34, Brown was elected governor of California, the nation's most populous state. While governor, he pushed controversial programs that have since won broad acceptance, starting with his assertion that in government, less is more. He was reelected four years later by the biggest margin in state history.

His priorities included many of the policies now taken for granted, including coastal protection laws, farm workers' rights, alternative energy programs, sexual freedom, and public education. He was an early opponent of nuclear power. In medicine, he helped to open doors to alternative medicine practitioners including lay midwives and acupuncturists. During his tenure, state funding to the arts rose more than ten fold. His appointments to California's Supreme Court included the first Latino, the first African American and the first woman, the late Rose

Bird, who also was the first woman to serve as the state's chief justice.

While his public life has been largely political, his private life has been largely spiritual. He studied for the priesthood at a Jesuit seminary but left before taking his vows. After losing a U.S. senate race to former Governor Pete Wilson in 1982, he went on retreat in Japan for half a year, then worked with Mother Theresa in India.

His impatience with big campaign donations and corporate greed are legendary and became major themes in his 1992 presidential campaign. While he remains refreshingly skeptical about the future of the Internet, he was online throughout our interview, occasionally checking his e-mail on the PC on his desk. At one point, he went on the Web to retrieve information for me about educator Seymour Papert, a leading researcher in the area of computer-based learning.

A few weeks after this interview, Brown hosted a high-tech summit in Oakland, exploring ways that technologies like the Internet can help create new jobs, improve public schools, and bridge the growing "digital divide."

What do you personally use the Internet for?

Mostly for e-mail and researching items from time to time, looking up cases—legal cases, articles, subjects, addresses.

How much would you say you use the Internet weekly or monthly?

A few hours, it depends. I don't distinguish the Internet from newspapers, magazines, and other sources of information. It can be handy when you need something very quickly and you don't have time. It's one of the tools to find things out.

You've talked about corporations growing and taking control over a lot of things in our lives during the past few years. Some of the particular comments I recall are about the environment. One of the things I looked up was a speech you gave on your 'We the People' program about methyl bromide. You talked about the power of people buying, and mobilizing power around that. These are themes that occurred to me as I look at my book. People don't have to buy from one source. They don't have to vote for a candidate based on a piece of junk mail they got. They can research issues if they want to.

They can, but the schooling and the organization of social life creates embedded dependency. The habit of looking stuff up for yourself is not one that is widely distributed, much less encouraged through the growing up process.

I sense with 90 million Americans using the Internet that this seems to be changing. A lot of people are turning off their TVs and looking up information, doing research. Don't you think that's an encouraging sign?

The theory would be that you can look up candidates and make up your own mind. But the fact of the matter is the candidates with the most publicity and the most money generally prevail. So that's not user-activated information. That's candidate-inspired manipulation and media control. So we're not at any tipping point from economic interest, advertising, passive reception changing over to consumer-activated choice. There are hundreds of millions of dollars in advertising to make sure that doesn't happen.

You've encouraged a lot of people to mobilize on a grassroots level a lot of times over a lot of issues. I see the Internet as a tool that could be used in that regard. Have you ever considered it that way?

Oh yeah. It could be. It's waiting for that to happen. There are a lot of people out there. There's Ralph Nader, there's Greenpeace, there's Public Interest Research Group, and there are lots of potential activist leaders. So far the Internet is more of a self-enclosed memo system. It's not this wideband mobilization technology. It's physically possible to do this, to reach out to millions of people.

What do you think it will take?

It will take issues. I believe it's going to come off of television. It's going to come off of some events, like some economic dislocation that could stimulate a lot of political organizing. But today we have a very demobilized electorate. Consumer choices are fairly well driven. We don't have small companies growing. We have big companies growing. We have more companies gobbling up other companies. Oh, there always seems to be plenty more starting, but Microsoft certainly seems to be the major influence when it comes to personal computers. And that indicates to me the power of centrally controlled money.

We have seen an awful lot of start-ups, including here in Oakland and elsewhere in the Bay area—with people just starting companies on their credit cards or with pocket cash or money from relatives—that have grown up and done very well. And there are other companies that have had a firmer start, like Amazon, which didn't exist six years ago and now is valued greater than Barnes & Noble.

Oh, that's a convenience to go look up books. I went to look up one myself yesterday. And eBay, where you can go and buy stuff. There's so much! It's a Tower of Babble. It's a tool that's growing up fast.

**To back up a minute, you were talking about what
kind of a political or social event it would take to
stimulate that kind of action where people would
get interested and start organizing on the Web.**

The central fact in politics is you have 100 million people
voting for president. You have 10 million people voting for governor of California. That's too many people to talk to. It's too
many people to mail a letter to. That means that mass media—
The Associated Press, large newspaper chains, television networks—set the tone.

Theoretically you can set up a Web page and you can find
out about Mr. X or Ms. X. But it's not happened yet. It's not been
a tool. Maybe we'll find out that one of the candidates for president will raise $20 million over the Internet. That still will have
to be stimulated through the media.

The potential is there; it's not spent yet. It's a potential
that's still in the potential stage, not in the realization stage. But
yeah, I think it could happen this year; it could happen in the
next five years.

**Let me take a consumer issue, like the methyl bromide
case, where you were telling people 'Look, maybe you
can do without some strawberries for a while,
or maybe buy less almonds.'**

Well, that doesn't affect the market. Society moves in
waves. There's a drift when things are moving to specific consumer style. Then things will drift slightly this way, slightly that
way. To interrupt that flow is only possible through some dis-
ruption: a war, a famine, a volcano, an earthquake, or some
social upheaval. Everything is incremental as far as I can see.
Music moves in a certain direction. Fashion and building styles
move in a certain direction. So there's an order to social and
commercial organization. And that order is not going to be
affected because you have a tool called the Internet.

The Internet is embedded within the existing structure: the grand global marketplace. The technology called the Internet is inside that. The global marketplace is not inside the Internet.

That's an interesting distinction, and I know there are people who'd debate you on that.

Where are the ideas? What are we interested in? What do we use the Internet for? They use it for games. They use it for sports. They use it for stock quotes. They use it for sexual images. They use it for what? To order airline tickets? To buy things?

Let's say you use it to buy things. So the Internet is going to make cheaper what is already created as being needed. Most of what is needed is arbitrary and beyond the bare necessities of food and shelter.

It could be used as a database for housing. It could be used as a resource for education in the schools.

Fine. Why aren't schools on the Internet? Why isn't first grade through college all on the Internet? Plug in first grade reading, first grade spelling, first grade history. Does it exist?

I think it will exist.

I think it will. There's a book right behind you. [Seymour Papert's *The Children's Machine: Rethinking School in the Age of the Computer*]. He believes technology is inconsistent with the current structure of school as it's now organized. Yes, you could animate a good deal of education and then people could get it off the Internet. That could be done. School districts could do that for the kind of money they spend anyway. And the teachers could be coaches, could be mentors, could be counselors. Peer learning. All of that could be. But it doesn't exist today.

**That sounds like a very positive thing.
Is that something you're pursuing?**

Yeah, I'm looking into that. I'm exploring that possibility. In fact, I'm waiting for an e-mail from Seymour Papert right now with some materials.

**On a related note, you could use it for
other social functions, like health care.**

You could diagnose yourself if you've got a problem.

**You can at least get a good clue about what's going
on and some quick access to information.**

Yeah, you *should* get that. You could render the expert claims subject to popular analysis. Yeah, that's good.

**Let me ask about an economic issue. We all love the
local bookstores, but they're feeling a lot of pressure
from commerce on the Internet. At the same time,
the Internet's creating a lot of technology jobs in the
area, so it's good for the economy in that regard.
How do you view some of those things?**

Well, you can't stop it. It's like the global marketplace. It's just moving until it bumps up against a superior force or it exhausts its current pattern. It's not subject to rhetorical blockage. It's like King Knute taking to the tide, saying don't come in. The tide doesn't listen to King Knute. The marketplace does not listen to politicians. Return on investment drives investors. That's in charge. We're observing this experiment.

Let's talk about art and the more creative side of life. There's an awful lot of that on the Internet. That part is not highly commercialized. It's a lot of organizations supported by donations that are putting up the art and making it accessible to millions of people. Do you see that as a benefit you can use in this city to help enhance the cultural environment of the city?

I see it in the education field as a way to supplement home schooling, to restructure the existing public schools, opportunities for training, access to literature, commentary, conversations, billboarding, notices, observing—it's a quick guide you can look to for movies, art shows, restaurants, woodworking, handicrafts, whatever. It's a dynamic, interactive billboard plus library, and that's what it's doing. It's like going to be a big library. It's not as good as a big library in some respects, but it's better in others.

I think it's going to be several years before we totally integrate the Internet into our lives. It appears there are still just as many people flying around on airplanes. The number of cars grows in California at least three times the growth of the population.

That's an amazing statistic.

Yeah! Cars grow at 7 percent, the population at less than 2 percent. The birthrate in America is about 1 percent, a little more, and the immigration in California brings it up to 2 percent

So telecommuting . . .

That should slow it down. But it's not doing it yet. There are plenty of roads, there's pollution, there are parking lots, and there's a lot of physical movement of stuff. Theoretically, the Internet is just going to be moving electrons, bits of information. But we're not there yet. I would assume there's going to be an increasing etherealization of humans. Paolo Saleri talks about etherealization—that's his word, not mine—where things get less material . . . more brain power than bulk power. Theoretically, that's what we're doing.

You have a reputation for being a very spiritual man. One of the things I sense lacking in our communities today is spirituality. I don't mean that in a religious sense. I mean that in a much broader sense of bringing people together, or sharing a common spirit about life. In one way, the Internet tends to isolate people. It leaves them at a desk in their homes. On another level, it helps to create communities by bringing together those who might not have known about like-minded people or have been able to share their thoughts. 'Community' is one of the most popular uses of the Internet.

I think the encounter through the Internet is different from the encounter in person. You get a message, you don't know if it's male or female, from Europe or Indonesia or next door. When you disembody the exchange of messages, you get communication, not conversations. Computers can communicate. Only people can have a conversation. This is input and output. That's not what human beings do. I don't believe conversation is input/output. But I think computers are input/output.

So there's a dehumanization that goes along with this, or a different kind of community.

I view it as a different kind of communication, like a letter.

It's not like a letter. A letter is embodied. A letter has paper. It's in ink or pencil. It has a certain style. It's physically expressible, observable. The Internet is the same text, the same font. It's machine created. There's not as much presence in e-mail as there is in the letter, much less the personal conversation.

So maybe this is all moving us to look more to a different kind of human contact. Sentences. Thought streams. But not the give and take of the presence. There's no 'presence' in e-mail. It's sent when nobody's there. I want that e-mail later. . . . Something else is happening. There's not a simultaneity. So that's different. I like to print out e-mails if I want to think about what they are saying.

I heard Mr. Microsoft, Gates, say if something is three pages, he wants it in hard copy. So much for the paperless office.

You're being, I think appropriately, skeptical.

Well, I see this as a powerful tool. It's alive on my desk. I see it right now. Here's the note from Mr. Papert. We can see what it is, and that can have an impact on the schools. So there's power there. But I think human beings reside in a physical place, not in cyberspace.

Cyberspace is a medium. You can send a glider through the air. You can move a flat pebble across the water. You can roll on wheels. The Internet is a means, is a medium. But it's not god. It's not art. It's not another human being. It's not a city. It's not a village. It's not a house. It's not a telephone. It's not a bar. It's just a machine that can access text or pictures.

Let me ask you a little more about the potential for power. You recognize it's a powerful medium.

I recognize that somebody is going to organize through the Internet, but it will have to be a very powerful, emotional cause. Or it would have to be someone who can spend tens of millions of dollars on TV and says, go enroll, and they could keep it going. I think you need physical clusters of people to satisfy what human beings are looking for, even though the Internet can call people to those physically present meetings. So it is like the telephone. It's like a bell. But it's a step beyond all that because it speeds up things.

It abbreviates. It's an abbreviation of human experience. It's a screen with dots. It's a flow of bits and inputs.

It's a piece of equipment.

It's not equipment. It's software, a network.

**It's a network of machines with a
human body behind each one.**

It's a network of human nodes that don't want to get out of
the loop.

**What kinds of things would you like to see
happen with the Internet hereafter?**

I'd like to see schooling made accessible through the Internet, as well as many forms of training. I'd like to see many of the
mundane activities, whether it's shopping or checking of schedules for movies, messages—bringing the Internet into full use
for human beings. I'd see that as a real positive, as a plus, and it
will grow because it does make sense.

You can go to Amazon.com and get 20 percent off and get
it delivered. I want to go browse a bookstore for the environment, for the people, for the ambiance, to see what somebody
else's judgment is. With 40,000 books, a bookstore can have a
function of presenting a type of book consistent with the character of that bookstore. I suppose the Internet can create the same
kind of thing. You can go to a spiritual book page, you can go to
a granola-off-the-trail page, you can go to a left page, right page,
fundamentalist Christian page, Islamic page. That presents
itself. But then people want to get into the mosque or the church
or the restaurant and experience it directly, physically.

The Internet is like gnosticism. The Internet is like direct
contact with the higher knowledge, with no intermediaries, no
literature, no clergy, no sacraments. But it's also disembodied.
That's why gnosticism was declared a heresy, among other
things. So this is a partial.

Maybe with 12 billion people on the planet we'll evolve a
species with less physical presence so that we can be compatible

with the atmosphere we're given. With genetic engineering and designer babies and the rest of the things that are coming down the road, it's hard to know where the Internet will fit into that.

Maybe people will have brain implants to substitute for the lack of imagination. Who knows? You can think of whatever sci fi nightmare, or vision, or utopia, and it's possible. It's not going to stand still because of some nostalgia for the way it was in the village, even though for a long time to come people are going to be drawn to physical contact situations. Why do we go to coffee shops?

People like to be together. Mammals need contact. That's why when ducks go paddling across the lake, they go in formation. The same thing with human beings, even if we get wired to the Internet. So it's one of those things. It has to be situated in the human environment.

When I go on the Internet, to use one example, to shop, I find a wide array of stores, a lot of them tuned to people who want specific types of things, people who may be spread out across the country. But you can get them into this one store on the Internet. I think that can happen a lot of ways, in terms of politics or schools or even religious beliefs.

Yes. It's a tool in that sense. You can find organic food on Webvan.com. You can get yourself organic meat from a farm over in Bolinas. You can't get that at your local Lucky store. Craft is something that is not commodified. So that's something where if the Internet can extend the market to that, it may well support more craftspeople, more artisanship. That will be good. There's lots of potential here.

PAUL ERDMAN

Author, Economist, and International Financier

Many people think of economist Paul Erdman as an international financier and best-selling author. I think of him as a smart, creative guy who knows how to live well.

He's written nine books, including *The Set-Up, The Silver Bears, The Crash of '79, Zero Coupon,* and *The Palace.* Together, his books have appeared for 152 weeks on the *New York Times* bestseller list.

As a journalist, he's written for *The New York Times, Washington Post,* the *Financial Times* of London, and the *Nihon Keizai Shimbun* in Japan. He also hosts a San Francisco radio talk show called "Moneytalk". Erdman writes a regular column for CBS. Market-Watch that has tackled everything from the effect of China's deteriorating environment on its economy to the internal politics of Europe's central bank.

Erdman also is an international financier who once founded a Swiss bank. He serves on the board of advisors to the School of Foreign Service at Georgetown University. As you'll see in our conversation, he's also a tech-savvy Internet buff who has figured out how to get online to check his e-mail from Moscow to Beijing.

You're very familiar with the Internet. But what do you personally do on the Internet? What do you use it for?

When I get up in the morning, I take a trip around the world. I start with the *New York Times* and the *Washington Post*—not the *San Francisco Chronicle*—and a couple of sites like the Bloomberg site and a couple of other ones. Then I move to London to read a couple of papers there. You know what I mean by 'read.' I just go through them quickly. Then I move to Paris, move to Hamburg, to Frankfurt, and to Dusseldorf. Then I move to Zurich. Then I move to the Nikkei—I used to be a columnist for them for many years in Tokyo. I use the Nikkei and one of the dailies, but the Nikkei is usually enough. You have to pay for it now—so what—and then I move to Hong Kong and more or less have my platter full. And then I read the funny paper—the *Chronicle.*

As I move through, I develop themes in my head. I say: 'Aha! This is a theme.' I don't print it or anything. I put it in my suitcase, the theme being the end of the world is near, or whatever it may be. You get stuff that is complementary as you move around, but with a different point of view.

So in one hour, I'm up to speed like gangbusters. It's amazing. It's something that's new under the bloody sun. And I actually look forward to doing that. And then after I've done that, I check the e-mail, people making smart-aleck-or-not remarks about my articles. I answer every one of them, very briefly, and I hope very politely. And I turn on CNBC and I get the real time on this sort of thing. And if I'm doing something for Market-Watch, I'll sit down and draft it right then and there, let it sit for a half-hour, and then finalize it and ship it out.

So that's how my day starts with the Internet.

Is there anything else you personally do on the Internet?

I do 95 percent of my correspondence in e-mail. I only shop for books on Amazon.com.

You haven't done any online trading yet?

That's coming, for damn sure. Because I always do my own stuff anyway. I just haven't gotten around to it.

I don't even talk to them. I just say 'Do it.' At the end of January, I said, buy me some Brazil stock. And the guy laughs. And I say, 'Look you son of a bitch, don't laugh, just buy it.' And that was at 9½ and I looked now and it's 15. That's the stuff you should do, just use your instinct and go with it. So you make a couple of boo-boos? So what?

John Chambers from Cisco Systems is predicting that the Internet could have $3 trillion in e-commerce by 2005. That strikes me as a huge figure because we were at virtually zero five years ago. I imagine a lot of that will be in the United States. What do you think of that?

You just have to look at the penetration. And you have to look at society. And you have to look at people who use credit cards, and people who still use cash. And then we're light-years ahead of everyone else.

Let's take those one by one. Let's look at retailing for example. You're going to have a lot more people shopping online and a lot fewer people buying things at the mall. They'll still go to the mall, I suppose, at least to look at things. But when they decide what books they want, instead of lugging them home, they say 'Gee, I can just order that online from Barnes & Noble or Amazon or somewhere.'

I've never thought of it the way you've been thinking about it. I would first start off with what *wouldn't* you buy [on the Internet]. At first, there were some of these ideas that you're going to use the Internet to buy groceries. But I don't believe that. When you go to the grocery store . . .

. . . you want to squeeze the melons?

Yes, you want to squeeze the melons. To buy that stuff [on the Internet], it doesn't make a whole lot of sense. It doesn't make a whole lot of sense to buy liquor or beer on the Internet for exactly the same reason. So there's a whole category I think you have to leave out of this. Are you ever going to buy a house on the Internet? I don't think so. You'll shop, but I don't think you're going to buy. It will lead you, maybe, to the broker who has the house, but the transaction is going to happen on Earth. Are you going to buy a car? Maybe. I'm not quite sure. I think you're going to do a deal on the Internet, and then you'll go to the dealer and the car will pop up there.

Or maybe they'll bring it to your house.

Yeah, that's better.

There's that commercial on TV where Saturn has the dealer coming to a dorm room, delivering the car like a pizza. . . .

That I believe. And then you come to everything in between: refrigerators, air conditioners, books, for damn sure. And this is where the guy asks which stock you're going to buy and the smart guy says American Express. And there's some truth to that, too.

I was at the BookExpo America in L.A. and there were several transportation companies among the publishers offering their services because, well, how do you deliver all those books?

This [the Net] is now the catalog in the sky. Catalog sales have done well across the board, and I think as everyone becomes more computer literate, it's going to take a while. Men—and I hate to put it this way—are fairly computer literate. Women, in general, are not as computer literate. I know this because I just bought my wife an iMac just to get her over it, and she loves her iMac, but still she's not up to the speed where she would try to buy anything up there. So there's a factor there, and it's women who do most of the buying.

**So it may get harder for certain types of retailers.
There will always be some of them, but a lot fewer.
If we have $3 trillion in online commerce, and even
a small percentage of that is retail, it's not inconsiderable
as to what effect it will have on the retail sector.
If there's even a 3 percent reduction in sales in stores,
that's got to have an impact on real estate. Do you agree?**

Totally. Exactly. If you're putting together a REIT [real estate investment trust] that has a lot of strip malls, forget it. It's almost that simple. I totally agree with you.

**Well, what kind of an impact would that have?
Strip malls were one of the big investments of the 1980s.**

I should note I'm on the board of a couple of real estate investment trusts, so I'm speaking not only out of self-interest, but experience. That ain't the right stuff to be in lately, you know. The right stuff to be in is the stuff we have been in—rental apartments in Las Vegas and the Midwest and so forth.

What you are suggesting makes total sense to me. If you think of the evolution over time, from when you and I grew up with mom-and-pop stores, and then the big downtown stores—the Macys—and then the flight to malls in the suburbs. And now it's a flight into the sky, in a way, isn't it? And we saw one after another wither on the vine. I wouldn't say the withering of the mall in the suburbs is going to be complete, but the mold certainly is going to be affected, beyond any doubt.

And the social consequences of this are kind of strange. You and I don't hang around in malls, but teenagers love it.

I suspect there will always be malls for those and other reasons. There are people who just like to go out and shop. They love to go out and paw through merchandise. I suspect we'll see stores become more like a display counter. People will go out to sample the goods, to try something on, to choose a color that goes with their hair. And then they'll go home and order the same merchandise over the Internet, maybe from the same store. Maybe they'll go to Macys.com and place the order there and have it delivered to their home so they don't have to carry it themselves.

I agree, and I think it's really very odd that the ones that are behind the curve are the Macys of the world. I suppose their original calculation was they didn't want to undercut their store sales, but by now they should be reaching the conclusion that if they don't undercut their own store sales, somebody else is going to.

Well, that brings up an interesting point. The online companies are undercutting the brick-and-mortar companies, and the newer online companies are undercutting the older online companies. Obviously, if you're Amazon.com and you don't have a retail store, you have a much lower overhead.

That's for damn sure.

Then you should be selling those books at much closer to the wholesale level. You have a good service, you're providing support, you're arranging delivery service.

So you're going to have a markup, but because you have much lower costs, maybe it's only 10 percent. So you should be seeing lower prices, right?

I agree with you, especially if you use Japanese inventory systems—just in time and so forth. And the ultimate beneficiary is—your point—the consumer.

The other thing is, why doesn't Macys.com get into this? There is a Macys.com, but you have to wonder how loyal they are to it, because they are undercutting the brick-and-mortar store, they are going to have to narrow their profit margin. Right now, that might not be too painful, but down the road, there may be a Murphys.com that sells the same merchandise without the big brand name but at a lower price. Do you think the price competition will hurt them?

I think they believe the rate of change will be much slower than what you're talking about. You're citing the $3 trillion and they're saying, 'Forget it, ain't gonna happen. We're gonna move somewhat away from the status quo, but not much. Therefore, we're going to put our money behind brick-and-mortar competition, Macys versus Gimbels—as if Gimbels still existed. And we're not going to worry about these Amazon dot things because that's a fantasy of these people who don't live in the real world.' You think there's some of that going on?

I think there's a lot of that going on. I think this is what held Barnes & Noble back for a while.

And now their site is very good, woo! Better in some ways than Amazon. I went up there once to check, naturally, on my books. They've got every book I wrote and in every version, including audio and big print and all that. It's amazing. Better than Amazon.

That's another thing I'm writing about, competing on service levels. You compete on price, you compete on service, you compete on variety. You have to have every book Paul Erdman ever wrote. You have to have reviews . . . .

And believable reviews! Not like what Amazon got caught on! [Referring to the incident in which Amazon admitted receiving revenue to promote particular books.]

That's right. You have to be objective, journalistic. You have to be a good merchant, a good corporate citizen. Once again, I think consumers come out the winner there because they're getting more selection, more service. And if you're not pleased, it's all too easy to go somewhere else. I mean, if you get there and say, well, I don't see the book by Paul Erdman that I want, it's very easy to see if Amazon has it.

I think on the Internet, if you get disappointed once or twice [by a merchant], you're never going to go back again. If you're in a mall, you keep walking by the place. But on the Internet, you never have to go back. You are your own master about where you go to.

Good point. That's a real difference. So it's very important for service to be high, for customers to be satisfied, and to compete on price. Now, this infers that over time, large retailers, with Macys being the classic example, could lose a lot of market position, a lot of market share. And the value of a brand name could be diminished.

And that's the greatest thing going for them on the Internet, brand name. Maybe I'm wrong and maybe I'm not wrong. Amazon built a brand name from nothing. But Macys, compared to Murphy's clothing—sorry, but I'm gonna check out Macys!

You'll be back! Actually, I think that's right. I think people will first go to a brand name they know. But as they become more comfortable, I think they'll be more willing to try out an Amazon, a Travelocity. I never thought even two years ago that I'd be buying airline tickets from Preview Travel or Travelocity. But when I call up the airlines and get Muzak in my ear, it seems like a delightful alternative.

Well, I'm a bum there. I go to both of them—Preview and Travelocity—and check out everything. But then, I have a problem; I'm not going to fly in the back of an airplane. I never did and I'm not going to start. If you fly first or business class, they can't help you. So I go to American Express and I buy a two-for-one. I buy a real fare and my wife goes for nothing. But someday, someone's going to cater to me, and undercut American Express.

The business travel market seems ripe for it.

Sounds like a great business!

Let's talk about wages. If you have a lot fewer stores out there, you have a lot fewer clerks working in them. Now being a store clerk isn't a highly paid profession anyway, and a lot of these clerks will move to the Internet. What do you think will happen there?

Retail store clerks are going to go the way of bank clerks. The Internet is going to displace retail clerks just like the ATM displaced bank clerks.

That's a huge number of employees, isn't it?

A huge number. But I think you've seen an indicator of what will happen because of the banking industry. You're onto a very fertile subject here!

Yes, it grows. And I want to talk about politics, too. This book isn't just about business. It's the way media reacts to all this, too, because the Internet is an interactive medium. When I think of a presidential election and I see a seven-second sound bite on TV, my guess is that people will go onto the Internet and will want to hear more. They'll want to hear what the context was. So it seems like this could change politics.

I doubt it. The people you're talking about watch McNeil-Lehrer. You know how many people watch McNeil-Lehrer versus Dan Rather or Oprah? It's a minuscule percentage. I'm sorry to give that answer. In other words, you're suggesting they get the teaser and want the depth.

Now the interactive element, that's something else. I think you have to go beyond the technology we're talking about today. You've got to go into this streaming stuff and beyond that. You've got to talk about when the Internet and the computer screen become one and the same—totally integrated.

Now we're talking something else again, big time something else. Because that is when you're going to have—I don't know what—the interchange of 'talk radio' will take on a whole new dimension there, and I think *that* will change politics.

That's probably just around the corner with digital TV. By 2006, all analog broadcasting will cease and we'll all be on digital TV. We've seen these big cable mergers that say, clearly, this is going to be an interactive system. And you're going to have the opportunity to do instant polls: 'How did the president do today? Vote now! Press 2 on your console.'

I would bet that in 25 years or less, we're going to vote over the Internet. It has to become integrated. It has to be a totally familiar tool for the simplest person—anyone can operate it. Then it will probably start at the very local level, you know, local school boards, municipal bond stuff, and rise from there. Because with bond measures you have to get 66 percent approval so you want to draw in as many voters as you can, and that will be the way to do it if people have a few brains.

We've talked about Microsoft's domination of the desktop, but I don't think many people consider the monopoly they could create in television if every couch potato in America is using a Windows CE device to watch TV.

I don't want to give advice to you, but I think your analysis group should pay a lot of attention to this and think this sucker through. Everybody wants to bust up everything. But I think in the long run, this could be very good for us, the United States.

Why do you think that?

We serve as the model for the entire world, and the widening of the bandwidth means Americans are going to serve as the role models for the world as we take a quantum leap in what we call this information age. This gives us an advantage over everyone else in every respect, in a political sense, in an economic sense, in a financial sense, everything.

What do corporations need to do to protect themselves, and what happens if they don't? Is this going to be a big change for the economy over the next few years?

Damn right. The only defense is offense. Absolutely. Offense is the name of the game. And damn the cost. The name of the game is not making profits, but expanding your base and improving your quality. As long as you keep expanding your base and improving your quality, you know damn well in the end, you're going to be a winner.

It's a good part of it, I think. In the early stages, especially, you've got to grab the real estate while it's available.

Exactly. I tried to explain this on the radio this morning. Only in America do you have Internet stocks with hugely exaggerated value. You can print your own money—exaggerated value dollar bills. And then you can buy real stuff, or semireal stuff. And then you get this magic mixture of *uh* and *uh*.

And it's an interesting currency, to be sure. There's a lot of speculation on whether the value of this new money is going to hold . . . And the effect on the economy as you generate this wealth out of thin air . . .

You go into budgetary surplus!

Meanwhile, some of the brick-and-mortar businesses, which seemed very solid just a decade ago, suddenly is very threatened.

That's creative destruction!

But that's scary, isn't it? Economically, where's the wealth, where's the value? And it's hard to justify the Internet stock valuations based on any mathematical models, so what does that do to the overall economy when you say the gross domestic product is X trillion dollars?

You *are* creating value. I just told you how I start my day. Twenty-five years ago, if I were to start my day that way, I would require access to the public libraries of New York, London, etc., and everything I'd be reading would be two weeks old. I hate the word 'new paradigm,' but there is really something going on here.

And the information age creates wealth in the sense of efficiencies that add to our productivity, which has been achieved through our economic growth in this decade. We didn't recognize until lately that there has been an upward shift in productivity. And the big puzzle today, as Greenspan said and as [San Francisco Federal Reserve president] Bob Parry said, is whether this upward shift is permanent or temporary. And the Fed policy of the future is dependent on whether the board of governors or Greenspan personally comes to the conclusion that all we've been talking about today has resulted in an upward shift in labor productivity and, therefore, despite a very tight labor market, the Fed will not have to brake the economy in a major way, because most of the gains are coming, not because of labor inputs, or lack thereof, but because of productivity growth. And all we've been talking about affects that.

Also interesting is that the values we've been talking about belong to the individual. The value of your day has improved because you can surf the world in an hour. That's a value that you inherit.

And I also can talk to the world in a half-hour. I send you a story, you post it, and in a half hour, people are e-mailing me from Moscow and Zurich and Sao Paolo. Could that have happened ten years ago? And am I adding to their knowledge pool and their efficiency and their productivity? One hopes so. In other words, we talk about efficient markets, right? Well, knowledge equals efficiency.

'Empowerment' is another one of those words like 'paradigm' that we're tired of using, but it fits here. You're empowered to look at all these newspapers, voters will be empowered to discuss issues or vote instantly,

**shoppers will be empowered to see a better selection
at lower prices. A lot of this value seems to
be shifting toward that end of the board.**

The Chinese are empowered, as Eastern Europe was, to understand our thoughts, and we're free to understand theirs, so that misconceptions about each other don't lead to situations like we got trapped in in Yugoslavia.

**That's a very good analysis. It shrinks the world.
I wonder if it makes it tougher for software and some
of the other U.S.-based industries to maintain an
edge over the rest of the world.**

Well, I don't think so, because when we go back to AT&T and Microsoft, or you go back to a piece I wrote for Market-Watch [in May 1999], they missed every boat. *Every boat.* I mean, there are no other Microsofts or AT&Ts out there, and now these guys are teaming up? If I were the rest of the world, I'd say, 'Oh, man! Look out!'

**There *is* a danger of hyping this, too. I think we all went
overboard with interactive television back in the early 1990s.
Pacific Telesis was talking about how it was going to build an
interactive TV system in California by 1997 and it never
happened. Telesis was broken up into AirTouch and the
company that is now owned by Southwestern Bell, which is
in no mood to build an interactive television network. They'll
probably get into interactive services through another level.
And that's another great subject: how traditional phone
companies are going to have to compete over some
sort of broadband network with new competitors.**

Yes, that's an absolutely whole new world that is going to come very quickly. Who's going to deliver what to your house? I live on a ranch, so I'm very interested about what they'll deliver over satellite. And I think everyone could deliver everything. But that's going to move very, very rapidly.

And America has almost a lock on all this stuff. You saw how we tested our weaponry in Yugoslavia. That's not necessarily a good thing, like the way we used graphite bombs to wipe out their power grid. That's cute stuff, right? Or our B2 bomber. We won't even let any NATO aircraft near those things because it is so good.

Does America then become the one superpower for the twenty-first century until someone else catches up?

Yes, for the first quarter, at least. I was in China, and, boy, this is 1.2 or, if you count it right, 1.4 billion people. It's a nation that has good universities. It has embraced technology and capitalism, no doubt about that. I would say the second quarter is going to be a two-superpower world—China and the United States. Thank god we recognize that and we remain fully engaged. We should. My feeling is, from the Chinese side, they have a fondness for America. Even from a century ago, there's always been a sort of affinity.

We haven't talked much about Europe. I think we all see some holes in their strategy, but I think the European community has gotten their interest rates together much more so than I ever expected.

Me, too.

They have a common currency. And when you put the whole thing together, that could become a mighty economic engine . . .

. . . if the corporations there join the modern world. I have been involved in investing there for a long time. You take a firm like Phillips or Siemens or British General Electric—they should be right up there, but they're not. Or Marconi, but they're not. Or Ericsson, but they're not.

Well, you've got to give the Europeans credit for developing the GSM standard for cell phones.

I give them enormous credit for the euro. That is the biggest economic innovation for the second half of the century. It's unbelievable. You have a guy like Tietmeyer watching over this thing and Duisenberg from Holland.

On a social level, we were talking about how the broadband will give the United States an edge because the rest of the world will have to catch up on installing cable. It takes a long time to get homes hooked up to cable, as we know. Does this mean the third world will sink further economically?

No, not necessarily. Because you have leapfrogging. You had, in many countries—Eastern Europe is the best example— no phone system. Now you can walk down a street in Warsaw or Moscow, and everybody has a cell phone. China, too.

So, if you can get wireless broadband that would really shrink the world.

And we're going to do it, we're going to deliver it. Slowly, we get monopolistic power. I'm not one of these gung-ho America types, but still it pleases me a little bit.

BARRY DILLER

Chairman and CEO of USA Networks, Inc.

As computers, television, and the Internet converge, nobody has a better view of the growing demand of high-quality, interactive programming than Barry Diller, the chairman and chief executive officer of USA Networks Inc.

The e-commerce and media company was formed in February 1998, seemingly to take advantage of the commercial opportunities on the Internet. Its entertainment assets include the USA Network, SCI FI Channel, USA Broadcasting, Studios USA, and USA Films. Its commerce activities include the Home Shopping Network, Ticketmaster, and USA Networks Interactive. USA Networks Interactive, in turn, includes the Hotel Reservations Network, SCIFI.com, and the Internet Shopping Network (ISN). And the ISN controls FirstAuction.com and First Jewelry.com. Finally, the company controls Ticketmaster Online-CitySearch Inc., an Internet company focusing on community content and ticket sales.

Clearly, Diller is betting heavily on the Web, and Diller has a knack for being right. As chairman of Paramount Pictures Corporation during the 1970s and early 1980s, he was credited with bringing that company back to life with a steady string of box office hits and shrewd investments.

From 1984 to 1992, as chairman and chief executive of Fox Inc., he did what many skeptics said couldn't be done by successfully launching a fourth U.S. television network. In 1992, he proved himself right again, preaching the virtues of home shopping as chairman and chief executive officer of QVC, Inc.

In 1995, he became chairman and chief executive of Silver King Communications and chairman of the Home Shopping Network. A year later, Home Shopping and Silver King merged with Savoy Pictures Entertainment to form HSN, Inc.

In addition to his corporate interests, the San Francisco native is unusually active in community programs, serving on the boards of the New York Public Library, Conservation International, the Museum of Television, and New York's public television station WNET. He's also a member of the advisory board for the Center for Health Communication at Harvard University's School of Public Health.

First, I'd like to ask about your personal use of the Internet.

I use it for communication. It has replaced the telephone as my principal communication device other than sitting with people in a room and talking. It has certainly surpassed the telephone, both internally and externally. But mostly internally in dealing with the people in this company of ours.

USA Networks has experience with online consumers, home shopping, reservation and ticket sales, entertainment, and more. I'm interested in how you plan to bring those things together as media converge.

Our take on this is there is a new convergence. It's entertainment, information, and direct selling. We think that over a period of time that advertising is on a long, slow arc to direct selling as machines become more capable of putting goods and services and consumers together in a much more seamless way than they have in the past.

Our company is divided into old and new media. And the old media—the television production, distribution, etc.—as well as the retailing business of HSN is on its way to being connected to this new media, which is CitySearch, the Internet Shopping Network, and other vehicles of ours. And we think that stitching across those is the work of the company for the future.

We think that's how these products will come together.

You have a very impressive history of making things work when people didn't think they'd work, like starting a fourth network, or home shopping, or Paramount. Now we hear some skepticism about whether e-commerce will really take off as much as people think it will. What's your sense here?

It's inevitable. It's simply inevitable. But these things take longer than the swift-moving media takes to hype them. It will be three years, five years—my cycle is a three-year cycle for almost everything—and I think we have some years to go before electronic commerce is going to be seamless enough, and easy enough, and ubiquitous enough, for people to get it in their rhythm.

It takes time. Even though people move more swiftly today, and they do, it takes time. Most people, and I mean way up in the 90s [percentage], would look at the process of buying things online—e-commerce—as 'why would I want to do that? I go to the store to do this and do that.' They'd say it's much too difficult: 'I don't want to do that.'

But I don't think that means anything. I think that's only what people say today because their rhythm is not in concert with these boxes, these machines.

So you're talking about a change in consumer behavior being the key factor here?

Of course! People say: 'Gee, I know how to do *this. That's* hard.' And it *is* hard. As we all know, it's really harder to get in a car, drive, park, and do all those things than it is to spend six gnarly minutes getting out your credit card, inputting the data, and going through a lot of multiple screens. It's confusing now, but that will change.

It seems like broadband is coming in pretty quickly and. . . .

No, it isn't.

Well, tell me why you think that. It seems certain we'll have a couple of million people within a year or two.

Oh, a couple of million. But we have a hundred million television homes. This is hardly serious. Eventually, broadband, of course, will be what we all have. Well, I don't mean all. . . .

A vast majority?

No, no, no. Say 50 percent. That's a huge amount, even in cable terms, which now reaches 65 percent of homes. It'll be in a lot of homes, but not for another three to five years.

And by 2006 we'll be on digital TV. Do you think, by then, the home TV will really be an interactive computer?

Yes. Now, you have to define computer. Will it have a keyboard? Will you use it like you use a computer? No, I don't think so. I think it will be point-and-click with a wand like you now have to change channels or change systems.

And I don't think it will be used for writing. I don't think you'll type things in and out. By then, you might have voice recognition and things like that. But I still think there will be separate uses for computers and for television systems. The television will be more a computer than the computer will be a television set.

So, when I go to do my taxes, I'll still go into the den and work on a PC?

Yes, I'd think so. Like anything, you'll be working close and it will be an extension—like it is now—of the writing tablet, the typewriter, the computer. They're extensions of each other. I don't think it becomes the interactive, big-screen, fully integrated device with lots of services; I'm talking about audiovisual services, etc., that will be probably be delivered through some integrated system, likely something separate from the PC.

When you talk about a wand, one of the images that comes to mind is somebody watching home shopping, and you see that necklace you like and you just click on it. And, at that point, you *won't* have to enter your credit card.

No, all that stuff will be worked through. Fairly soon—within the next year or so—the e-wallet will be fairly well developed where you really will have it embedded in your PC or your small appliance, your PDA or whatever it is. And it will execute these transactions and bill you accordingly.

You remember that line from the early 1990s, about how you'll have 500 channels?

I was there when it happened. Dr. John Malone, 1992, Western Cable Show.

Now it seems like there's almost a limitless choice. I loved that Qwest commercial that has the guy checking into a dusty motel and the clerk says the rooms include every movie ever made at any time. I wonder if you really think we're heading to the point where we'll have an almost limitless choice of entertainment and shopping options?

Yes, inevitably.

You're best known for your work in entertainment, but you're also known for having a strong social conscience. I wonder how you think these choices are going to affect some other areas, such as education or politics.

It's very hard to do it with education. The *New York Times* had an article about a new company that will provide online education to five big institutions. I think that is inevitable. I don't think electronic commerce is going to replace bricks and mortar. Nor do I believe the institutions are going to go out of business. But I think a lot of our work is going to be done online.

I think it's a remarkable development that you could have so much more exposure to the education system than you get by attending school.

I've talked to a number of people who say it would be wonderful to have a school in a box, but there are so many regulatory obstacles to it.

Yes, it's very hard to do, but I think it will happen.

As far as politics, I think doing referendums online is going to change things. How and in what way exactly, I can't predict. It's going to be interesting to watch it unfold.

**Do you think wireless will get to the point where it
will offer the same types of services?**

No. I think wireless will develop, but I think it will be much
slower.

**How do you view the competition between DSL [digital
subscriber lines, a broadband service generally offered
by phone companies] and cable [the higher capacity
service offered through cable companies]?**

Its cable's to lose. Cable has the advantage and it may waste
the advantage, in which case the RBOCs (regional Bell operating
companies) will emerge. But it doesn't appear to me that will
happen. I think cable's got the advantage.

PAUL SAFFO

Director of the Institute for the Future

We all wonder what tomorrow will bring. Paul Saffo makes a living thinking about it.

He's Director of the Institute for the Future, an organization founded in the late 1960s to provide strategic planning and forecasting services to government agencies and corporations.

Saffo holds degrees from Harvard College, Cambridge, and Stanford. He's written numerous essays that have appeared in such publications as the *Harvard Business Review, Wired, Civilization, Fortune,* the *New York Times,* and the *Los Angeles Times.* His essays also were published in Japan in book form as *Dreams of Silicon Valley.* He's also authored *Road from Trinity.*

In addition to his role at the Institute, Saffo serves on the AT&T Technology Advisory Board; the World Economic Forum Global Issues Group; and the Stanford Law School Advisory Council on Science, Technology, and Society.

Like most people with an intimate working knowledge of technology, Saffo is excited about the Internet's potential to bring change, but wary of the potential for the abuse of its power. Due to his profession, he's much better versed than most technologists to speak specifically to how the Internet is likely to surface in our day-to-day lives.

How do you personally use the Net?

I live on the Net. I've had an e-mail address on my business card since 1983. It's actually kind of a weird thing for us at the Institute. One of our founders was Paul Baran, the father of packet switching, so electronic communications is pretty deeply embedded in our genes at the Institute. They did the first conferencing experiments on the Arpanet way back when. So we've always used the technology while observing the technology and using it in our research. I'm really dependent on it. I do tons of my research and, like everyone else, I do lots of shopping, and basically everything.

Now, not everyone else is doing a lot of shopping. I do a little bit and other people are doing a little bit here and there. Would you say you do the bulk of your shopping online?

I don't buy groceries yet, because the Web delivery services are just shopping. But I did well over three-quarters of my Christmas shopping last year on the Net. I buy a lot of books and one or two things per week. I used a lot of catalogs before and now I get impatient if I can't go to their Web site and do it.

You are a futurist?

I am a forecaster. There are people who call themselves futurists, but it's a term I'm very uncomfortable with because the term actually has a pretty sorry history in this century. One of the first rules of forecasting is to never allow your opinion of what you think *should* happen interfere with what you think *will* happen.

One of the things I'm doing is looking at how things like the telegraph and the telephone and radio came to be adopted. I've been surprising myself with some of the numbers. For example, it took 28 years before radio became a commercial medium.

Most ideas in the history of technology take 20 years to become an overnight success. Technological change is extremely slow, even today. The Internet took 20 years to take off.

**And we're really not there yet.
I get the feeling we're just starting to take baby steps.**

Oh, yeah. At the moment, I feel like it's television in 1951, it's PCs in 1981. The revolution really hasn't started. It's not that the revolution arrives, or we're waiting for it to arrive, but you have things come along that transform the environment. When we made the jump up to 28.8 modem speeds, that was a transformative event in communications. Broadband is a transformative event for the obvious reason that it has the bandwidth, but more importantly it typically turns out it's the nonobvious thing that is the most important about technology and the nonobvious thing about broadband is that it's always on.

You don't hang up a broadband link. It's always leaking bits off the wire or the fiber. And that means the moment someone has a broadband setup—right now, if you use a PC it's not quite this way, the moment you have a permanent, 24-hour-a-day link to the Internet, it means you're always going to have bits leaking into your house and people are going to find ways to use those bits—a very practical, pragmatic aspect. Maybe you're not a day trader, which I think is an enormous amount of folly, but you pay a lot of attention to your stocks and you're watching things carefully. Right now, you've got to dial into the Net. Imagine that your system is always connected to the Net, but you get alerts, like you get in the office. But in your house, you're in the kitchen and your telephone rings and it's your computer calling you to tell you something just happened in your Schwab account.

That always-on feature is really going to turn the Net upside down. It's almost as big as the shift from e-mail–centric to Web-centric on the scale of change, but it means there's a very aggressive shift from the asynchronous—the store-and-forward world—today, to a synchronous world, where everything is very much real time. E-mail is store-and-forward. The Web is actually store-and-forward. It's this warehouse in cyberspace and on one side people shove a bunch of stuff into the warehouse, and on the other side a bunch of people visit the warehouse and look at the stuff and fiddle with it.

I was thinking of it in a different way, as a passive versus active thing. What you're describing is a more passive environment, where you're always hooked up to the Web and you have agents alerting you to various things.

That's right. When the devices start coming without off switches, then you know something is going on.

Have they?

Well, the router I have in my house or a 10-base T-hub doesn't have an off switch. Routers are always on. So it's just barely beginning to start, but it will accelerate. [Editors note: Routers are components that direct data through a network, distributing it through a hub.]

It's more like a refrigerator?

Yes, in many ways. The definition of an appliance is that it doesn't have an off switch. It's always ready to use and always active.

The other thing that's going to be important that I'd watch is ICQ, the buddy system on AOL. You put your buddy list up and any time you touch the Internet, those people get a message saying that Paul's on the Web. It's enough of a problem that I know people who use pseudonyms because they don't want their relatives bugging them. It's happened to me. You get on the Net to do stuff and your phone rings. You know, 'Hey, I saw that you were at your computer.' But that to me is the thin edge of a wedge that will mean some fundamental changes in audio. We can begin to glimpse the death of dial tone. IP-based [Internet protocol] audio communications isn't telephony. It's something else.

In IP telephony, it isn't that you have a phone connected to your computer and you dial it and it rings on the phone connected to the computer of the person you're trying to reach. Internet telephony becomes like ICQ where you're working away, someone sees you're there, and someone just goes *bong* on your screen and says, 'Hey, I saw you're at work,' unless you have a 'do not disturb' light on. That's a big deal, a very big deal.

These sorts of things will take a while I know.

It's about a 20-year road.

Do you care to give us a few forecasts as to what we might see by the year 2010 in terms of those things I mentioned?

By 2010, the main event won't be digital technology. The hot thing's going to be biology and genomics. Kids. By 2010, teenage hackers are going to want to be hacking molecules, not bits. The Internet won't be hip. It will just be part of our lives. It's not that this stuff disappears. It will keep happening. Some things are very slow. People sort of woke up to this recently. The phone's been around for a hundred years, but half the people on the planet haven't yet made a phone call.

The way to think about it is we're standing on the threshold of real Internet appliances, broadband diffusing outwards. Broadband will happen fairly quickly in major urban centers.

For the next five years, it's broadband, it's appliances, it's IP in everything. Moore's Law not only keeps driving the price of chips down, but most people don't really understand what Moore's Law means at a device level. It's not that the chips get smaller, it's that the circuits get smaller. The chips stay the same size and that means there's empty real estate on the chip. And the companies, in order to differentiate themselves from their competitors, scratch their heads and say, 'What can we stick on the chip now?' And so, we're seeing the kind of penetration where the entire PC is on the chip. There's a professor at Stanford who has a Web server that's the size of a pack of cigarettes. It's an entire PC and a hard drive, small enough to get lost in a briefcase, and it's connected to the Web.

So we're driving these systems down to where a single chip gets so cheap that a manufacturer says, 'I'm going to put an IP chip into my ice box, my washing machine, my cell phone, and I don't know why, but I can say it has IP inside.' You know, right now, how 'dot-com' sells? If you have IP inside, it's a little like 1963 when you advertised on the front of your radio how many transistors it had. The moment that happens, then things start getting real interesting because people start connecting those devices to the family Intranet and they probably don't even realize it. You just buy the appliance and plug it into the wall and they just go and find each other over the electrical wire, or you run a wire to a box on the wall where your broadband comes in, and it has enough smarts to look for other appliances and negotiate. That's the sort of stuff that will happen in the next five years.

I wonder if we'll also get to a computer-everywhere environment, where we don't need to carry around computers because they'll be everywhere, like telephones. And you can access your directory that way.

Yes and no. That notion has popped up in a couple of different forms. Ubiquitous computing was the most recent form. It's not that we'll carry fewer computers with us. In fact, we're already in danger of carrying so many electronics on our person to be nervous in lightning storms. But the devices we carry will tend to be smaller and lighter. We'll carry more of them. But they will be in much more constant communication with the computing environment we move through.

So it's the kind of world where you still carry a cell phone, but the cell phone as a built-in GPS [global positioning satellite] chip and, if you're willing, and maybe even if you're not, people will call you with 'specials.' Or you'll have a beeper with a GPS chip and you'll be walking through Chinatown and it's about 5:30 and the restaurant down the street beeps you and says it has a special. It's that sort of thing that will happen.

We're talking about the apparatus without talking about the uses. I hear a lot of folks say different things about how they expect the Internet to evolve. What I come away with is that it will be user-defined; it will become what you want it to be. But I've heard people say it will be taken over by TV networks that will shift it to a passive medium. And other people say, 'No, no, no, it will always be an independent thing.' Where do you fall along those lines?

We tend to put inventions into the service of preserving cherished old habits. That's why tract houses in Silicon Valley have mansard roofs, designed for the Normandy coast before the invention of central heating. We tend to use this stuff for very conservative activities: How do we manage the family, how do we stay in touch with kids? So we'll continue to do that. The newest technologies will continue to be put to the service of fulfilling the oldest human desires and needs.

People talk about the Internet as the neodemocracy, or that it will be taken over by corporations—as long as it keeps moving forward quickly, there'll be a space for small players. Will the big TV players get in? Of course they will. On the passive and active thing, we're all a mixture of passive and active. Way, way back, in 1982, Mark Heyer—he was at Sony at the time, he's now in Palo Alto—was the first to say, look, there's a taxonomy of hunters, grazers, and browsers. Just as in a savannah, there's a lot more hunters than browsers and more browsers than grazers. Hunters are people who go out there and get what they need; they bid on eBay. Browsers are not tracking stuff down, but they're selective within eyesight—'I think I'll go to this site or to that site.' And grazers just chew up whatever's in front of them. We're all mixtures of the three types. We don't spend all our time being hunters. And the Internet is going to reflect that. There'll be a lot of sites that are grazer oriented.

One paper I read recently suggested that bandwidth is being quickly usurped and that it should be rationed or sold at bids, that people willing to pay the most would get the most bandwidth and a kid downloading a video game would be out of luck until the bandwidth was cheaper. Is that even within the realm of possibilities? Do you see that happening at all?

It's just such a patently absurd idea. I'm not a rabid free-market kind of guy, but market forces work pretty well, and there's a lot of incentive to put more fiber in. You can carry the volume of the entire radio spectrum on a single fiber. We'll always feel like we're about to run out of bandwidth. There's no doubt about that. I don't see it exactly as a world of bandwidth to burn—there'll be some pain and the like. But the last hundred years make it pretty clear it's going to keep getting cheaper. Bandwidth rationing? Maybe that will happen if some recombinant DNA researcher is stupid enough to build a bug that eats fiber. Then we've got problems.

Internet2. Is it working? [Internet2 is a research project focused on the next generation of Internet technology].

It's cool! When they put up Internet2, there was a pretty substantial commitment. I forget what the schools had to pay, but it was something like a half-million dollars. They thought they'd get the usual suspects: CMU, USC, Berkeley, and Stanford. They got something like five times the usual number of schools signing up as they thought. I think that's a real sign that Internet2 is a happening thing. Internet2 isn't quite here yet for most of us, but it's quite real in academic circles.

Let's talk about agents for a little bit, and bots. First, could you talk about the difference between agents and bots?

Well, agency is probably the superset of things like bots. I sort of think of bots as agents who need adult supervision. They're the first, baby steps toward having autonomous agents cruising the Web, which is an idea that's come around a couple of times. Bots are not there, but they're useful. At least I don't have to watch them every second.

When people talk about a shopping bot, they're really thinking about an intelligent agent, aren't they?

Yeah, people are going to push toward that. It turns out there are a lot of silly little details. But the broad elements you need to do that are around: expert systems and AI to give the devices personality. The difficulty is in traversing the Web, and in software compatibilities. As Marc Porat at General Magic was the first to make explicit, the moment you have something autonomous, the real challenge is clearly defining the limits of the autonomy and making that autonomous thing accountable. If you launch an agent out there, you better make sure you know what it's doing. It's 11 PM, do you know where your agent is? Those are the small things that will hold it up.

As they get refined and as we move forward over the next few to several years, I could see agents taking on a lot of the tasks that people do now on the Internet.

Well, there are two companies to watch. The first is Time-Dance. It has a group calendar scheduler—we've followed that technology closely. It's the first one I've seen that really makes a lot of sense. It doesn't require you to synch your Palm Pilot or anything. It's an agent. It just doesn't look like one. In the shopping area, a company called QuickBuy in Boston has a really interesting technology it calls buycons. It's an extension of XML that allows you to put things on your Web site for sale and that little book is actually a buycon. So I cruise in, throw it in my shopping cart, and then I go off to another site, get another buycon. Basically, it's like cruising through a big department store where you pay when you check out. And you could put intelligence into the shopping cart, saying what book I want. And maybe it's a sophisticated algorithm that doesn't just go by price, but do I get frequent flyer miles? It can munge things through and tell me where I get the most benefit. So it's happening, and it doesn't have to be an explicit agent that pops up on your screen. There are companies like NetSage and Extempo that are trying to put personalities into software, to try to convince you to have a conversation with a piece of software.

Well, if you have a shopping agent and you can say, 'I want Paul Erdman's last book,' doesn't that deflate the modeling for a lot of e-commerce companies? Does it result in a world where there are just razor-thin margins and companies have to compete on that?

You'll see margins disappear on some things, but it just means we'll find something else that can't be subject to razor-thin margins. Business has always been a process of responding to changes. The printing press in the mid-1400s led to the explosion of mercantile capitalism in the early 1500s. The same sort of stuff will happen today.

The prices of some things have plummeted because of the Web. On the other hand, there are some things we can now sell on the Web that we couldn't sell before. I saw a bunch of people on eBay bidding on a book. And this lucky, happy buyer spent $130 for this particular book. At the exact moment when the bid closed, I went over to ABE and Bibliofind and found nine other copies of the same book for between $20 and $60, all in better condition than the book the bidder bought. This is a case where someone could have gotten a better deal—saved $100—without moving a single muscle below the wrist. And the bidding went on for days.

Our lives have become so busy, but it seems like many of the things we're talking about are going to empower people by giving them more time and more options. You mentioned shopping and even grocery shopping, and bargain hunting.

Once upon a time, people went to banks to get loans and we've left that behind. Some people get loans from their credit cards now. You don't even go into the bank. You pull money out of its wall at the ATM. I think in ten years we're going to look at the idea of going to the market to buy paper towels and ordinary staples and say 'We did that once? What a crazy thing!' Some people will still do it. It's kind of like pay phones. Now we have cell phones. There are still pay phones, and they're still used by people but . . .

. . . it's fading.

Yeah. Lines at pay phones! The same sort of thing will happen with shopping. We're going to avoid the kind of shopping we don't want to do, but still go into supermarkets. You'll say, 'Well, it's Thursday night and I don't know what I want.' So you'll cruise the aisles and look at the steaks and stuff, but it's the stuff you want to do. It's also the kind of world where, with IP devices, the washing machine service people will call you, you don't need to call them. You'll pick up your phone and they'll say, 'We need to be at your house tomorrow,' and you'll ask why and they'll say 'Your washing machine called us and it needs servicing.'

Or your washing machines calls you and tells you when it arranged its own servicing.

Yeah! The one thing people are still worried about is having people come into their house, so it'll probably call the company.

I know people who were big fans of Amazon a year ago, and swore they'd never buy a book another way, and now they're coming to me and saying 'Gee, have you been to the Barnes & Noble site lately? They've really improved it a lot.' It occurs to me companies are really going to have to bend over backward to keep customers, that they'll have to come up with better prices and better service and constant improvements.

That's why I wouldn't bet against Jeff Bezos, because Jeff's kept his loyalty up with constant changes and improvements.

Loyalty can change with lightning speed. The whole system is set up to encourage people to switch. But it also means businesses will get more creative in finding ways to keep people from switching. More and more transactions are being determined by externalities. Once upon a time, the transaction was determined by the object of the transaction, the service being provided. Now there are ring upon ring of externalities. I'll use this credit card because I'll get frequent flyer miles, for example.

I think we could see more competition in politics, too. Right now, it's very easy for a candidate to get on TV and give the seven-second sound bite.

The technology changes the political environment. Kennedy was the first telegenic candidate. Before him, and people don't realize this, Lyndon Johnson's technological advantage was he was the first candidate to use a helicopter. He was everywhere in Texas, because after the Korean War helicopters were just coming into civilian use. We have yet to have the first Web-genic national candidate. I think I know who it is . . . Jesse Ventura.

Will the Web lead to better political decision making? I watched someone pay an extra $100 for a book when a better deal was one click away. Are they really going to look at the politics? My nightmare here is that it leads to worse decision making. That it overloads everyone on politics and the people who end up making the most use of the Internet are the talking head morons on AM radio.

Now you said that's your nightmare. Let's look at the flip side. What's your dream?

Well, I think it will be really broken at the national level, but I think it's really going to work at the local level. The Internet is going to get people engaged in local politics in a way they never have been in the past, because local politics never had an efficient means of getting the message out. Nobody reads the local papers, which are dying. If communities put up community Web sites, people can look at the bulletin boards, the agenda.

Then you say, what happens if it doesn't work on the national level, but it works on the local level? Well, that accelerates the devolution of power from the national level to the local level. Net-net, bottom line, the result may actually be possible.

So more people have more control at the local level, and the local level has more control. We talked about agents and nightmares. One of the nightmares for me is that everyone has access to different technologies and agents, and you have all these agents and counteragents running around. While you're trying to get more power over your life, other people are also trying to get more power over your life.

I'll tell you the place you're going to notice it. When broadband arrives, you have information appliances. You reach the point where refrigerators have touch screen and an IP address and you can use it for a family message center and it's dinner time and the refrigerator screen chimes because MCI knows it can get you there to switch your IP service. With a pipeline that is always on into your house, marketers and advertisers—even though it's not in their interest—are going to try to figure cunning new ways to tunnel themselves right into your fortress of solitude.

Let's talk about privacy, starting with cookies and working up to a massive invasion of privacy. How do you feel about cookies? Almost everybody I read says cookies are good for the consumer. I've seen that hundreds of places. Do you agree?

Well, they are good in that they remember where I've been on the Web before. But I'm really old-fashioned about cookies. I always leave my cookie alert on. But it's irrational because you look at this line of code and you say, well, what the hell does this do? And I always click 'OK,' and there are only a couple of instances where I backed out of a site.

Privacy means different things to different people. I think privacy in this age goes back to the roots of how it was articulated by Louis Brandeis. It isn't about people snooping, it's about 'just leave me alone. Don't call me during dinner.' Privacy is 'Yes, you can have my confidential information, but don't give it to somebody who's going to bug me, or who's going to screw up my life.' I think we're going to get back to that kind of definition of privacy, and that companies will discover that confidential information about people is a dangerous thing.

Like what kind?

Personal health information. Like if you're HIV positive and your insurer lets that out and your employer finds out and fires you, or your friends find out and you're subject to ridicule.

Do you think we'll see situations where it turns out certain companies are collecting detailed information on what people eat, what they do, what shows they watch, and that sort of thing? And will they be compiling it on individuals themselves as opposed to aggregating it?

Oh, the temptation is there. The next time you're on the freeway at rush hour, look around and count the number of idiots endangering their lives and the lives of others, and for what, three minutes of saved time? People can be idiots, even in situations that threaten their lives. It's even more true that people can be idiots in business. You look at some of the things businesses do and you say, why?

A case came down recently about a retail chain where managers were keeping records about the ages of employees and, when they downsized, started eliminating jobs in departments in a way that was prejudiced against older people. How stupid can you be? It's like people have lapses of intelligence, normal ordinary people. You see it in business, guys who are committing fraud. They know they are going to get caught, but they do it anyway. Or politicians. People are stupid. And the rest of us are always going to have to be alert to the consequences.

Are we heading for a better world or a worse world— purely on the technological aspects? I won't even go into the biological dangers out there.

We're heading into a world where the technology gets easier to use and there's more technology. And the consequence is it gives us more choices. So from that point of view, it's a more complicated world. It's the kind of world where the consequences can be much greater than ever. Give your electronic agent the wrong instructions when you're a day trader doing futures trading of pork bellies and you may discover that a truck pulls up to your driveway the next morning with a truck full of pork bellies.

It's the kind of world of surveillance where if a kid steals a candy bar or pushes a classmate, suddenly his parents could have a suit. So it's a world where the consequences of a mistake get steadily higher. That's a very different world than we live in.

And with more choices?

It overwhelms us. The more choices we have, the more intelligent we have to be about the choices we make. The price of choosing badly is higher than ever.

You almost make this sound like a very negative thing. Is that your view?

No, not at all. I think it's a positive thing. It's not that the technology appears in a vacuum and drops in on us. We have time to coexist with it. One of the amazing things to me is that consumers have learned to memorize and remember their PINs and to keep them secret. That's amazing. In the 1950s, if you asked people to do that, they would have looked at you like you were an alien.

Look at the automobile. Think what it takes to drive a car. It actually takes quite a lot. It's not just getting in the car and going. Even that takes quite a lot. But you have to deal with auto dealers, you have to deal with a bank for financing, you've got to understand enough about repair to know when to send your car in, you've got to pump your own gas, monitor the oil, know the traffic laws, and have some common sense about driving—which many people don't have. Look at the two-second rule: watch the car ahead of you, see a point it passes, count to two. If you crossed that point before two, you're too damn close. But we've figured out cars, and we'll figure out computers.

Life will get more complex. But we will become, as individuals and a society, more sophisticated. Does life get better or get worse? It mostly stays the same, but the details differ.

WEB RULES
Conclusions and Challenges

Not long ago, I waited in a long supermarket checkout line as a rude clerk chatted with coworkers, oblivious to the growing irritation of her customers. This went on for about five minutes while shoppers shifted from foot to foot. Then, after finishing with one customer, she stopped checking entirely for an extended conversation with the bag boy about his plans for Friday night.

As other customers muttered about the bad service, I looked at the woman who was now first in line. She was a slightly built immigrant in her mid-30s with a crying baby in her cart. She seemed nervous, as if she was uncertain whether to try to say something to the clerk in her limited English. Instead, she remained quiet, her eyes cast at the floor as the baby howled and the clerk gabbed on and on.

We are the immigrants in cyberspace. Like any customer faced with rotten service in a store down the block, we have every right to expect good service from the companies we deal with, and companies have a responsibility to deliver it. Unfortunately, like the young mother in my checkout line, we haven't yet learned the rules of power in this new realm. We haven't yet mastered the customs of our new environment. And we don't know what's acceptable and what's not.

This is a pivotal time for consumers, and for those who hope to win their favor.

With the growth of the Internet, consumers have a chance to change much of what they don't like about the political, social, and commercial institutions around them. But this opportunity won't last for more that a few years. By then, the customs of the Internet could be well established, setting new expectations for customer relationships and social interaction.

In these final pages, I'd like to bring together some of the ideas we've examined and offer consumers, companies, and lawmakers a map to follow as they move along this course. In writing these Web rules, I was inspired by our own history and by the comments of the women and men I interviewed for this book. You're more than welcome to second-guess me, but I implore you to exercise your new power—as a consumer, as an investor, as a leader—to help set the tone for the coming age. These thoughts fall into two major areas: social and commercial. Each arena will take a different level of participation.

SOCIAL IMPACTS

Among social institutions, the potential for change is hindered by a lack of economic incentives, a mind-boggling array of regulatory roadblocks, and the self-serving nature of bloated bureaucracies.

Not surprisingly, the slowest growing areas of the Internet have been education, grassroots politics, and social services. You don't have to gaze into cyberspace to see this is true. You only have to contrast the opulence of California's Silicon Valley with the rundown public schools and the pockets of poverty throughout the San Francisco Bay area.

For example, although California has been showered with riches as a result of the Silicon Valley companies connected with the Web's growth, the state's schools rank 47th among the 50 states in spending per pupil. While parents in wealthy areas donate computers to the schools, the poorest schools can't afford paint and basic repairs.

Over the long term, this inequity will undermine the great economic potential of the Internet by leaving us with a society where companies can't find enough skilled workers; where deteriorating social conditions will handicap profit growth; where millions of have-nots are disenfranchised from the democratic process.

Several of the leaders I spoke with while researching this book—including Ann Winblad, Jerry Yang, and Oakland mayor Jerry Brown—seemed doubtful when I asked them about the probability of change in these areas. None seemed confident change will come easily or quickly:

- Winblad said there's little interest in backing companies focused on the education market because of the tight budgets within the schools and the intense regulations that surround public education.
- Brown, who made a name for himself by challenging the status quo, correctly observed there's been little change so far as a result of all this talk about the Internet. He said big money drives change.
- Yang said the technology industry could help create the framework for bringing the Internet into more classrooms, but estimated it would take a sea change in the regulatory environment before technology could succeed in the schools.

These comments are more reflective of the magnitude of the challenge than anything else. To be sure, this will be one of the greatest tests for our society in the coming decade, but it is one area where we don't dare fail.

Each of us can have a real impact on education, for example, by demanding that legislators and educators provide:

- Standardized K–12 curricula through the Internet, replete with study plans for teachers and automation to help administer tests and grade papers
- Network-based interactive software to supplement the efforts of classroom teachers by making learning as much fun for children as a video game
- A regulatory environment that encourages parents, investors, and educators to build new types of schools that incorporate new technologies

Companies anxious to build a healthy economic environment online need to recognize there are those who share these concerns in the brick-and-mortar world, where the companies' very real customers face very real problems.

On the network, we're all connected, and the brilliant future that glimmers ahead of us could easily be dimmed if we ignore the socioeconomic dangers before us.

COMMERCIAL IMPACTS

In the commercial realm, competition will generate furious fighting among companies for the hearts and minds of consumers. And consumers have an opportunity to tell these companies exactly what they expect in terms of service, selection, and price.

Consider some of the things we've heard from those who are busy setting up shop on the Internet:

- Jerry Yang, cofounder of Yahoo!: "It's one thing to say we're going to protect the consumers, but if you try to cheat them or do something they're not comfortable with, they'll just go somewhere else."
- Venture capitalist Ann Winblad, whose firm has bet tens of millions of dollars on Net start-ups: "The companies

have already learned that the major reason we as entrepreneurs have an advantage over everyone else is that we have surrendered to the consumer. We said 'We know if you don't like us, we're out of business.'"

Over the next several pages, I'll offer ten rules for companies. These are, by no means, intended to be the ultimate guidelines—those will be established by the consensus of consumer demands. But companies who follow these guidelines will have an easier time adjusting to this marvelous new age.

1. Consumers Are in Control

On any commercial Web site, assume consumers are in control. The site should be set up to accommodate their needs, using an interface that makes it easy to shop. Consumers should let the site know what they think, and merchants should listen carefully and respond quickly. Polite but vocal protests should result in rapid change from shopkeepers anxious to attract and retain a clientele because the customer is always right, again.

2. Prices Should Be Attractive

We've talked several times in this book about the reduced costs that businesses face on the Internet. We've also talked about the current, heated competition among companies to stake out turf in cyberspace. This has led to several situations where retail stores in cyberspace have dramatically cut prices to attract shoppers and fend off competitors. Some companies like eBay or Priceline.com have set up their businesses so that customers set the prices by bidding on merchandise or offering a given sum for a particular good.

Consumers should expect this type of behavior to continue for the next few years as companies build up a solid base of regular customers. Then, we're likely to see an effort to raise prices at the largest retailers. Why? Because:

- Shareholders expect their companies to make more money each year. Most Internet retailers have operated at a loss in the early going, but that can't continue for long.
- Cybermall operators will raise rents, and that cost will be passed along to consumers.
- Retailers competing on the Web will add extra services and "bonuses" for shoppers in an effort to retain them. Consumers will pay for them.

But consumers don't have to pay the higher prices, because there will continue to be new competitors on the Internet who'll be happy to get the business. Consumers may have to re-register at a new store, but they're likely to find similar goods at better prices.

3. First-Class Service Is Expected

Nobody is more essential to the long-term success of a merchant on the Internet than the customer. Given that importance, consumers should expect first-class service. Just like price, service will be one of the key points of competition between retailers and other service providers on the Web.

If consumers want to shop at 3 AM, the store should be ready to accommodate them. If they're not happy with the service, they should go somewhere else. Odds are, they'll find other companies very eager to win their loyalty. While consumers tend to trust brand names they know, there are myriad new brands on the Internet that provide top-quality goods and services. Consumers should get to know some of them. Remember, the Internet is a new world, so we should expect to try some new things.

4. Offer Strict Privacy Policies

If consumers don't see a merchant's privacy policy clearly displayed on the home page of the site, they may go somewhere else. Most sites will ask you to accept "cookies" on your computer. These are software codes that will continue to feed information back to the merchant about your preferences. While this will, over time, help the merchant identify your likes and dislikes, it also gives them access to information about your household you might not want everyone to know. Many sites promise that this information will be kept confidential and only will be "aggregated" for use in developing advertisements, improving services, or working with its business partners. But there is little case law on what will happen if that promise is broken. Some companies on the Internet may be in other countries, making it difficult to take action against those who sell confidential information.

Consumers always should have a right to refuse cookies and other restrictions.

5. Offer Strong Return Policies

What if consumers don't like the merchandise once they receive it? What if a new book is missing pages? What if Aunt Sarah hates that brooch? Can these things be returned? Who pays the shipping charge?

I was impressed recently with this guarantee from a retailer: "No sale is considered final until you're completely satisfied." Amen to that.

6. Avoid Added Costs

Don't you hate it when you shop for a car and the salesperson tells you it costs one price, then—after you sit down to sign the papers—adds in five other charges to drive up the price 10 percent?

Many prices quoted on the Internet don't represent the final price. Often, companies add charges like shipping costs that may vary depending on how quickly you want the product and where you live. In comparing prices, consumers should remember to look at the bottom line, and merchants shouldn't try to hide it.

7. Are You Offered "Frequent Buyer" Perks?

As noted earlier, many companies are already offering "bonuses" for loyal customers. These are similar to frequent flyer miles paid out by airlines. The costs of these programs, however, will be passed along to consumers in the long run. But if consumers buy a lot of goods from a favorite merchant, it's reasonable to expect rewards.

8. Who's Running the Shop?

With so many new brand names on the Internet, it sometimes seems like a sea of strangers. And it is. Many of those companies are owned by firms customers have dealt with for years. Others are trustworthy newcomers, eager to impress with their service and prices. But there also are a goodly number of fraudulent merchants, and consumers need to watch out for them.

Consumers should expect the merchant to answer these questions: Where is the company located? Who owns it? How long has it been in business? If any of that information is hard to find, consumers should be ready to move on.

9. (Most) Bots Are Our Friends

Companies and consumers will soon be using a lot of bots. They'll help consumers find the best bargains, and they'll help merchants keep up with competitors in a way that should end up helping consumers.

Consumers should beware of merchants that don't allow bots, and of unsolicited bots that may be in the service of an unscrupulous merchant. Consumers shouldn't completely trust bots until they get to know them:

- Where do they come from?
- Do you have any common acquaintances?
- Are they of "good character"?
- Who do they work for—the mall, a given retailer, a bot service, or you?

Similarly, consumers should ask retailers if they have any policy on bots. Some stores may ban bots, particularly bots generated by a competitor. There may be a good reason for this: Bots could be used by one retailer to compete unfairly with another. In any case, make sure you approve of the store's policy.

10. Money Talks

Many retailers advertise that other shoppers love them. Who cares? What matters is that the individual consumer likes them. If shoppers have any hesitation about making a purchase over the Internet, they won't do it. Hopefully, they will tell the merchant why they chose not to make the purchase.

A quality merchant will pay close attention to customer feedback and will change any nonessential policy that is turning away shoppers. Consumers will assume the merchant is there to serve them. Any dissatisfaction is sufficient reason to go elsewhere.

CLOSING THOUGHTS

The United States has prided itself on setting an example for the world in democracy and, more recently, in technological advances. Now, as these two elements come together, some of the Web rules I've proposed may seem extreme to some companies and consumers.

Consumers who've forgotten that they are always right may feel uncomfortable telling a merchant to change a policy, cut prices, or increase selection. But they now have that power.

Retailers who've long been able to set the level of expectation for their customers may be shocked to find out that consumers are expecting better treatment in the future. And they may be out of business if they don't deliver it.

Social institutions, particularly the public schools, may be surprised when citizens band together to demand more for their tax dollars. If these institutions wish to survive, however, they should embrace this change and remember that the taxpayers are their bosses.

Is this all pie-in-the-sky thinking? No.

Consider this: In China today, relatively few people have computers or access to the Internet, or even phones. It's not uncommon for many families in one village to share a computer, if one is available at all. Yet consumers there are embracing the power of the Internet, setting their own Web rules.

The Falun Gong, a social movement that mixes religion and politics, has already attracted tens of millions of members with the help of the Internet. In one instance, 10,000 of the group's members showed up for a protest in Beijing, catching government bureaucrats by surprise. Its leader was later branded public enemy No. 1 by the government, which labeled the Falun Gong the gravest threat to Chinese stability in the 50 years of Communist rule.

Thousands of the group's members have been detained by the government, hundreds were packed off to labor camps without trial, more than 100 were charged with serious crimes against the state and at least 5 have died while in custody.

I won't judge the merits of the group or the extraordinary response of the Chinese government. I will only ask this: If it is possible to stir that sort of social action in a country where group members risk arrest and punishment, what is holding back a consumer revolution in the U.S.? Nothing.

Nothing, but the consumers themselves. The Web rules are in their hands.

INDEX